# LANGUAGE AND LIFE ON OCRACOKE

# LANGUAGE AND LIFE ON OCRACOKE

## *The Living History of the Brogue*

Jeffrey Reaser, Walt Wolfram & Candy Gaskill

The University of North Carolina Press
CHAPEL HILL

Manufactured in the United States of America

Designed by Lindsay Starr
Set in Miller, Cervo Neue, and Bourbon

by Rebecca Evans
Cover art: Ocracoke Lighthouse, Ocracoke Island, North Carolina.
© Adobe Stock / Jorge Moro

Library of Congress Cataloging-in-Publication Data
Names: Reaser, Jeffrey, 1976– author. | Wolfram, Walt, 1941– author. | Gaskill, Candy, author.
Title: Language and life on Ocracoke : the living history of the brogue / Jeffrey Reaser, Walt Wolfram, and Candy Gaskill.
Description: Chapel Hill : The University of North Carolina Press, [2025] | Includes index.
Identifiers: LCCN 2024062219 | ISBN 9781469685298 (paperback) | ISBN 9781469685304 (epub) | ISBN 9781469685311 (pdf)
Subjects: LCSH: English language—Dialects—North Carolina—Ocracoke Island | Ocracoke Island (N.C.)—Languages. | BISAC: HISTORY / United States / State & Local / South (AL, AR, FL, GA, KY, LA, MS, NC, SC, TN, VA, WV) | TRAVEL / United States / South / South Atlantic (DC, DE, FL, GA, MD, NC, SC, VA, WV)
Classification: LCC PE2927.027 R43 2025 | DDC 427/.9756184—dc23/eng/20250304
LC record available at https://lccn.loc.gov/2024062219

For product safety concerns under the European Union's General Product Safety Regulation (EU GPSR), please contact gpsr@mare-nostrum.co.uk or write to the University of North Carolina Press and Mare Nostrum Group B.V., Mauritskade 21D, 1091 GC Amsterdam, The Netherlands.

# CONTENTS

# ILLUSTRATIONS

FIGURES

# ACKNOWLEDGMENTS

WALT WOLFRAM

When you have interacted with an island community for more than three decades, taken more than a hundred trips to the island, engaged in a variety of research and engagement projects, taught in the school, attended special events, and simply hung out with folks who are celebrating or grieving, it is difficult to acknowledge all of the people who have helped in one form or another. Overall, the community of Ocracoke has been the interactional highlight of my career as a sociolinguist. At the same time, this extended engagement makes it impossible to name everyone who has assisted me on this decades-long journey.

In 1992, I was a new professor at NC State University. I did not know anyone at the university outside of a couple of linguists, whom I knew professionally. With my wife Marge, I decided to spend weekends traveling around the state to become acquainted with some different local regional and cultural communities. While explaining these weekend trips to a new faculty acquaintance, I was told to take a trip to Ocracoke, where "the people speak Elizabethan English." I immediately recognized that comment as a simplified, romantic myth often associated with long-term, isolated language varieties such as Appalachian English, but I was intrigued. And so I put Ocracoke, an island I had never even heard of before moving to North Carolina, on our itinerary.

I started asking colleagues in my department and students in my first class if anyone happened to know someone from Ocracoke. Fortunately, one student in class mentioned that her mother had gone to school on the mainland with a woman from Ocracoke, so I asked for contact information. The obliging student, whose name has been lost among the myriad of students taught over the years, led me to contact Elizabeth Howard, a matriarchal figure on Ocracoke who became our first interviewee—on a cold, blustery Friday afternoon in December 1992. She was friendly, lively, and talkative as she recounted stories of her life on Ocracoke in a unique dialect that was quite unfamiliar to me. I was hooked!

It got even better when a faculty member at NC State, Dr. Lucinda (Cindy) MacKethan, told me that she and her husband were close friends with O'Cocker David Esham and his wife Jen. David had worked with John at a Raleigh accounting firm until he became homesick for Ocracoke, and so the Eshams moved back to the island as new owners of one of the old motels, the Pony Island. David was the kind of character no one ever forgets, walking around the island in bare feet, full of sass and vigor—often with a paper cup containing a mixture of Canadian Club and island water. It is hard to imagine two more appropriate people than David and Elizabeth Howard to start a study, and both remained in close contact as my team and I started our inquiry. They were the type of O'Cockers the island should never forget, and they helped introduce us to many other community members we eventually interviewed.

In February 1993, I brought a class of five students from a research seminar class to do a week of interviews with islanders. It was a risk, as we had only one participant, James Barrie Gaskill, who agreed to an interview, but we went nonetheless. I learned a lot on this first research trip, including that calling in advance and setting times for interviews was not the way requests worked in the

Ocracoke community. Early in the week, I was invited to a small gathering with David and Jen Esham. Included in the party were “Uncle Wallace” Spencer, a crusty “old salt” islander, and his artist wife Barbara Gainey, all gathered for a dessert set up by my new colleague Cindy MacKethan and her husband John. Marge and I brought one student, a likeable, gregarious young man by the name of Chris Craig, and we were evaluated in terms of our acceptability as a crew of researchers “from off.” As the evening wore on, Uncle Wallace took a liking to Chris and invited him into his back room sanctuary to talk to him about the island. In fact, he liked Chris so much he gave him an unused pair of shoes than Chris shined up and wore for months—even though they were two sizes too big. The shoes signaled our group’s acceptance, and we left the island at week’s end with more than forty interviews through the personal friend-of-a-friend technique often used for interviews in the field of sociolinguistics.

During more than three decades on Ocracoke, our team—which has expanded to include Dr. Jeffrey Reaser—has transitioned from “researchers from NC State” to friends, colleagues, and advocates, especially with the O’Cockers, the term used to refer to residents who can trace their island heritage for centuries. Folks like David Esham, James Barrie Gaskill, Rex O’Neal, Rudy Austin, Chester Lynn, Vince O’Neal, Isaac “Ikey” O’Neal, Kenny Ballance, Maurice Ballance, Candy Gaskill, Essie O’Neal, Elizabeth Howard, Rena Dell Garrish, Trudy Austin, Lou Ann Gaskins, and many others, who were there that first week, became friends whom we love to visit. In the time since that first trip, a couple of hundred NC State students and some prominent linguists have also accompanied us over the years, and all of them were as intrigued as we have been. The first few groups of students were led by (now) Dr. Natalie Schilling and Dr. Kirk Hazen, who spent most of their graduate programs doing research there. Dr. Schilling has written three of the chapters in this book (chapters 12, 14, and 15), which have greatly enhanced this story of the Brogue. As the community received many new Latino residents, Spanish language experts

Dr. Maria Coady and Jodie Roberson visited the island with us and wrote the bulk of chapter 22, which describes the Spanish language landscape of the island.

Dr. Jeffrey Reaser started his excursions to Ocracoke as a graduate student in 2000 and has been a vital collaborator ever since, developing the curriculum on dialects and language into a full-fledged unit now endorsed by the North Carolina Department of Public Instruction. As far as we know, this was the first unit of its type in the United States, and it currently continues. The curriculum unit was developed for the eighth grade; in fact, one current Ocracoke teacher, Katie O'Neal, was an eighth-grader in one of our early classes and later returned to teach it with us when she was studying at NC State to become a teacher. For more than three decades, we have taught the curriculum mostly with two teachers, Gail Hamilton in English and Language Arts and Gwen Austin in Social Studies, both of whom have been gracious and supportive of our work. Ocracoke has been blessed with some great teachers dedicated to all of their students. We are also grateful for the proactive support of the school leadership, including past and present principals Leslie Cole and Jeannie Owens.

Other Ocracoke institutions have proven essential to our work on the island and to this book. These include the Ocracoke Preservation Society (OPS), the *Ocracoke Observer*, and the *Village Craftsmen* newsletter, written by the talented historian and writer Philip Howard. I contacted the OPS during the research first trip to the island in 1993 and have worked with them on several unique projects, including the development of the "Dialect Room," which has played our Brogue documentaries continuously since 1995. Special thanks is due to DeAnna Locke, who has been a friend and advocate from our early visits, and to all of the leaders of the OPS, including Amy Howard and current director Andrea Powers. The OPS is the one of the most proactive historical societies we have encountered in our research throughout North Carolina. The members' love for the island's history and culture have resulted in a rich archive that has proven essential to our work on the island.

Ocracoke has many talented artists, and while we would have loved to have featured many of them in this volume, we have opted to use mainly photographic portraits by the incredibly talented Ann Ehringhaus, who generously shared her art with us for this project. In fact, she relentlessly tracked down film negatives from nearly three decades ago so that we could include portraits of O'Cockers who have passed away. Ann's art and generosity makes this volume all the better. We also wish to acknowledge Danica Cullinan, one of our multitalented videographers who has helped compile the video vignettes that enhance the book as well as creating the maps in chapters 4 and 6. Brody McCurdy is due sincere thanks for his incredible work making all the audiovisual enhancements work and for designing the website that accompanies this volume. Thank you to Owen Reaser for coding the website and to Adeline Reaser for making all the QR Codes. Finally, thank you to NC State University for hosting the book's website and for its role in supporting the research that made this book possible.

It has been a pleasure working with the staff at the University of North Carolina Press, and we are grateful that they continue to be a partner in our celebration of North Carolina's linguistic heritage. Lucas Church, especially, has helped us with every step of this project, while also being patient and flexible as it has evolved into a different book than the one we initially pitched. Thomas Bedenbaugh and Mary Carley Caviness also provided critical support and guidance throughout this project. Drs. Lucina MacKethan and Jennifer Cramer reviewed an early draft of this manuscript and provided invaluable guidance and comments that have enhanced this work. We also want to thank Bailey Brown who helped organize, format, and edit an early version of this manuscript.

In this version of a "book on language and life" in Ocracoke, we have enlisted Candy Gaskill as a coauthor. Candy hails from a long-standing Ocracoke family and became one of our friends during our initial visit. While Jeff and I have now been hanging around the island for decades, we are still—and always will be—*dingbatters*, outsiders whose observations need critical guidance by those who have experienced community life throughout their lives. Candy and her family certainly qualify as guides, and we are most grateful and appreciative of her insight and knowledge. She has offered an invaluable insider's perspective on our observations.

One of the commitments of our linguistic research is to share the knowledge we have gleaned not just with a specialized group of linguists, but with the people who have shared their language and life with us. As one scholar put it, "If knowledge is worth having, then it is worth sharing." This is our third book on Ocracoke, and we have published more than fifty technical articles on the Brogue in linguistics journals, but this book is dedicated to the community and to the many people who are curious about this distinctive language variety, regardless of whether they have had any technical training in linguistics.

This new book represents one heartfelt way to express dimensions of our gratitude as linguists and friends to the community for all it has done for us. From the onset of our work on Ocracoke, we have been involved in the community, from connecting with the school where we teach annually to participating in the many facets of the Ocracoke Preservation Society and other local events. These activities have involved giving annual porch talks and presentations, constructing museum exhibits, producing documentaries and oral histories—and even clearing the grave site of the only African American family to live on Ocracoke since the Civil War. We have enjoyed an extensive partnership with the community, one that is far more extensive than what is usually witnessed in sociolinguistics. It has been a special gift of friendship and favor that this community has afforded us, and we hope that we have given Ocracoke something in return for their indulgence of our fixation on the Brogue. Our goal all along has been to provide a better understanding—from the far past into the foreseeable future—of this very special place and people.

—Walt, on behalf of Jeff and Candy

# PREFACE

In the following, we share information that we hope enhances your enjoyment of the story. Perhaps the first and most important thing we wish to highlight are the more than eighty QR codes found throughout the volume. We encourage you to follow these links because we believe that dialects are best experienced when they can be heard. The content can be accessed by using the camera app of any web-connected device (i.e., a tablet or smartphone) to scan the QR code or by following the accompanying URL. All the media content for this volume is organized by chapter and hosted on the accompanying website, ocracokebrogue.com. Additionally, on this website are two oral history projects in their entirety, *Ocracoke Speaks* and *Ocracoke Still Speaks*, and links to two documentaries, *The Ocracoke Brogue* and *The Carolina Brogue*.

In writing this book, we have departed from some traditions of academic books. Perhaps most obviously, we have not included full citations and or a bibliography. When we have quoted from other sources, we have offered sufficient information for the reader to recover the source, but we have forgone full citations of works of technical linguistics and other sources as we felt they would detract from the reader's experience. If you would like specific references to any of the more than fifty linguistics articles we have written on the Brogue, please do not hesitate to reach out to the authors. We have also tried to avoid linguistic jargon and complex statistical analyses except when intentionally making a point about the scientific nature of our discipline.

Additionally, we have written in what we believe to be a casual tone, rather than what is found in typical academic publications. We would love to believe that our writing is as playful as the islanders' speech, but we know that we have fallen short in that regard. This admission is a second reason to engage the linked audiovisual content. Should you not have the time to access the accompanying media, we have done our best to represent the dialect in examples using spelling-pronunciation conventions of standardized English, even while acknowledging that such practice offers only an echo of the voice and overlooks important linguistic nuance. Except in cases where we explicitly reference pronunciations in an extended passage, we have used standardized English spellings for the transcripts of narratives, despite the fact that these usually contain a rich assortment of dialect features. When you listen to these narratives, you might notice that we have edited slightly the textual renditions of what was recorded. This editorial touch is always very light and involves such things as removing hesitations ("uh" or "um"), repeated words, false starts, and so on. We do this merely to improve the readability of the text, not to pass judgment on the spontaneous speech of those quoted.

Finally, we have written this volume as a series of twenty-four short chapters, each centered on a thematic question. Our goal was to write a linguistics book that you could deem "a good beach read." On the beach, you might read a chapter before dozing off for a nap, going shelling, or hopping in the ocean. Because of this, each chapter is meant to be more or less self-contained. You can read the book in the order we present it or skip around. For example, we fully expect many of you to start with chapter 5, "Is the Brogue Pirate Talk?," because why wouldn't you? In order to make each chapter its own story, some information and quotations are repeated among some chapters, though we signal in text these repetitions in case you want to visit a chapter you may have not yet read.

In case you do read the chapters in the order that we present them, you can expect the following organization: We start by imagining the experience of a tourist coming to Ocracoke for the first time. These opening three chapters investigate who the Hoi Toiders are and what it means to be a community member. From there, the next three chapters (4–6) investigate the facts and fictions surrounding the Brogue's origins. We then pause our explicit discussion of the dialect to ask some more general questions about how and why it is important to study dialects. These chapters (7–9) use the Brogue as the illustrative dialect, and so the reader will learn more about the dialect while also learning about the fields of linguistics, dialectology, and sociolinguistics. Chapters 10 and 11 return to investigating formal aspects of the Brogue, pronunciation and grammar, respectively. Chapters 12 to 15 take a sociolinguistic approach to the dialect; these chapters examine the social meanings of language forms as they relate to categories such as gender, islander status, identity, and local culture. For example, chapter 15 investigates what you can learn about island history and culture by looking at the local words and phrases used to describe weather. Chapter 16 offers a linguistic interregnum, as it documents residents' stories of Dorian, the worst weather event ever recorded on the island.

The remaining chapters investigate some critical language questions and stories. Chapters 17 and 18 discuss what the Brogue was like before tourism and how it is now changing, leading into chapter 19, which documents our efforts to teach about the Brogue to the current students at Ocracoke School. Chapters 20 and 21 document some incredible, little-known histories of African Americans on the Outer Banks, including the story of Muzel Bryant, who passed away weeks shy of her 104th birthday as the last remaining member of an isolated African American family on Ocracoke. Chapters 22 and 23 take up the newest linguistic narrative on the island, the arrival of Spanish to Ocracoke, and how the linguistic landscape has shifted. We conclude the book with our reflections on three decades of engagement with a small, island community, and what that tells us about the future of the Brogue. The subtitle of our book tips our hand just a bit, as we truly do see the history of the Brogue as a living history. It is our hope that our readers will come to see themselves as agents who help write that history, either through preserving or appreciating the island's unique cultural resource.

The first goal of this book is straightforward. We simply wish to share knowledge about what is perhaps the most unusual dialect of American English. There is a belief among academics of all stripes that the world would be better off if the general public understood more about their particular field of inquiry. In that sense, we do hope you will learn more about linguistics from reading this book. As we indicated in the acknowledgements, and as we hope the entire book shows, we have a deep love for Ocracoke, its people, and its languages. A second goal, then, is to share this love with as broad an audience as possible. While we can argue the merits of sharing knowledge, it is hard to argue the merits of sharing joy. It is our sincerest hope that reading this book opens up some new appreciation for this unique place, people, and language, whether you have lived there your whole life or have yet to step on the white, sandy beaches of Ocracoke.

# LANGUAGE AND LIFE ON OCRACOKE

*Chapter 1*

# DO THEY TAKE AMERICAN MONEY OVER THERE?

Intrigued by the fact that it consistently ranks among the top ten "Best Beaches in America," you plan your first trip to Ocracoke, North Carolina, a fourteen-mile-long island forming part of the Outer Banks that separates the Pamlico Sound from the Atlantic Ocean. This island with an unusual name (pronounced just like the vegetable and the soda, *okra* + *Coke*), unconnected by bridges or tunnels to any other land, remains one of the most remote places in the state. You arrive at the ferry terminal in Swan Quarter, having driven through some of the most historically isolated parts of the state, where the farming of cotton, peanuts, and soybeans is possible largely by digging deep channels to drain the black soil so that fields are not too swampy. The 220-foot-long Silver Lake ferryboat seems impossibly large for the brackish waterway stretching out from the terminal. (Figure 1.1 shows the very first ferry used to shuttle people to and from Ocracoke.) Somehow, the tan-uniformed ferry workers efficiently load fifty vehicles onto the boat, skillfully packing cars with scarcely enough room for passengers to squeeze between them as they mill about the deck. The smell of diesel quickly follows the growl of the engines, which nearly drown out the captain's welcome via the intercom. He notes that the twenty-seven-mile trip should take about two hours and forty minutes, and that the vessel, even fully loaded, can operate in a mere six feet of water.

FIGURE 1.1. Modern ferries have come a long way since the original Frazier Peele ferry, which began service in 1950. Photograph courtesy of the Ocracoke Preservation Society

Up the staircase at the center of the vessel, you find a sundeck. The breeze is not quite enough to alleviate the heat of the day, so you step into the air-conditioned lounge and find a seat by the window. As more passengers arrive, voices fill the space, and you cannot help but overhear the conversations. One family is reminiscing about their previous vacations; another group seems to be catching up during what must be the only time of the year they are together; a third group is excitedly discussing favorite places to eat. You make mental notes to seek out some fig cake and Ocracoke clam chowder. The conversations share a clear reverence for Ocracoke; they describe a unique and deeply loved place. One group of passengers in particular draws your attention. Their voices are robust and distinct, full of energy. There is something familiar about the dialect, but you cannot quite place it. Is it from somewhere in England? Maybe an Irish accent? Welsh? Could it be Australian?

## WHERE ARE Y'ALL FROM?

The group's hearty laughter makes them seems approachable enough, so you decide to get an answer to your gnawing question. You greet the group and then make the same mistake as hundreds of tourists before you, by asking, "Where are y'all from?" The response, "right here," accompanied by uproarious laughter, leaves you disoriented. This mistake is so frequent that it is part of island lore, passed down by O'Cockers—Ocracoke residents who trace back their family lineage on the island for generations.

So universal is this experience that our video and audio recordings from the island have more examples of this anecdote than any other topic. For example, James Barrie Gaskill notes, "I have a lot of people asking, 'Are you Australian?' . . . I don't know what an Australian is supposed to sound like." Rex O'Neal shares a similar sentiment: "I have a lot of people who think I'm from Australia or Ireland, yeah." So common is this confusion that one resident, Chester Lynn, decided to play a trick on some fellow travelers on a guided trip to Israel: "A lot of people that was, you know, from the United States, they thought I was from London. Matter of fact,

I picked a map up real quick and looked and told them for half the trip that I was from this little town outside of London, and they believed it."

To hear residents talk about being mistaken for non-US natives (from *The Carolina Brogue*), visit www.ocracokebrogue.com/chapter/1/QR1-1.mp4.

Americans are not the only ones fooled by Ocracoke natives. In the 1990s, we brought famed British dialectologist Dr. Peter Trudgill to Ocracoke. He took back some speech samples of native islanders to Essex, England. He mixed these samples with others from five English dialects from around the world. The people who listened to these recordings unanimously, but incorrectly, reported the voices from Ocracoke were British in origin, most commonly suggesting they came from southwestern England.

No other dialect of American English is routinely interpreted as being non-American. Among the features that seem to lead listeners to this conclusion are the distinctive way that locals pronounce their *r*-sounds in words like *year* or *car* and the pronunciations of certain vowels, most notably the way they pronounce the long i vowel in *high tide* as "oy," or "hoi toid" (high tide). This pronunciation gives islanders one of their nicknames, *Hoi Toiders*. "Banker speech" is another term for the dialect, but locally, the term *Brogue* is the most commonly used moniker. The exact path of this term into English remains a linguistic mystery, but there are some known steps along the way. The first documented use of the term in English describes the coarse shoes of highland Irish and Scottish folk. This untanned leather shoe was called a *brog* in Irish, which derived from Old Irish *bracca*, the same root that gives us English *breeches* as a type of pants. It is possible that the term *brog* eventually extended in meaning, referring to the whole person —including their speech—rather than just the iconic footwear. The term entered English in the early 1700s, where it came to be used for any highly distinctive dialect, especially the English spoken in Ireland and Scotland. Because the Ocracoke dialect is both distinct and reminiscent of some distinct dialects in the British Isles, it makes sense that the term *Brogue* has stuck. Islanders seem to have embraced it heartily, as this reflection from Chester Lynn shows: "It's the way your ancestors had been taught. And so that's the good part now with the Brogue is that people understand that, you know, it was the family's descent and the family's legacy that went on. It wasn't that it was bad English, it was just a different English."

To hear Chester Lynn reflect on how the Brogue was viewed (from *Ocracoke Still Speaks*), visit www.ocracokebrogue.com/chapter/1/QR1-2.mp3.

## TRAVELING TO ANOTHER WORLD

Distinctiveness is just one part of the dialect's intrigue. The rich history of pirates in the area, including the infamous Blackbeard, has led some to speculate that Hoi Toiders sound like the pirates of yesteryear. Others have claimed the island, settled by Europeans in the early seventeenth century, has preserved Elizabethan or Shakespearean English. Neither of these assertions is quite correct (see chapters 5 and 6 for more on these topics), but they do accurately capture the fact that the roots of the dialect are deep, rich, and fascinating.

Ocracoke's allure is multifaceted. Because the island is accessible only by boat, it has an exoticness that makes visitors and would-be-visitors feel they are going someplace quite different. So much so that first-time visitors treat Ocracoke as though it were a different country rather than an island off the North Carolina coast. Candy Gaskill offers a lighthearted perspective on outsiders' perceptions: "They always ask the guys on the Hatteras Ferry whether we take American money over here. I don't know where they think they're going, but they always want to know if we take American money." Dale Mutro describes visitors by saying, "I think they think that we're the outback or something, in the lawless land or something."

What gives Ocracoke this otherworldly feel? Certainly, the geographic remoteness and the unique dialect contribute, but there are additional factors. The island is routinely described as a quaint fishing village, which is both truth and fantasy. Commercial fishing, long a pillar of the island economy, is now practiced by just a few islanders, but the maritime past is indelibly imprinted on the island, and the local fish house remains a prominent landmark on the harbor. An additional contributor to Ocracoke's quaintness is that it has no chain restaurants or stores, and it remains walkable and bikeable, though more recently, scooters and golf carts seem to have become the preferred mode of transportation in the village. This is not to say the island lacks modern conveniences. Mobile phone coverage now reaches out to the beach, the hotels have high-speed internet, and the island boasts many excellent restaurants and bakeries. There are museums, shops, a hardware store, gas station, grocery store, brewery, local music and theater venues, and more. It is simply a fact that contemporary Ocracoke relies on tourism rather than commercial fishing to fuel its economy. To first-time visitors, the island's allure usually centers on its sixteen miles of immaculate beaches, the crown jewel of the Cape Hatteras National Seashore. The white sand beaches are protected from development, so swimmers and sunbathers can enjoy the environs without houses in sight. The remoteness of the island and the plentiful beaches make it possible, even in the height of tourist season, to find your own patch of sand away from everyone else. This wildness is what led Dr. Beach (a.k.a. Stephen Leatherman) to name it 2007's "Best Beach in America." In 2022, Dr. Beach again named it the best beach, making it a rare repeat winner. Leatherman writes about Ocracoke, "It's my favorite getaway beach. Here you will find some of the wildest beaches in the country."

Others come to the island for the world-class fishing. Since Ocracoke is located near the Gulf Stream, sport fishermen seek mahi-mahi, tuna, grouper, swordfish, marlin, and other large catches. From the beach, surf fishers routinely catch dinners of drum, Spanish mackerel, and bluefish. The Pamlico Sound offers a wealth of marine life, including clams, oysters, shrimp, flounder, scallops, and blue crab. The fall months also attract duck hunters, rounding out the island as a sportsman's paradise.

## CULTURAL TOURISM

A less obvious but no less important part of the tourist economy is the local culture, and perhaps there is no more iconic cultural marker of Ocracoke than its dialect. Candy Gaskill, longtime proprietor at Albert Styron's Store, a (now closed) popular tourist stop near the lighthouse, recalls how visitors would come into the store and demand that she perform for them:

> This man and woman walked in, and I was like, "Hi, how are y'all," you know, and they walked around and stuff and everything, and the lady come up to me and said, "Speak!" And I said, "Excuse me?" She's like, "Speak!" And I said, "What do you mean, speak? I'm talking to you right now." "No! You have this way that y'all are supposed to talk down here. Speak." And I'm like, "Ma'am, this is the way I talk. I've lived here thirty-some years," I said, "and I've always talked like this." So that was basically the story: She wanted me to speak and I got ready to say, "Well, you gonna give me a biscuit and I'll be glad to speak."

To hear Candy Gaskill tell this story (from *Ocracoke Speaks*), visit www.ocracokebrogue.com/chapter/1/QR1-3.mp3.

Whatever initially brings visitors to the island the first time, chances are they return to the island because of the people. In our trips to the island over nearly thirty years, we have increasingly come to appreciate the humor, grace, and hospitality of community members, and to admire the community's resourcefulness and resiliency. The stories of Ocracoke form a rich history. They capture both the routine and the profound, and many are steeped in island humor, an attribute that is venerated among O'Cockers. Collectively, they tell the story of a people who are persevering and generous. They include stories of heartbreak, such as those that describe the destruction of Hurricane Dorian in 2019, the worst natural disaster ever recorded on the island (see chapter 16). But they also include stories of inspiration, portraying a community that has flourished through hardship, devastation, and change.

It is tempting to see the island as stuck in the past, but this is not a fair interpretation. While the past is an important cultural currency for islanders, they and their community have embraced the changes of the modern world. Like many other areas of North Carolina, Ocracoke is now an increasingly diverse place. Beginning in the 1990s, Spanish-speaking immigrants began moving to the island. They now make up an important contingent of the island's population, and they continue to shape the community's living history.

This book is about that living history, as told through the lens of the dialect's past, present, and future. We start this journey in the past, with the story of how Ocracoke got its name. As with many Ocracoke things, there is lore and there is reality. One story of the name's origin attributes the coining to Blackbeard. Charlie Williams recounts the story this way: "Well, they always said that Blackbeard laid out here in the inlet. He found out there was a Lieutenant Maynard, I reckon, was after him—I believe that's the way it is. But he wanted to get going, he wanted to get out of the inlet. When the rooster crows in the morning, it's getting closer to daylight. So he said, 'Old cock crow!' And after that the old cock crowed and he went out. But they changed the name around—*Ocracoke*. That's what I always been taught."

To hear Charlie Williams recount this apocryphal story of how Ocracoke got its name [from *Ocracoke Speaks*], visit www.ocracokebrogue.com/chapter/1/QR1-4.mp3.

As creative as this etymological origin is, it is ultimately merely a fanciful legend. Maps from 150 years before Blackbeard harbored on the island designate the inlet and island with a variety of names, including "Wokokon," "Woccocock," "Oakacock," and "Okercock," meaning that the name was established before Blackbeard could have coined it in 1718. There are two likely sources for this name.

The first possibility is that the island was eponymously named after the Indigenous Wococon, a Siouan group that lived in what is now central North Carolina; but the geographical distance makes this unlikely. The more likely explanation is that it derives from the Algonquian word "waxihikami," which meant "enclosed place" or "stockade." One explanation for how Ocracoke earned this name is that the island rises a little higher than other nearby islands, and, as such, harbors a more substantial tree cover, making it more "enclosed" than other places along the Outer Banks. On early maps of the area, directions for navigating the Hatteras and Ocracoke Inlets sometimes begin by instructing sailors to locate the islands' "Hommocks." *Hommock* in this usage refers to a heavily wooded area. For example, on an 1853 map produced by the United States Coast Survey, the "sailing directions" instruct captains to locate "the remarkable round Hommock on the North Eastern side of the entrance." A second topographical feature, what is now Silver Lake, may also be the source of the name. Though Silver Lake has been enlarged from its original form, the harbor is visible on early maps as an enclosed, protected space. It is probably this harbor, located on the sound side of the island and protected from the ocean's wind and waves, that led to the Algonquian people's labeling it "waxihikami." As described below, that name eventually changed into "Ocracoke."

In North Carolina, many place names reflect the Indigenous populations' legacy. Along the Outer Banks and in the eastern mainland of North Carolina, many place names derive from Algonquian tribe names, including the Pamlico Sound, Roanoke, Waccamaw, Cape Fear, Core Sound (from the Coree Indians), and Neuse River (From the Neusioc Indians). Many other place names derive from Algonquian words that describe an area's topography or other geographical features. *Hatteras*, for example, comes from an Algonquian word meaning "less vegetation," *Currituck* comes from the word *carotank*, meaning "land of the wild geese," and *Chicamacomico* means "place of sinking sand." *Ocracoke*, as noted above, seems to have come from an Anglicization of *waxihikami* (stockade or enclosed place), which, had by 1590 become Anglicized and was written as *Wokokon* (see fig. 1.2), with variant spellings such as *Wococon* on contemporary maps.

The shift from Wokokon/Wococon to Ocracoke seems to have happened gradually. Historical maps gradually dropped the initial *w* from the spelling and eventually introduced the *r* that the name now carries. The first process stems from a common practice in English dialects whereby word-initial *w*-sounds are lost, as in the transformation of *young ones* to *young'uns*. The latter is a little trickier, but it is not uncommon in English for an *r*-sound to be added where there was not one previously, as can be heard

FIGURE 1.2. Part of "The carte of all the coast of Virginia" (1590), by Theodor de Bry, showing the original Anglicized spelling of the island as "Wokokon." Courtesy of the North Carolina Collection, Wilson Special Collections Library, University of North Carolina at Chapel Hill.

in the common dialect pronunciation *warsh* for *wash*, or in the phrases *the idear of it* and *vanillar ice cream*. Finally, the loss of the *n*-sound from the end of *Wococon* also reflects a pattern seen throughout the history of the language, whereby word-final sounds are dropped. Though historical documents provide no clear timeline for these changes, old maps indicate that it is likely the loss of the *w* and *n* happened relatively early—by 1676—and before the intrusion of the *r*, which became consistent around the 1850s. The modern spelling first appeared on a United States Coast Survey map in 1856 titled "Preliminary Chart of the Sea Coast of North Carolina," and this spelling then quickly became the standard.

It seems fitting that the island's name and the local Brogue tie in so strongly to the place's past. In some ways, the island simply but methodically collects things—shipwrecks, pirates, shells, artists, and even linguists (i.e., people who study languages and dialects)—creating an evolving and complex milieu. Not everyone stays, or returns, but for those who feel the island's gravity, the pull can be strong. As Candy Gaskill describes it, "it's one of those places that you either love it or hate it. And the people that love it, it does; it gets in your blood and it's just like, it stays there. It's like your blood. It's like the salt gets in your veins and just—you just can't get it out. It doesn't make no difference where you go." In this book, we try to honor the voices and stories of community members who have been generous with their time and trust. It is their generosity, history, and good humor—not the miles of pristine beach—that truly makes this remote island with the funny name such a draw for people. So, no matter where you are or where you have gone, we hope that this book makes you feel the pull of the island just a little more strongly than you already do.

*Chapter 2*

# WHO SPEAKS THE BROGUE?

It can be dangerous telling someone what dialect they do or do not speak. A Southerner being told they sound like a Yankee? Well, them's fightin' words. Instead of directly answering the question posed by this chapter's title, we examine some of the terms islanders use to talk about community insiders and outsiders: Ocracoke natives, transplants, and, of course, tourists. Because dialects are fundamentally about defining who is in versus out of a group, it should be no surprise that group labels are an important component of all dialects. When you ask Americans about who speaks differently, it quickly becomes apparent that they have little difficulty dividing people into groups, be they groups in the immediate, local context, or groups across the country. It is unsurprising, then, that there are labels for these groups. As is typically the case with language, these labels become imbued with feelings about the people they describe. In many cases, the labels for groups imply a way of speaking, but even more so, a way of being, that is, a set of traits or characteristics.

Sometimes these different ways of speaking can be substantial, but other times they may be imperceptible to those outside of the local community. For example, people who live in Robeson County, North Carolina, around a hundred miles inland from Ocracoke, are readily able to identify local Lumbee Indians, African Americans, and whites by dialect alone; however, if you ask people from the state capital, Raleigh, to categorize these people by listening to them talk, they cannot do it. Lifelong residents of the Outer Banks tell us that they can pinpoint a person's native community just by hearing them talk. For example, native Ocracokers can often tell a person from Harkers Island and vice versa. But they also claim to be able to differentiate folks from Hatteras, Frisco, Buxton, and Avon, four communities spread across just seventeen miles of Hatteras Island. As linguists, we are not exactly sure what they hear that leads them to these judgments, but we also are not going to tell people that they lack this ability. Subtle differences can be important. Older O'Cockers maintain they could once tell a Pointer from a Creeker (two different parts of the Ocracoke community; see the next chapter for more on these terms) by the way they talked.

## NOT EVERYONE WHO LIVES ON OCRACOKE IS AN O'COCKER

Every March, when we teach our dialect curriculum to eighth-graders at the Ocracoke School, we start by getting to know a bit about the students. We often ask them to raise their hands if they are O'Cockers (originally a shortened form of *Ocracoker*, pronounced "OH-cock-er"). Inevitably, a number of hands go up. Almost immediately, a few students begin vociferously objecting to some of their peers' raised hands. What is going on here? To many people, including the students with improperly raised hands, it seems like an O'Cocker must simply be someone who lives on Ocracoke or, perhaps, has lived on Ocracoke for all or most of their life. However, native islanders have a much narrower definition for the term and reserve it for people whose families have lived on Ocracoke for many generations. A few decades ago, only residents who had both maternal and paternal island lineages could claim the title O'Cocker, but the frequency of marriages to non-islanders has eroded this requirement. Now, residents can claim the title O'Cocker as long as one side of the family has substantial island roots.

What exactly defines "substantial" remains a topic of debate among islanders, but generally speaking, those with substantial island lineage are those who know enough family and island history to recognize that it is "substantial." Islanders take this label seriously. In a few cases, islanders whom we thought could claim O'Cocker status have refused the title. In one case, a member of the Howard family, the family that purchased Ocracoke in 1759, told us that he did not use the term for himself because his parents had moved him away from the island prior to his birth. He returned to the island to live as an adult, but that was not enough to make him feel like he could adopt the term. This is not to say that non-O'Cocker residents are not important community members, but there is an obvious kinship visible whenever two O'Cockers get to talking, which is visible even in photographs, such as figure 2.1. Oftentimes, the rate of speech increases and the Brogue thickens, sometimes so much so that non-O'Cockers are left wondering what they are saying.

The term encompasses more than just family heritage; it also implies an orientation toward the community's history and culture. O'Cockers all serve as island historians, to one extent or another. Storytelling remains an important part of island life, and the oral histories passed down among generations honor the lives and stories of important community figures, living and deceased. Having grown up on the island, they inherited island ways and the island spirit. Generations of isolation have forged a resourceful independence among island families. O'Cockers would do anything to help a fellow O'Cocker, and just about anything to help anyone else. It is

FIGURE 2.1. O'Cockers Candy Gaskill (left) and Chester Lynn chat outside Albert Styron's store. Photograph by Ann Ehringhaus.

not uncommon for O'Cockers to have substantial skills in fishing, gardening, cooking, canning, and fixing darn near anything. Many of them are also adept at carpentry, plumbing, electrical work, car repair, and other mechanical skills. It did not take us college professors long to recognize we were some of the dumbest smart people on the island. In fact, iconic O'Cocker David Esham made this exact comment to Walt on one of the latter's early visits to the island, saying he was "the dumbest smart person he had ever met."

So, what about those non-O'Cockers who have lived a significant part of their lives on the island? These residents may claim terms like *islander*, *community member*, *year-round resident* (to contrast with those who have vacations homes), or even recently, *Ocracoker*, but they cannot lay claim to the term *O'Cocker* without the family heritage. A number of non-O'Cockers become critical parts of the community, and O'Cockers often acknowledge their integration into the community with the phrase, "They weren't born here but they got here as soon as they could."

## NAMES FOR PEOPLE FROM OTHER PARTS OF COASTAL NORTH CAROLINA

Every state has stereotypes about neighboring states. Any Tar Heel can list many things wrong with *Sandlappers* (i.e., residents of South Carolina)—all born out of a good-natured rivalry, of course. Southerners could levy an even longer list about *Yankees*—maybe not exactly born out of good-natured rivalry. The same holds true for cities and towns, not just states. Residents of Raleigh, Durham, Chapel Hill, and Cary, North Carolina, all have ideas about how people from each of the other communities act. On a larger scale, we all have ideas about what people from New York City or San Francisco are like. In Ocracoke, some of the closest neighboring communities are described in ways that poke fun at the people who live there. Though only twenty miles away, Hatteras is more easily accessible than Ocracoke and, over the years, has attracted a number of wealthy residents. When Ocracokers interacted with these transplants, they often found them to lack the sensibilities of those who had a family history of living on the Outer Banks, earning them the name *Hatterassers*.

One of the next towns heading north along the Outer Banks is Avon, formerly known as Kinnakeet. Residents from this town were called, predictably and innocuously, *Kinnakeeters*. O'Cockers often saw these folks as lacking common sense. Instead of a playful name, as in the case of Hatterassers, O'Cockers relied on a rhyme to capture the Kinnakeeter's essence: "Kinnakeeter yaupon eater." Yaupon is a native, small evergreen shrub. Its bitter leaves are boiled for a medicinal tea that, if strong enough, would induce vomiting. As such, only an idiot would actually eat yaupon unless they were purposely in search of a stomachache. However, we do recommend that you sample the teas that include yaupon from the local coffee and teashops on Ocracoke. Just do not be a yaupon eater! Residents from more distant parts of the North Carolina coast are grouped into a few categories. Generally, people from places like Atlantic, Sea Level, Stacy, and Davis—that is, the towns between Cedar Island and Williston, are called *Core Bankers* or *Core Sounders*, despite living on the mainland of North Carolina. People from farther south of the aforementioned communities, for example, people from Marshallberg, Harkers Island, or Beaufort, North Carolina, are more likely to be called *Downeasterners*.

To hear Clinton Gaskill talk about how to cure yaupon for tea (from *Ocracoke Speaks*), visit www.ocracokebrogue.com/chapter/2/QR2-1.mp3.

## NAMES FOR TOURISTS

It should not be surprising that tourists have accumulated various monikers over the years. Some of the terms Outer Banks residents use for outsiders are highly localized while others vary in frequency by community. In the southern Outer Banks, especially in Harkers Island, the term *dit-dot* has been used for many years. This term comes from Morse code, which uses combinations of two sounds called a dit and a dot to communicate messages. Morse code is notoriously difficult to understand, just like the mainlanders were to the residents of Harkers Island. Ocracokers tell us they are familiar with this usage, but they do not use it themselves. Also common in the Core Banks is the term *woodser*, presumably to describe someone from where there are many trees, that is, farther inland. One resident noted, "Ever since I can remember, somebody not from here was called a *dingbatter* or a *dit-dot* or a *woodser*. People not from here is called woodsers too. And I asked, uh—I asked daddy one time, I remember when I was young, I said, 'Daddy, why does Charlie call that crowd woodsers?' That was his Daddy. He said, 'Cause that's somebody from inland, not from the—not from the Banks and around the water.' That's why old folks used to call 'em woodsers." A final term used by much of the Outer Banks is simply *from off*. As one resident of the Core Banks described it, "If you're not from here, anyplace else in the world is 'off.'"

To watch Core Sounders talk about various words for people from "off" (from *The Carolina Brogue*), visit www.ocracokebrogue.com/chapter/2/QR2-2.mp4.

More locally, on Ocracoke, those from off used to be called *foreigners* or *strangers*. In fact, the oldest residents of the island still use these terms to describe both tourists and non-O'Cocker residents. But the terms have fallen out of use among the younger generations of islanders.

No term for tourists has had more staying power than *dingbatter*, the term that eventually usurped *foreigner*. The story of the term *dingbatter* is almost as interesting as the stories O'Cockers tell about dingbatters. Linguists often claim that popular media does not play a big role in spreading language features, but in this case, it is appropriate to look to television. Broadcast television arrived on Ocracoke as early as the mid-1950s and was widespread in the community by the early 1970s. The television was becoming an increasingly prominent fixture in Outer Bankers' homes when *All in the Family* hit the airwaves in 1971. The show lasted nine seasons, but its linguistic legacy persists. In the show, protagonist Archie Bunker (played by Carroll O'Connor) commonly referred to his wife Edith (Jean Stapleton) as a "dingbat" when she displayed a lack of common sense. Though the term existed well before the show, island residents found the use of the term a fitting description of the gullible, often naive tendencies of some tourists, and *dingbatter* was born.

Every islander has a story about dingbatters. Rex O'Neal captures a few common dingbatter tendencies, saying, "What's a dingbatter? He's really not a bad person, he's just an outsider that comes in and asks—and asks you where the lighthouse is . . . when he's standing right in front of it. [Or he] points out over the Pamlico Sound, say, 'Is this the Atlantic Ocean?' [Or asks,] 'What time does the four o'clock ferry leave?'" Chester Lynn tells a similar story about dingbatters' inability to find the lighthouse. While working at the Island Inn, Chester would frequently field questions from tourists about directions to the prominent landmark. Many times, the same tourists would come back swearing the lighthouse was not where Chester said it was. His response: "That lighthouse has been down there about 175 years, and I haven't seen them come up the road with it yet."

To watch Rex O'Neal talk about the silly questions of dingbatters (from *The Carolina Brogue*), visit www.ocracokebrogue.com/chapter/2/QR2-3.mp4.

To hear Dale Mutro recount Chester's story of the dingbatters who couldn't find the lighthouse (from *Ocracoke Still Speaks*), visit www.ocracokebrogue.com/chapter/2/QR2-4.mp3.

Dale Mutro recalls a story of a would-be tourist's troubles reaching the island. One car would "come up to the front [of the line for the ferry] and it'd turn around and get in the back." When asked what he was doing, the driver responded, "Well, I saw these other ferries come in and I didn't want to go to any of those places." Dale explains, "You know . . . some of the ferries are named after people but most of them [are named after places like Roanoke, Cedar Island, and Hatteras]. He said he doesn't want to go to any of those other places, he wanted to go to Ocracoke." The driver mistook the vessel names for their destinations, and missed a number of ferries to Ocracoke while he waited for the one named "Ocracoke."

To hear Dale Mutro recount the full story of the dingbatters who couldn't figure out which ferry to take (from *Ocracoke Still Speaks*), visit www.ocracokebrogue.com/chapter/2/QR2-5.mp3.

Other dingbatter tendencies include riding a bike—or driving a golf cart—in the middle of the road, often with a line of cars waiting behind. David Esham offers one final encapsulation of dingbatters: "I don't mean they're dumb, they just don't know any damn better. A real true-blood dingbatter is someone who would see the [tire] tracks going across the beach and would go across there in a car. And think he could go where a four-wheel drive [vehicle could go]. That is a real dyed-in-the-wool dingbatter." Dingbatter has persisted for a half-century, and its use remains strong today. There was a brief period around 2010 in which younger islanders used *touron* (a blend of *tourist* and *moron*), but that term's usage seems to have ebbed, leaving *dingbatter* as the term islanders use to name those who lack island sense.

The term is not restricted to Ocracoke and is quite prominent elsewhere in the Outer Banks. In the southern part of the Outer Banks, where there are fewer tourists, the term is used slightly differently. Ocracokers use the term exclusively with island visitors, but elsewhere, the term can be (lovingly) applied to even long-term residents. In one excellent encapsulation that we included in the documentary *The Carolina Brogue*, an island native appears alongside an older gentleman who had moved to the island decades ago. The younger man says, "This is a dingbatter. He married a Downeast woman. . . . He's from Kenosha, Wisconsin. Now, this is what we consider a dingbatter, a damn dingbatter." The older gentleman responds, "I've been here since before he was born." To which the younger native remarks, "It doesn't matter." Though this usage is not common in Ocracoke, it does highlight nicely that there is something unique about those from traditional island families. Here, the term marks a distinction like that of *O'Cocker* versus *island resident*. Both live there, but only one has a family history that is intertwined with island history.

To watch a vignette in which Core Sounders describe other residents as dingbatters (from *The Carolina Brogue*), visit www.ocracokebrogue.com/chapter/2/QR2-6.mp4.

Once on island, you may find additional names for locals. As noted in the next chapter, there are names for different parts of the village, and some of the traditional labels for the groups of residents, such as *Pointers* and *Creekers*, have long been used to differentiate, respectively, those who live near the lighthouse (Springer's Point) from those who live across the harbor, which was previously called Cockle Creek. Though locals swear there used to be dialect differences between these parts of the village, we never had any luck identifying what features distinguished the two groups.

Finally, just as terms for outsiders can capture a range of attitudes about others, there are also terms used to capture a sense of closeness among insiders. The term *buck* or *bucky* is used for a man who is a good friend, while the term *puck* or *pucky* is used for a woman who is a good friend. The latter term can also be used to denote someone's romantic partner, as in, "Melinda is his puck," to mean that Melinda is his girlfriend or wife, not just a good friend. *Buck* does not get used in this way and is actually more commonly used by men to denote their other male friends, as well as a term of address, as in, "What's up, bucky?" or "Hey, buck!"

## WHAT'S IN A NAME?

The labels people use to identify other groups are seldom neutral. In some cases, they may be playful, but even these carry some social commentary. As linguists, we feel strongly that ethnic and regional groups ought to be able to name themselves, so when the Cherokee or Lumbee tell us they prefer *Indian* to *Native American*, we adhere to their preferences. But what if you have been called a *dingbatter* and would prefer a less judgmental label? In this case, the term is not used to denote some unchangeable trait like heritage or skin color. Instead, it is a term that reflects something you did or said, so it may be worth pausing and reflecting on what you did that caused others to label you in this way. Though we have certainly committed plenty of dingbatter offenses over the years, our engagement, promotion, and love of the community have resulted in few people calling us dingbatters—at least not to our faces. O'Cockers and Ocracokers are a generous lot, and respect for the island's way of life will go a long way toward ingratiating tourists to the natives. Being called a dingbatter is just an invitation to learn more about the local ways of life.

*Chapter 3*

# WHAT WORDS DO O'COCKERS USE TO TALK ABOUT OCRACOKE?

Ocracoke village is a relatively small place, just over four square miles. Perhaps the two most distant points in the village, Howard's Pub and the very end of Harbor Cove Lane, are a mere 1.6 miles apart by road. That does not mean the island is an easy place to navigate. Maps are ubiquitous on the ferries as well as in retail outlets across the town. Modern visitors have it easy. Although the national emergency number, 911, was established in 1968, it was not until the Wireless Communications and Public Safety Act of 1999 that many communities, including Ocracoke, were required to name local streets to help 911 emergency response. And it was not until 2005 that the town erected street signs consistently throughout the village.

Prior to formalizing the street names, locals typically referred to streets by people who lived there (e.g., "Tom Neal Drive" or "Winnie Blount Road") or an important landmark (like the school, water plant, British Cemetery, or poker house). Following the government's directive to formalize street names, the community created a street-naming committee, consisting of Kenny Ballance, Darlene Styron, James Barrie Gaskill, and Ellen Marie Fulcher Cloud. They formalized many of the traditional names and formalized others, such as Poker Players' Road. The committee's finalized naming scheme caused little consternation, which does not mean all the residents abandoned the traditional names. One of the village's main roads is now known as Sunset Drive. It connects Back Road to the Jackson Dunes and Oyster Creek sections of town. Many residents still refer to this road as Ammunition Dump Road; this road was the first paved road on the island when, in 1942, the US Navy paved it to allow access to an ammunition dump near what is now Oyster Creek. The modern moniker was proposed by Lloyd Harkum, a non-resident developer, which might explain why locals have been reluctant to adopt it.

The island's most iconic landmark now resides on the aptly named Lighthouse Road, but this renaming almost did not happen. The road was also traditionally called Point Road, named after another important island place, Springer's Point. The street-naming committee recommended the latter name become the official name for the street but changed it to Lighthouse Road after a number of residents objected, claiming they had officially designated their property's address as being on Lighthouse Road.

Perhaps no collection of street names is more confusing to visitors than Beach Road, Old Beach Road, Ocean Road, and Ocean View Road. Not one of these roads currently connects to a beach or allows for a view of the ocean. All of these names predate the current street-name configuration of the island. You might think that Old Beach Road was an ocean access road that previously existed but no longer takes you to the beach. In fact, the beach referred to by "Old Beach Road" was not a beach on the ocean, but Bald Beach, an elevated series of sandy dunes near where the Pony Island Inn sits today. It was actually from these dunes that one could see across the marshes all the way to the ocean, which explains why Old Beach Road and Ocean View Road are adjacent. Ocean Road, which is across from School Road, led to the ocean at one time, but that access has long been closed. Beach Road is perhaps the most inaptly named of all. It is a short road behind the bank, not attached to any beach or beach-like area. The road was named in the early twentieth century by promoter of the island, Robert Stanley Wahab (1888–1967), perhaps as part of a development scheme.

The street names of Ocracoke commemorate a wonderful list of notable island individuals, families, fauna, and flora. In fact, a list of street names might make a good checklist for visitors to learn more about the island. While it is no mystery where names like Cedar Drive, Fig Tree Lane, Fish Camp Lane, Horse Pen Road, Live Oak Road, Pintail Road (a type of duck), Widgeon Woods Road (another type of duck), or Terrapin Drive come from, each of these names offer visitors a chance to learn a little more about the island's fauna and flora. Philip Howard maintains a delightful history of every street name on his Village Craftsmen website, but visitors may reconstruct some of the history on their own by combining their observations with a sense of curiosity.

## A WALKING TOUR OF OCRACOKE

Modern GPS systems and signage make the island easily navigable. But they may impede one's understanding of the island's geography and the town's layout. If you travel south on NC Highway 12 from the Hatteras Ferry terminal, the layout is predictable and intuitive. The water to the left is the Atlantic Ocean and the water to the right is the Pamlico Sound. Just before reaching the village, the road sweeps dramatically to the right. Many underestimate just how substantial this turn is, so they can be forgiven when they get to the lighthouse, which is to the left of the highway, and assume that the water they see from there is the Atlantic. It is not. Any water seen from the village is actually the Pamlico Sound.

To get the traditional island experience, put the phone away. Start at the main ferry terminal at the southern terminus of Highway 12. Looking at the harbor, you will find yourself staring at Silver Lake, which is obviously not a true lake. Prior to the dredging of the harbor in 1938, the area was a wide but shallow inlet called Cockle Creek, or simply *the creek*. In fact, ask a local for directions and they are more likely to use the term *creek* than *Silver Lake*. This usage of *creek* reflects a Briticism still in use today, where it denotes a narrow area of water where the sea flows into the land, or an inlet. A number of similar creeks can still be seen along Highway 12, north of the village. The creek was perhaps the geographical anchor point, and used as the basis for two distinct areas, Around Creek, which was the northeastern side of the creek, where the school and community store reside today, and Down Point, which was the southern side of the creek, home to the lighthouse and, historically, Albert Styron's Store. As noted previously, when we first started conducting interviews on Ocracoke, residents informed us that Pointers and Creekers sounded different from each other. Though we never uncovered any linguistic differences between the groups, it does speak to the community's understanding of its neighborhoods that they would hear differences in the voices of neighbors. Connecting Silver Lake to the Pamlico Sound is *the ditch*. From the ferry docks, the visible spit of land across the ditch is known as Windmill Point.

To listen to residents talk about the difference between Creekers and Pointers (from *Ocracoke Speaks*), visit www.ocracokebrogue.com/chapter/3/QR3-1.mp3.

As you travel up the highway, around the harbor, you have Nubbin's Ridge to your left, just beyond where the Anchorage Inn sits today. On an island where the highest point is twenty-eight feet above sea level, even small topographical changes are noteworthy. Walk past British Cemetery Road, which would take you back to

North Pond, a little bay popular with kayakers. Continue winding your way around the harbor until you get to Fig Tree Lane, where you go left and then take the right onto Howard Street, named after the Howards, a prominent island family. Howard Street started its life as a footpath before being widened in 1835 and made a public thoroughfare. It used to just be called the *Main Road.* Now it is one of the last remaining unpaved roads on the island and offers a glimpse into a not-too-distant past (see fig. 3.1). The sandy way is capped by a soaring live-oak canopy and is bordered by a number of tidy family cemetery plots, which chronicle a more than 300-year history of life and death.

Howard Street dead ends at the Methodist Church, which is adjacent to the school. If you turn right and walk back toward the highway, you'll find that School Road ends just feet away from where Lighthouse Road begins. Continuing your journey, you are now walking through the Down Point area, also called Cat Ridge, the second of the two historically main areas of town. About a tenth of a mile past the Assembly of God Church (also called the Lifesaving Church), the road loops around to the area's namesake, Springer's Point, which just so happens to be near the infamous Teach's Hole, where Blackbeard was killed. Springer's Point, in addition to being a common landmark for giving directions, is home to a preserve with a footpath through some dense vegetation that allows visitors a chance to imagine the island's wildness in the early days of its settlement.

Returning to the highway, where you continue north, you are now about to navigate one of the sections of town that tourists find most confusing. Two "newer" sections of the village, Oyster Creek and Jackson Dunes, flank the third original neighborhood, Up Trent. All these sections can be accessed by walking left on Back Road and then taking a right on Sunset Drive (aka Ammunition Dump Road). At the end of this road, you will find Cutting Sage Road to your left and Trent Drive, the namesake for the area known as Up Trent, to the right. Following Cutting Sage Road around a corner, you'll start to see a series of manufactured channels for boats. The process of creating these channels is called

FIGURE 3.1. Howard Street today preserves the traditional style of Ocracoke's roads. Photograph by Jeffrey Reaser.

*breakwatering* by the locals. Channels were dug into the marshy land, shoring up buildable lots. Permanent barriers were erected to keep the sandy soils in place and to create mooring docks for boats. A breakwater is anything intended to stop the water, so even using sandbags to stem the surge of a hurricane is known as breakwatering. This is an extension of the general use of the term *breakwater*, which usually means a permanent structure, but it is also unique in that the word is used as a verb instead of as a noun.

Just past the corner, you will come to the intersection of Cutting Sage and Cuttensage. This intersection probably delights us linguists more than the typical visitor, as there is a little linguistic playfulness found here. Both streets are named after a plant traditionally called *cutting sedge*. The linguistic play is not the change from sedge to sage, but the so-called dropping of the final *g* in the word *cutting*. In fact, the word *cutting* does not contain a *g*-sound at all, but what linguists call an engma (phonetically, /ŋ/). The difference between this sound and the *n*-sound is small, with the latter being made with the tongue behind the teeth and the former made with the tongue further back in the mouth on the palate. Alternating between the words *kin* and *king* should result in a sort of seesaw motion of the tongue as it moves between these two places of articulation. When we look at these two street names phonetically, we conclude that they differ in this one sound. When two words differ by only one sound, linguists call them minimal pairs. Minimal pair analysis is a core methodology in describing a language or dialect. The delight is simply this linguistic knowledge encoded in what might otherwise be thought of as confusing street names.

Crossing over the bridges out toward the sound, you will pass by a number of streets named for iconic island families, including Esham Lane, O'Neal Lane, Styron Lane, and Gaskill Lane. There are many more families and characters to learn about by taking notice of the street names. When the road ends, you might be surprised to learn that you are just a few hundred yards from North Pond, which was observed near the beginning of our journey. Despite this proximity, no roads connect these two sections of the island. It takes a 1.6-mile walk or a 0.25-mile boat ride to get from one to the other.

Here ends our guided tour. There is plenty more to explore and we encourage you to do so. Use your phone not for directions but to take pictures of the village, paying special attention to street signs. Take photos of them so you will be reminded to learn more about the Bryant family, pompanos (a fish), the Odd Fellows Lodge, or any other signs that pique your curiosity and lead you to learn a little more about the island's history. Good luck finding your way back!

We often remember the directions that we received when we first arrived on the island in the early nineties, "Take that road there until you can't go anymore. Turn left on the dirt road and go around a bend and over three small bridges. When you can't go any farther, turn right, and the poker house is the last on the right." And that summarizes how many locals will still give you directions.

## NAVIGATING OUTSIDE THE VILLAGE

When we first started doing fieldwork on Ocracoke, we relied on the locals to tell us who else we should track down for an interview. On one such occasion, we were told we really need to talk to a certain resident, but he was up the beach. Given how often potential interviewees were away from the island or out fishing, we were thrilled to learn that a resident was just up the beach. Our excitement over tracking down the resident was met with confusion. Locally, the phrase *up the beach* means anywhere between Hatteras and Nags Head. Obviously, we did not interview the resident that day. Had the person been where we thought they were, that is, at the beach on Ocracoke, we would have been told he was "across the beach" or "over to the beach." Small prepositional differences make large geographical distinctions. In fact, the whole stretch of island—beaches, the campground, the pony pens—from the edge of the village northward to the ferry terminal is referred to as *down below*.

The term *away* is used to describe being anywhere in the world except on Ocracoke. You can be away up the beach, away to the mainland (used particularly for the non-island parts of North Carolina), or away to anywhere else in the world. Native islanders occasionally move from Ocracoke for a period. They are usually described as *living away*. For example, if an island kid were to attend college at NC State, locals might say, "Katie lives away to Raleigh." This phrase—*live away*—can also refer to a period of time, as in, "They lived away after they got married." Or a combination of place and time, as in, "They lived away to Nags Head for a few years." You can also be away to *down sound*, which refers to the areas near the Core Sound, such as Cedar Island or Harkers Island. Interestingly, as far as we know, you cannot be away to up sound. This term *away* captures something of the indelible imprint of home on islanders: there are only two places in the world, home and away.

The island itself has a number of topographical features with special names. The first part of this chapter detailed places such as the Creek, the ditch, Silver Lake, the Point (Springer's Point), Teach's Hole, and various ridges. In addition to these, older islanders use the term *hill* to refer to a sand dune. A few notable hills include Loop Shack Hill, Styron's Hill and Billy Goat Hill. This usage of hill is seen in conjunction with another toponym oddity at the Hammock Hills Nature Trail, just across from the National Parks Service campground. The history of this term is investigated more in chapter 4, but locally, the term *hammock* is used to refer to a grove of trees. Locals may refer to places such as Cedar Hammock or Old Hammock.

A favorite local pastime involves *taking a scud*; that is, taking a trip around the island. While you can take a scud through the village, most often your scud would take you out to the beach. With the proper permit and vehicle, of course, you might drive across a number of *camel humps* or *camelbacks* (raised sections of sand, caused by the tide) on your way to *South Point*, the southernmost tip of the island where the "channel" connects the Atlantic Ocean with the Pamlico Sound. Here you can look across the channel to Portsmouth. With binoculars you can even pick out some of the old structures on that island. Established in 1753, Portsmouth was, at one time, one of the largest settlements on *the Banks*, and was home to more people than Ocracoke. The last residents left the village in the early 1970s, when the island became part of the National Parks Service. Should you decide to take a scud on the beach, we recommend you pay close attention to the tidal charts. It is better to go at ebb tide (low tide) than to get stuck out in a flood tide (high tide).

If you wish to take a closer look at Portsmouth, you might take a scud over to it. Yes, you can also take a scud by boat. Most of the time, if you are taking a scud by boat, you are just cruising around. You might stick to the *back of the island* (the sound side) or venture out along *the front of the island* (the ocean side). Ideally you would do this on a *slick cam* day (when there's "no waves whatsoever"), but definitely do not try it on a day when "it's blowing harder than a popcock."

To hear islanders describe the use of phrases like "slick cam" and "blowin' harder than a popcock," visit www.ocracokebrogue.com/chapter/3/QR3-2.mp4.

## WHAT TO NOTICE ON YOUR VISIT

In our modern world, place-names might seem like a simple necessity of getting around. But the reality is that nothing is named without some sort of reason, be it historical, cultural, or personal. One of the joys of Ocracoke's place-names is how clearly they illustrate the changes to the island over the past century. Hills and ridges have been leveled, hammocks cut down, and ammunition dumps (mostly) cleaned up. They also highlight what is locally essential: family, heritage, remembrance, and respect for the local environment. In one case, they reflect the islanders' love of language play. This chapter offers only the tip of the iceberg with respect to naming, but we hope that it has sparked a curiosity, much like what the island's place-names sparked in historian C. A. Weslager, who visited the island in 1949 and embarked on a survey of place names, published in the *North Carolina Historical Review* in 1954. So taken by the local names, he wrote of the island, "Perhaps there is no better example in America of the place-name pattern of the earliest English settlers which, due to the isolation of Ocracoke Island, escaped mainland political influence for more than 200 years and still survives." Closing his article, Weslager looks to the future, "If we may be permitted to speculate—we may expect the older place names to be blotted out and supplanted by newer ones." Weslager was correct in that a few names have been replaced, but the biggest change is not one of replacing, but forgetting. There are now very few locals who know all the named bars, shoals, reefs, holes, swashes, creeks, hills, beaches, rocks, lumps, grasses, hammocks, castles, points, woods, ponds, and islands in and around Ocracoke. The community has taken steps to preserve this history. One example was a 2003 publication (now out of print), *The Complete Illustrated Map of Ocracoke Island*, by P. L. Len Skinner and D. Gorman Wells. Another is a digital humanities project called Ocracoke Navigator. While the website does contain commercial offerings, it foregrounds mapped historical content, free audio walking tours, island information, and historical photos. Though the phrase "island time" is mostly associated with a slower pace of life in places like Hawai'i, it is a nice reminder of the hidden richness that emerges when visitors slow down a little and give in to their curiosity about the people and places all around them.

*Chapter 4*

# IS THE BROGUE SHAKESPEAREAN ENGLISH?

When Walt Wolfram arrived at North Carolina State University in 1992, a few of his colleagues told him he needed to visit Ocracoke Island because the older residents there still spoke Elizabethan or Shakespearean English. The theoretical history for this belief is simple: The island was settled by British citizens who left England around the end of Shakespeare's life (the 1610s) for places like Jamestown. These settlers eventually made their way to present-day Ocracoke by 1715. These English transplants then, the story goes, lived in isolation, preserving their Shakespearean English until the tourism boom started in the mid-twentieth century. This lore lives on today; the internet is rife with reputable news outlets with headlines that perpetuate the myth, such as the 2019 BBC article "The US Island that Speaks Elizabethan English," which includes the line "The island's isolation preserved the Hoi Toider dialect, a mix of Elizabethan English, Irish and Scottish accents, and pirate slang" (pirate slang is addressed in the next chapter). An educational media site, Open Culture, conveys a similar perspective in their posting "Meet the Americans Who Speak with Elizabethan English." Then there is this intriguing 1997 headline from the *Baltimore Sun,* "Dialect Mommucked by Tourists' Language: The Endangered Tongue of Ocracoke Island, N.C., Still Cherishes Words Left Over from the Days of Shakespeare." The internet's iterations of discussion boards from Yahoo! to Reddit all have multiple threads treating this belief as truth. So, is it true? Well, mostly no, but like any good myth, it has a kernel of truth.

Consider the timeline of the claim. If we are being persnickety, the first permanent English-speaking colony in what is now the United States, Jamestown, established 1607, was settled during Shakespeare's life, but after Elizabeth's life (1533–1603). But this does not really undermine the veracity of the claim, as those early settlers at Jamestown—some 1,400 people by 1622—would have learned their language squarely in the late-Elizabethan period, and, generally speaking, people's dialects do not change substantially once they reach adulthood.

While this timeline reasonably supports the idea that the early setters could have transplanted Elizabethan English to the new world, the linguistic reality is murkier. Specifically, the question must be asked, what exactly is meant by Elizabethan English? For many people, the answer is the language of the King James Bible, which was commissioned in 1604, shortly after Elizabeth's death, and completed in 1611. The history of this volume is remarkable and involves spelling mistakes and corrections, printing press disputes, fires, disputes over profits, debts, and countless arguments over translations. This turbulent history culminated with the 1769 publishing of the so-called Standard Text of the King James Bible, which is the version most people are familiar with if they are at all familiar with the book. As one might expect, between 1611 and 1769, the language continued to change, and what is recorded in the 1769 version, while certainly distinct from present-day English, is much more modernized than the text of the 1611 version. Thus, one of our anchoring texts for imagining what Elizabethan English was like was not actually written until over 150 years after the end of the Elizabethan period.

What about using Shakespeare's texts as an anchor for defining Elizabethan English? This is perhaps a better starting point, provided we look back to the earliest collections of Shakespeare's writing, such as the *First Folio*, compiled in 1623, seven years after his death. To the modern reader, the language of the *First Folio* likely seems homogeneous; however, to a linguist, it is clear that Shakespeare's characters were crafted to reflect the dialect diversity of his time. In fact, some characters even shift between dialects as a way of ingratiating themselves to others, usually as a means manipulation. There are a few points here. The Elizabethan English myth is built on the idea that it was a prestigious way of speaking, which would single out the dialect that was used among the social elites in the courts. These aristocrats were one of the audiences Shakespeare wrote for, and voiced in his plays, but they were not the majority of English speakers during that time-period. Just like today, dialect differences—both social and regional—were found throughout the English-speaking Elizabethan world. While there were a few social elites among the early arrivals to the New World, most of the settlers of the Outer Banks were not of this social class. In fact, the early settlers tended to be ship pilots and crew, fishermen, farmers, or debtors trying to avoid debtors' prisons. That is, working class rather than social elites. Even if the community's founders fit into the Elizabethan English timeline, they do not fit the social profile of what is thought of as the typical speaker of Elizabethan English.

To hear Ellen Cloud's account of the early British settlers from *Ocracoke Speaks*], visit www.ocracokebrogue.com/chapter/4/QR4-1.mp3.

At this point, you might be thinking, "Well, sure, it's not technically Elizabethan English, but isn't it still an earlier form of English preserved by the centuries of isolation?" The short but unsatisfying answer is, not exactly. As noted previously, the settlers who came to what would eventually be called Ocracoke hailed from disparate backgrounds. When groups of people with diverse dialects come to live in a place, there is often a period of language shift over a few generations whereby what was more diverse becomes more unified. Certainly, some of those early dialects would have been influential, but right from the beginning, Ocracoke would have developed a way a speaking that deviated from the various dialects that were brought to the island.

As we describe in more detail in chapter 6, the influx of settlers did not stop after the initial wave of settlers. In addition to the early English settlers, a second group had an important impact on the development of the Brogue. Between 250,000 and 500,000 Scots-Irish immigrants, mostly fleeing Ulster Plantation, arrived in Philadelphia between 1700 and 1820. It should be noted that *Scots-Irish* does not simply mean "Scottish and Irish," however. The term refers to diverse groups that emigrated from the Ulster Plantation. Many of these immigrants traveled the Great Wagon Road and settled in large areas of the Appalachian region. Others left by boat and settled along the Outer Banks, including on Ocracoke. The dialects that these speakers brought were quite different from the early English dialects that were originally brought to the island, and they resulted in some substantial changes to the local way of speaking. This "second settlement" period delivers a knockout blow to the claim that Elizabethan English has been preserved by the islanders.

Even without this second settlement, however, it is not the case that the original language of Ocracoke would have remained unchanged over the centuries. While isolation can slow language change, every living language is in a constant state of change. In a closed community, linguists still find substantial variation among the speech of individual residents. In fact, one study of isolated islands off the coast of Ireland even found there to be more linguistic variation in these small communities than is typical in much larger, more diverse communities. One theory as to why this is the case is that in a small community, everyone already knows other people's individual and family status, and so language is less important for conveying one's social identity. Regardless of the reasons, all available data point to the same conclusion: no living language is static, so there are exactly zero modern speakers of Elizabethan English found in Ocracoke—or anywhere else.

## WHAT WAS ELIZABETHAN ENGLISH LIKE?

Now that we have thoroughly rained on the Elizabethan English myth, imagine for a moment just what it would sound like if the residents of Ocracoke really did preserve Elizabethan English for all these years. Some of the language would resonate strongly with the Brogue, such as the robust pronunciation of the *r*-sound in words like *bear* and *fear*. Early dialects of the inland South tended to drop these sounds, much like modern broadcast British English (what is sometimes called Received Pronunciation or RP—think of the language heard from presenters on the BBC). But other language features would be glaringly different. Two of these are examined in the following paragraphs.

The Elizabethan English period saw an important grammatical shift take place. Prior to this time, English speakers used *you/ye*, *your*, or *yours* when addressing or talking about groups, similar to how Southerners might use *y'all*, *all y'all*, or *y'all's* today (or how Northerners might use *you guys*). For addressing or talking about a single person, these speakers would have used *thou*, *thee*, or *thy/thine*. Though initiated earlier, the Elizabethan period coincided with a major shift where the pronouns reflected not just the singular or plural nature of the subject, but also captured politeness. This system was identical to that used in modern Spanish or French, where speakers use *usted* as a polite version of *tú* (in Spanish) or *vous* instead of *tu* (in French). English speakers of this period often used *you* as a polite replacement for singular *thou*. This might seem backward at first, as many people think that *thou* sounds more formal than *you*. This is merely a product of familiarity. The only times we tend to encounter *thou* in our modern world is when reading one of these older, formal texts (like Shakespeare or the King James Bible). Any dialect that has truly preserved Elizabethan English would still be using *thou*, *thee*, *thy*, and *thine*.

Elizabethan English speakers also treated their verbs quite differently than we do in modern English. A phrase like "he jumpeth every time you sneezest" demonstrates this clearly. Again, this language might evoke Biblical or Shakespearean texts, and it highlights just how different the language of that period was from what we hear even in the speech of isolated communities. In this case, verbs in the present tense following second-person singular subjects (*thou* [informal] and *you* [formal]) required the ending *-est*, while verbs following third-person singular subjects (*he*, *she*, and *it*) took an *-eth* ending. In present day English, we maintain part of this convention, adding an *-s* to present-tense verbs following third-person singular subjects ("he *jumpS* every time you sneeze"). Curiously, the modern convention for third-person subjects (*-s*) is more similar to the Elizabethan convention for second person subjects (*-est*) than it is for third-person subjects (*-eth*).

Given all this proof that the "preserved Elizabethan English" belief is myth, why does it persist? Perhaps most importantly, it is a romantic myth that lends credibility to a unique way of speaking and living that is quite different from the norm; and it is a positive myth, since British English is still considered to be more prestigious than American English. There is no denying that part of the lore of Ocracoke is—for English speakers in the New World—its deep history. That cultural-historic tradition does include a distinctive variety of English; it does have some vestiges or older forms of language that have fallen out of use elsewhere. Some of these uses do extend to older forms of English that were used during the period inhabited by Shakespeare. So, there is a kernel of truth that is found in this statement.

## WHAT HAS BEEN PRESERVED FROM EARLIER FORMS OF ENGLISH?

In this section, we detail a few things that are preservations of earlier forms of English. Some of these features can be traced back to the Elizabethan period, but others cannot. In some sense, it does not really matter when the feature was used. What is important is merely that something once common in English has been preserved in Ocracoke—and sometimes other communities—while falling out of use in mainstream English. Many of these features are described in more detail in the chapters on grammar, pronunciation, and vocabulary, so here they are presented mostly as illustrations of the language fossils found on the island.

One grammatical feature that can be traced back to the Elizabethan age is the use of an *a*-prefix (pronounced "uh") with some *-ing* verbs, as in "She was a-hunting and a-fishing." Historically, this construction derived from the preposition *on* or *at*, which was used with *-ing* verbs. For example, Thomas Nashe's novel *The Unfortunate Traveler* (1594) contains the line "hee set before his eyes king Henrie the eight with all his Lordes *on hunting* in his forrest at Windsore" (emphasis added). That preposition *on* reduced to the "uh" sound and resulted in "a-hunting," which was then carried to the New World by the Scots-Irish and preserved in both the Outer Banks and the Appalachian Mountain region, as well as other remote regions. For this reason, the Brogue has more in common with the dialects of Appalachia than with those of the Piedmont, Coastal Plain, or Low Land dialects of South Carolina, such as that heard in Charleston, as is illustrated in figure 4.1.

A few pronunciation features found in the Brogue that were previously more widespread in many English dialects include the addition of a *t*-sound to the end of words like *once* and *twice*, which would sound like "oncet" and "twicet." A second preserved pronunciation is in words where the unstressed *o*-sounds at the end of words are changed to sound more like *er*, so that *yellow*, *fellow*, and *hollow* sound more like "yeller," "feller," and "holler." Finally, the collapse of some two-syllable words into single-syllable pronunciations, as in "far" for *fire* and "flar" for *flour*, can also be traced to an earlier, widespread usage that has subsequently changed in mainstream English forms. But none of these pronunciations can be thought of as Elizabethan in origin. Even the iconic vowels of the Hoi Toid Brogue were once more common, but, again, not Elizabethan in origin.

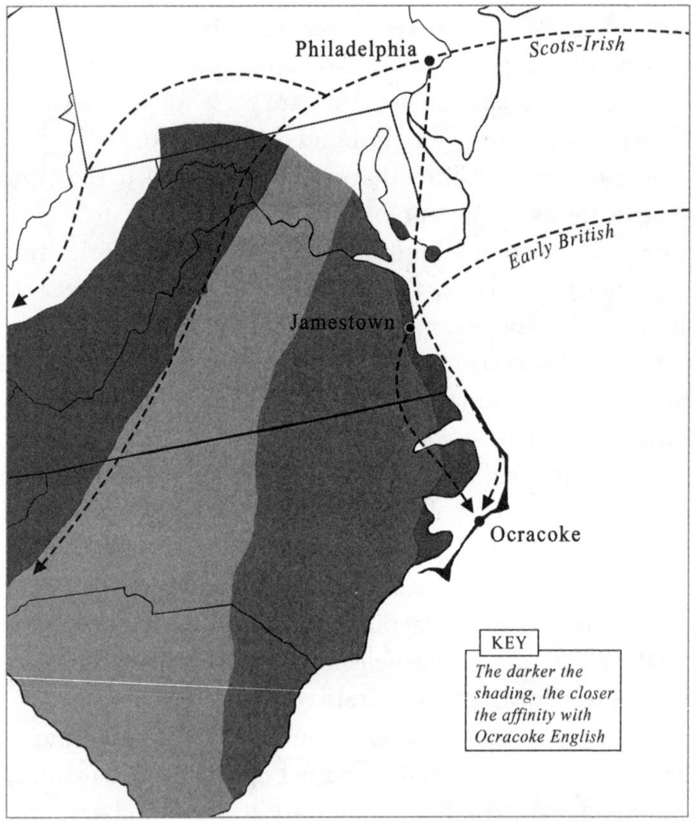


FIGURE 4.1. Ocracoke's Brogue has more in common with the dialects of Appalachia than those of the Piedmont or coastal South Carolina. Map drawn by Danica Cullinan.

Linguists often note that words are the easiest thing to add to a dialect, and dialects routinely add words related to the local environment, ecology, economy, and culture. However, in addition to these additions to the language, the Brogue has preserved a few words that have fallen out of use in other English dialects. One of the most robustly used examples of this is *mommuck* (also spelled *mammock*, *mommick*, *mommock*, and *mammick*), which locally means to harass, especially playfully, as in, "My brother was mommucking me all afternoon!" The term can also be used to describe being battered by storms, the sea, or other events, as in, "Dorian sure mommucked the island" or "I thought that storm was gonna mommuck me to death!" This is a word that was used in the Elizabethan period but has subsequently fallen out of use in most dialects of English. Shakespeare used it in his play *Coriolanus*: "Whether his fall enraged him, or how 'twas, he did so set his teeth and tear it; O, I warrant it, how he mammocked it!" This earlier definition—to tear or shred—was broadened on Ocracoke, where it tends to be used as a metaphorical tearing or shredding. With this in mind, the *Baltimore Sun* headline from earlier, "Dialect Mommucked by Tourists' Language" is, perhaps, cleverer than it seemed initially.

One additional vocabulary holdover from this period can be found on the little hiking trail located just across the highway from the National Parks Service campground. The name *Hammock Hills Nature Trail* may never have stood out as unusual, but it is a linguistic curiosity. This section of the island is the highest and most densely forested. As such, you would not be wrong to assume that it is a good place to hang a hammock (don't forget your bug spray!), but you would be wrong if you assumed that was the source of the name. While *hammock*—as in what you hang up between trees to relax in—came into English from the Spanish *hamaca*, English previously had the word *hummock* (which was often spelled *hommock* or *hammock*), which likely came from German *humpel* ("hump"). The *Oxford English Dictionary*—the preeminent historical dictionary of English—defines the original English usage of this term from the late sixteenth century as "a name given by mariners to a hillock, or small eminence of land resembling the figure of a cone and appearing on the seacoast of any country"—in other words, a raised area surrounded by a level surface, which perfectly describes Ocracoke's Hammock Hill.

Ocracoke has plenty of other old-timey-sounding vocabulary that is not Elizabethan. Islanders may use *tote* instead of *carry*, *poke* instead of *sack*, or use the term *begombed* (also spelled *begaumed*) to mean soiled with sticky residue, all of which evoke a previous time. A few terms draw from way earlier than the Elizabethan period, such as the term *token*, which in local parlance means "a bad omen or a sign of impending death." This specific usage can be traced back to the tenth century and seems to have fallen out of use in most English dialects by the nineteenth century. This example highlights something important about English vocabulary: most of the words we use in English today have a long history, and so we tend not to think of them as being associated with a specific time period. The only thing remarkable about *token* is that other dialects stopped using it. Many other words, like *cow* or *go* are just as old, but we do not note them as unusual, because they are still a part of the general parlance.

To hear Rudy Austin tell a story about a "token of death"[from *Ocracoke Speaks*], visit www.ocracokebrogue.com/chapter/4/QR4-2.mp3.

## IS THERE A DOWNSIDE TO THIS MYTH?

While there is nothing inherently harmful about this myth, on occasion visitors miss what is truly unique about the community when they bring their assumptions to the island. One humorous but somewhat aggravating example involved a television crew from the British Broadcasting Company (BBC) who came to the island believing they would be hearing Elizabethan English. What better way to capture the glory of an almost lost tongue than to have these speakers read the words of the Bard? The crew filmed residents of Ocracoke reciting lines from Shakespeare's plays, thinking they were capturing how the actors of the Globe Theater would have said those same words 400 years earlier. Comically, at least to us, some of the residents of Ocracoke put on their best British accents, not their Brogues, to read the lines. Others, however, found the request somewhat insulting and would have no part of it. The crew produced the story they assumed to be true, and missed entirely the reality of what was right in front of them. They thought the isolation was the star of the story when it was actually the local culture.

While we have not yet taken on pirate slang, what do we make of the BBC caption that described the situation as, "The island's isolation preserved the Hoi Toider dialect, a mix of Elizabethan English, Irish and Scottish accents, and pirate slang"? On the one hand, there is some truth to it. There are preservations from Elizabethan English and the Scots-Irish settlers. On the other hand, all dialects of English have preserved *most* of the language from the Elizabethan period, so the BBC's description is actually an apt description of all dialects of English. Certainly, there are differences in what has been preserved, what has been lost, and what has been changed, but no dialect can claim to have a monopoly on preserving the English of an earlier time. What is most important here is not the linguistic absurdity embedded in the myth, but the power the myth has for conveying something about the special status of residents of Ocracoke and their way of speaking. Saying it is Elizabethan English is really a way of saying "this inherited cultural history is important and should be celebrated." While that is not the sort of claim that lends itself to factual verification, we certainly believe it to be true.

## *Chapter 5*

# IS THE BROGUE PIRATE TALK?

If you read the previous chapter, you can probably guess the answer to this chapter's title question is "no." Or, at least, that it's not *just* pirate talk. But walking around the village, it is clear the community has embraced the pirate legacy from its early days. Vestiges of this heritage are manifested in Blackbeard's Lodge, the Pirate's Chest, Teach's Hole Blackbeard exhibit, the annual Blackbeard's Pirate Jamboree, and the 1718 Brewery. This last one might be less obvious, but it too is rooted in pirate history, as 1718 was the year Blackbeard was killed, right off the coast of the island. The brewery also uses imagery from Blackbeard's pirate flag on its merchandise, as do other businesses, including the Mexican food truck Eduardo's. It is clear the island—even its most recent arrivals—has embraced its pirate past. Did it also embrace any pirate language? It turns out the answer to this question is more complicated than a simple "no." Before we get to that question, we should take a moment to explore the pirate history and lore of Ocracoke.

## PIRATES ON OCRACOKE

The Golden Age of Piracy spanned roughly from the mid-seventeenth century to the early eighteenth century. During this time, Ocracoke Island became a well-known spot for pirates to replenish supplies, make repairs, and divide their plunder. The sparsely inhabited island, with its many creeks and coves, made for an excellent place to hide from authorities. But the big draw was the channel between Ocracoke and Portsmouth. Keep in mind that it was not until a hurricane in 1846 that the Hatteras and Oregon Inlets were opened permanently, meaning that there were no consistently navigable inlets from Ocracoke northward all the way to Roanoke (see fig. 5.1). This meant the channel south of Ocracoke was the major route for ships carrying goods to the mainland. The other primary way to access the mainland was via "haul overs," such as the one at what is now called Haulover Day Use Area, near Avon. Since this area is only 150 yards wide, it was possible to haul some small vessels from the ocean to the sound via rollers.

Stede Bonnet was one notable pirate linked to Ocracoke Island. Often called the "Gentleman Pirate," Bonnet had a secret hideout on the island. He was eventually captured and brought to trial in Charleston, South Carolina, where he was convicted and executed in 1718.

Edward Teach, better known as Blackbeard, was the most famous pirate associated with Ocracoke Island. But his operations were not limited to Ocracoke; his exploits extended throughout the Caribbean. Though details are scarce, his piracy may have only lasted a few years, potentially only from 1716 to 1718, during which he commanded the forty-gun vessel *Queen Anne's Revenge*. His ventures on the island were brief but profitable. On Ocracoke, he was known to blockade the entrance to Ocracoke Inlet and ambush passing ships.

In May 1718, Blackbeard blockaded one of England's most important ports in the New World, Charlestown, South Carolina, an audacious undertaking. His bold move initially paid off when, after threats of extreme violence, he bartered peace for medical supplies for his crew; however, this maneuver made Blackbeard a marked man. From there, Teach sailed to North Carolina. He spent time in other parts of coastal North Carolina, including Bath, but Ocracoke became his base. It was here that Lieutenant Robert Maynard tracked the pirate, and at daybreak on November 22, 1718, engaged

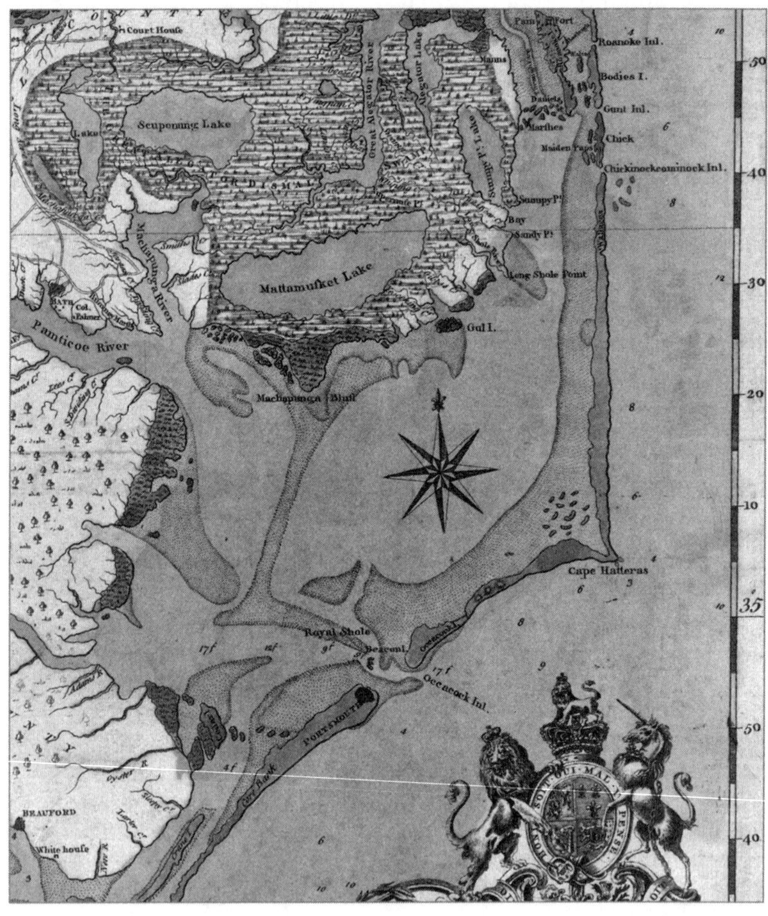


FIGURE 5.1. Detail of Collet's 1770 "A Compleat [*sic*] Map of North-Carolina from an Actual Survey" showing the Hatteras Inlet as closed. Courtesy of the Library of Congress.

him and his crew. The surprise worked, and though the battle was bloody on both sides, eventually Maynard and his crew killed Blackbeard. Maynard noted that Blackbeard's body had been shot five times and cut by swords about twenty times. They decapitated him, tossing his body into the inlet and keeping his head so as to be able to claim the £400 reward (the equivalent of £67,000 today, which would exchange for nearly $90,000).

This early morning battle has produced a local myth about the island's name. According to legend, Blackbeard arose and saw Maynard's approaching sloops. He tried to wake his crew, who were sleeping off the libations from the previous night. Unable to rouse a sufficient number of sailors, Blackbeard is said to have wailed, "Old cock crow!" in hopes that the rooster would crow and awaken the seamen. Though this story is apocryphal—Ocracoke in fact comes from the Algonquian Indians, as we explain in chapter 1—it does illustrate just how entwined pirate history is with the island.

To hear Charlie Williams recount this apocryphal story of how Ocracoke got its name [from *Ocracoke Speaks*], visit www.ocracokebrogue.com/chapter/5/QR5-1.mp3.

## PIRATE TALK

September 19 is International Talk Like a Pirate Day. Created in 1995 by John Baur (aka Ol' Chumbucket) and Mark Summers (a.k.a. Cap'n Slappy), the holiday began its rise to prominence after it was promoted by the likes of humorist Dave Barry and musician Tom Smith. Perhaps the moment that awareness of the day really soared was in 2008, when Facebook introduced a pirate-talk translation of the website. Instead of the traditional post-prompt, "What's on your mind?" the site asked, "What arrr ye doin' right now?" The "Home" link was relabeled, "Home Port," the "Friends" link became, "Me Hearties," and "Messages" became, "Bottle o'messages." A number of additional pirate-themed words and phrases appeared in other places on the site, including "News Ahoy!," "Plank Hangin's," "Ye hast invitations!," and "Crow's

Nest." In addition to the many idiosyncratic changes, a few patterns emerge that highlight just what people in the modern world think pirate talk sounded like. First, as illustrated in a number of examples above, we can conclude that pirates used *ye* instead of *you* and *me* instead of *my*. The former connects pirate talk with one of the Elizabethan English features discussed in the previous chapter. Second, pirates maintained verb endings similar to those used in Elizabethan English. This makes some sense, given that the Golden Age of Piracy, roughly 1650 to 1726, followed soon after Elizabeth's reign. Third, and perhaps most salient, it is clear that pirates had robust *r*-sounds in their speech, visually represented on Facebook with three *r*'s where standard English has just one, as in *arrr* for *are*. In fact, the *r*-sounds are so robust that they even show up where English has no such sound, as in "arrrnouncements" and simply as an interjection, as in "Arrr! Ye have been skewered by . . ." (this was when "poking" was still a part of Facebook).

The first two of the linguistic features described above are reasonably thought to be part of pirate talk, given the period under consideration here. The third one deserves just a bit more investigation. Before looking at the linguistics, it is worth asking, Why is it that we all know what a pirate sounds like despite—at least for the vast majority of people—not ever meeting a single real pirate? Cultural researchers suggest that the archetype for the modern notion of a pirate is Robert Newton's 1950 portrayal of Long John Silver in the Disney adaptation of *Treasure Island*. Newton was a British actor from Shaftesbury, Dorset, in the southwestern part of England. Located on the English Channel, this county, along with Devon and Cornwall, its neighbors to the west, was known as the home of smugglers and pirates. It is said that for his role, Newton simply exaggerated his West Country accent, including strongly pronouncing the *r*-sounds after a vowel in words like *bear* or *fair*. Even today, while much of British English now says these as *bea'* and *fai'*, most West Country dialects have preserved the earlier form with the *r* pronounced robustly. Newton's iconic portrayals of pirates did not end with Long John Silver, however. He then played Edward Teach (Blackbeard) in the 1952 film *Blackbeard the Pirate* before reanimating Long John Silver in the film *Long John Silver* and spinoff TV series *The Adventures of Long John Silver*. He is now the "patron saint of International Talk Like a Pirate Day," and his iconic portrayals of these pirates may be the main reason we all seem to imagine the same thing when it comes to pirate talk.

The language of the area Newton is from, along with the counties to the west, is referred to as West Country English, and was quite different from the English spoken in the Elizabethan courts. It is influenced by both Welsh and Cornish, two languages from different language families than the West Saxon language (a Germanic language) that provided the skeleton for modern day West Country English. Some of these differences are preserved in pirate talk, such as the generalization of "be" where other dialects use *am*, *is*, or *are*. Thus, phrases like "I be a swabbin' the deck" or "he be a tyrant" are rooted in historical linguistic accuracy. However, it is important to note that these constructions do not occur in the Ocracoke Brogue, so even if local pirates once used these forms on the island, they have not been incorporated into the Brogue as we know it today.

The iconic vowels of Ocracoke, as in *hoi toid* and the pronunciation of *sound* as *saind*, are a part of West Country English; however, given that many early settlers trace their lineage to the West Country, it is more likely that the vowels were transplanted by settlers than they were adopted from pirates. That said, these pronunciations, if used properly, would make one more authentic-sounding on International Talk Like a Pirate Day.

The *r*-sound is certainly the most iconic feature of pirate talk. Indeed, West Country dialects traditionally maintained a robust *r*-pronunciation (linguistics call this "rhotic"), even though it has been receding in recent years to align more with modern British norms. Ocracoke's Brogue is and has been a rhotic dialect, contrasting with many inland southern dialects. However, it is overly simplistic to say this is more evidence of the influence of West Country English forms, as even the dialects of London were rhotic during the time Shakespeare wrote and did not shift toward non-rhotic pronunciations until sometime later.

The most rhotic of all pirate expressions is the interjection usage of *arr*. This word can express approval, triumph, disappointment, warning, or any number of other things. It can sometimes begin with a *y*-sound, as in *yarr*. The *Oxford English Dictionary*, the most authoritative historical dictionary of the language, traces the origin of *ar* as an interjection (chiefly used in British English) back only to 1905. The pirate version, spelled with an extra *r*, is first documented in the *Daily Mail* on August 5, 1966: "[Caption to a cartoon showing a swordfish dressed as a pirate, addressing a smaller swordfish] Arr . . . Jim lad!" The next citation goes all in on the rhoticity and mentions our actor friend. Writing in the 1983 book *Children's Novels and the Movies*, Perry Nodelman notes, "For the last thirty years, Robert Newton in a three-cornered hat . . . his mouth half-smiling and half-sneering as he deliciously growls 'Arrrrh, me 'arties,' has been everybody's idea of Long John Silver." It turns out, again, that perhaps the most iconic example of all pirate talk was merely an invention by a charismatic actor from the West Country.

Though our modern world has a singular notion of what a pirate sounded like, there is a lot more to this history than simply assuming all pirates sounded the same. For example, it is estimated that around 30 percent of pirates were of African origin, including enslaved and non-enslaved Africans. Irish speakers also made up a contingent of pirates in the seventeenth and eighteenth centuries. In some cases, these Irish pirates began as indentured servants whose ships were pirated, with both human and nonhuman cargo taken. A few notorious pirates were also of different nationalities, including Olivier Levasseur, aka "The Buzzard" (French); Hendrick Quintor (Black Dutch); and Roche Braziliano (Dutch). Because pirating was so lucrative, pirates of the time came from all over the globe, including Italy, Spain, Portugal, Greece, China, Japan. And of course, though we tend to associate pirate talk with the speech of men, it should be noted that there were plenty of infamous women pirates, including Anne Bonny and Mary Read.

## PIRATE TALK ON OCRACOKE

Ocracoke's most famous pirate, Blackbeard, was thought to have been born Edward Teach in about 1680 (at least according to some histories). It was common practice for pirates to not use their real names, so Blackbeard's true identity and origin remain a mystery. It is thought he originated somewhere around Bristol, which is just north of the area typically associated with West Country English. In that area, there are several similar surnames, including Thatch, Thach, Thache, Thack, Tack, Thatche, and Theach, though Teach is the most common, which is why that is the spelling typically used for Blackbeard's ostensible given name. The pirate probably did not even use the name *Blackbeard* himself; the moniker comes from Henry Bostock, who was taken captive when Teach ransacked the *Margaret*, the merchant ship of which Bostock was captain. Bostock later wrote that Teach was a "tall spare man with a very black beard which he wore very long." This description inspired many posthumous portrayals, including Charles Johnson's 1724 description as "such a figure that imagination cannot form an idea of a fury from hell to look more frightful." Six years after his death, Blackbeard's notoriety began to eclipse his reputation while he was alive.

Just as mysterious as Teach's origin, then, is what Ocracoke's most notorious pirate actually sounded like. Regardless, what is clear from this brief history is that Blackbeard's—and all pirates'—legacy on Ocracoke is cultural, not linguistic. For example, Chester Lynn, from his family's long-standing legacy on the island, claims that a couple of his ancestors served with Blackbeard. Chester has salvaged antiques that came from Blackbeard's camp on Ocracoke, enhancing the legend of the infamous pirate on Ocracoke.

Pirates were simply too diverse as a group to support the claim that there even was something that could coherently be called "pirate talk." And the transient lives of these pirates probably meant that the islanders did not adopt many, if any, linguistic traits from them. None of this diminishes the importance of the pirate legacy on Ocracoke. Like any good history, there are larger-than-life characters, mystery, and intrigue. There are just enough knowns to weave the speculations into a fantastic tale, one that Ocracokers are proud of and occasionally exploit. Much like how their Brogue is a key part of O'Cockers' cultural capital, the pirate legacy on Ocracoke is one more piece of the lore that makes the island such an intriguing place.

*Chapter 6*

# WHERE DID THE BROGUE COME FROM?

The previous two chapters were about where the Brogue did *not* come from, but they hinted strongly at the answer to this chapter's title. This chapter offers a fuller history of the island's dialect, which is also a brief history of its people.

## WHY OCRACOKE?

Today, Ocracoke may be best known for its beaches, but early English colonists were less interested in working on their tans than they were in the strategic passage to mainland North Carolina between what are now Ocracoke and Portsmouth Islands. At that time, though there were small breaks in the chain of barrier islands north of Ocracoke, few of these channels were consistently navigable. South of Jamestown, Virginia, there were two channels that provided strategically important passages. One, a channel near present-day Nags Head, allowed passage to Roanoke Island

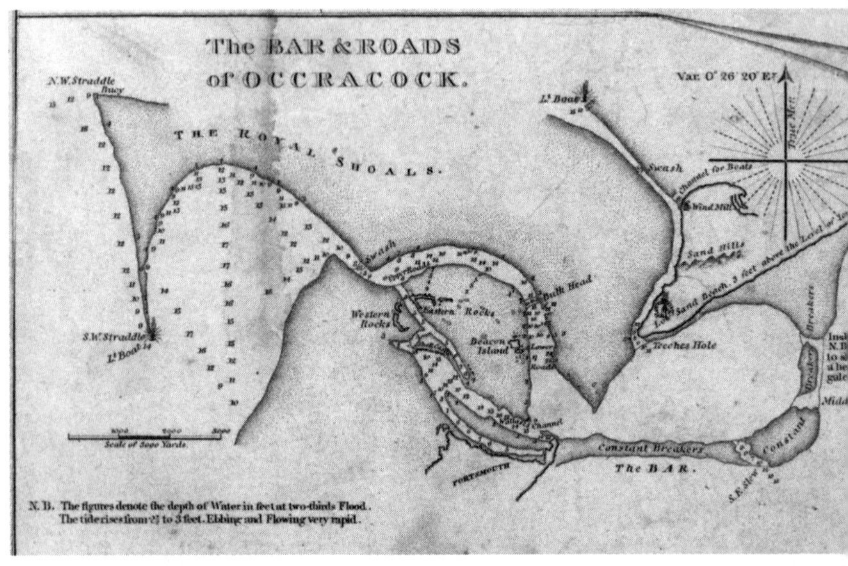


FIGURE 6.1. Inset map from William Hooker's 1846–1850 "Coast of the United States of North America from Cape Hatteras to Cape Fear North Carolina" detailing the channel's hazards. Courtesy of the North Carolina Collection, Wilson Special Collections Library, University of North Carolina at Chapel Hill.

(present-day Manteo) and, eventually, Edenton (established 1712). The other was the channel south of Ocracoke, which allowed access to the mainland, including the towns of Bath, the first permanent European settlement in what is now North Carolina, established in 1705, New Bern (1710), and Beaufort (1713).

The channel south of Ocracoke was not an easy passageway to navigate (see fig. 6.1). The tides could be strong and the water rough enough to conceal many obstacles. The North Carolina colonial government passed in 1715 "An Act for Settling and Maintaining Pilots at Roanoke and Ocacock Inlett [*sic*]" to ensure a continuous population of ship pilots to help boats navigate the channel. Pilot Town persisted as a hangout for pirates and ship pilots for a number of decades until it was renamed Ocracoke in 1753 and was recognized as a town that was home to some twenty to thirty families. This same year, Portsmouth was established on the south side of the channel.

## OCRACOKE SETTLEMENT

By about 1770, Ocracoke and Portsmouth were well-established communities. Essential for understanding the origins of the Brogue is tracing where these settlers came from. The oldest island families, with surnames including Bragg, Gaskins, Howard, Jackson, Stiron (spelled Styron today), and Williams, likely came from England through the Tidewater area of Virginia, which began to receive British settlers starting with the establishment of Jamestown in 1607. The exact origins in English of Jamestown's first governor, Sir Thomas Gates, and its most famous early citizen, John Rolfe (husband to Pocahontas), are disputed, which leaves their linguistic heritage mysterious. However, the dialects of the earliest settlers are not crucial to this history, as the mortality rate at the colony—from starvation, disease, and Indian uprisings—was so substantial that the colony's charter was revoked in 1624 by King James I. It was not until the mid-seventeenth century that Virginia's population began climbing quickly, growing from 8,000 in 1642 to 40,000 in 1677. This population included freed English, white indentured servants, and enslaved Africans. The English dialectal milieu of this period likely featured speakers of English dialects from southwestern England and East Anglia, the area just northeast of London. These regions were among England's most strongly seafaring regions, so it makes sense that they may have factored heavily in the settlement of the coastal areas of the New World. It is likely these dialects formed the backbone of the dialect that was brought to Ocracoke in the late seventeenth century. Irish immigrants also made up a significant proportion of the early arrivals in the Jamestown region. These settlers lived alongside the other groups and likely influenced the emerging dialect. Groups of early English and Irish settlers left Jamestown by boat and established enclaves along the coast. It is likely that this pattern of settlement gave Ocracoke the prominent O'Neal and Scarborough families.

A second linguistic influence on the island came later, when additional Irish and Scots-Irish settlers began arriving to the New World en masse, with the plurality arriving in the second half of the eighteenth century. The Scots-Irish were a diverse group bound together most strongly by Ulster Plantation, in what is now Northern Ireland. These settlers were driven from the Ulster Plantation due to religious tension, trade restrictions and tariffs, droughts, a bovine disease called "rot," and smallpox. They arrived primarily in Philadelphia, where most then moved inland and settled along the Great Valley, the fertile planes along the Susquehanna River. Eventually land ran sparse in this area, and later groups went farther south, settling in the Shenandoah Valley to the west and eventually followed the Great Wagon Road to settle in the North Carolina mountains. As land along the Great Wagon Road became more densely inhabited, other Scots-Irish immigrants left Philadelphia by boat and settled in the coastal communities, including Ocracoke. As Ocracoke and Portsmouth grew, they attracted settlers from other places along the Outer Banks and the mainland, including the Austin, Ballance, and Midgette families.

## THE REACH OF OCRACOKE ENGLISH

The history above suggests that the Brogue does not have a single source but is a mix of English dialects. Many of the most prominent features of the dialect can be traced back to two main sources: the dialects of the West Country of England and the Gaelic-influenced English of the Scots-Irish. Before examining these in more detail, it is important to consider the scope of this early dialect. Ocracoke might be the most well-known Hoi Toider community, but it is not the only one. Similar ways of speaking can still be heard in communities along the Core Sound, including Harkers Island, Marshallberg, Stacey, Sea Level, and Atlantic. Heading north, the dialects of

Smith Island, Maryland, and Tangier Island, Virginia, are also quite similar to what is heard on Ocracoke. We have even documented the Brogue in mainland Hyde County, North Carolina, among both white residents and the oldest African American residents.

To listen to speakers of Smith Island, visit www.ocracokebrogue.com/chapter/6/QR6-1.mp3.

To hear an elderly African American Speaker from mainland Hyde County who has elements of the Brogue, visit www.ocracokebrogue.com/chapter/6/QR6-2.mp3.

What we now think of as the Ocracoke Brogue or the Outer Banks dialect used to be spoken throughout the coastal areas of Virginia, Maryland, and North Carolina. Though geographically close, Charleston, South Carolina, had a very different history and dialect; instead of saying *time* as "toim," Charleston speakers would say something more like "tahm." The *r*-sound is another important difference. Throughout the Tidewater region, the *r*-sound in words like *far* and *mother* were pronounced, but in the areas around Charleston, SC, the *r* sound would be dropped, resulting in "fah" and "motha." Though not identical, the traditional dialects of North Carolina's Piedmont and Coastal Plain regions had more in common with the Charleston dialect than they did the coastal dialect, as was depicted in figure 4.1. As will be discussed below, because of the Scots-Irish influence both in the Appalachian Mountains and along the coast, the dialects from the two ends of the state have more in common with each other than they do with the dialects in between.

Today, it is almost impossible to hear the traditional Brogue along the northern Outer Banks. But the oldest lifelong residents of Hatteras still maintain a distinctly British-sounding pronunciation of the town as "Hah-triss" rather than the now more common "Hah-der-is." The story here is probably clear enough, but important: Tourism came earlier to places like Hatteras than it did to places like Ocracoke. Tourism is still not the primary economic driver in communities along the Core Sound or in Smith Island, Maryland. These places have remained insulated from the "dialect swamping" that inundated other communities in this region such as Hatteras and, more recently, Ocracoke. As for the communities in mainland Hyde County, echoes of the Brogue can still be heard in the white residents, but the African American residents have looked to the speech of more urban areas where models of speaking are available to index an African American identity. Chapter 10 investigates in more detail the historical usage of the Brogue by a Black island family.

## THE STORY OF THE BROGUE

Many of the pronunciations and grammatical patterns that make the Brogue distinct likely originated from English settlers from England's West Country and the subsequent Scots-Irish settlers from Ulster Plantation. A number of these are investigated in more detail in chapters 10 (pronunciations) and 11 (grammar). A few words can also be traced to these dialects as well. In this chapter, we highlight only a few distinctive features and trace their origins.

To understand the roots of Ocracoke's dialect, it is worth starting with the language picture in England during the period of British exploration and settlement. Though linguists quibble over precise dates, the Early Modern English period is bookended by two important changes related to literacy. The start of this period coincides with William Caxton's setting up the first printing press in England in 1476, radically changing the cost and availability of print materials. The period is bookended by Samuel Johnson's *A Dictionary of the English Language*, published in 1755. Both events would have acted to standardize language or slow language change. Essentially, the printing press elevated the dialects of London as the standard, and the dictionary standardized spellings that were largely unstandardized previously. Then, as literacy increased, these standards would become more important across England.

Despite these pressures, it is critical to note that at no point was all the English in England the same. Historical linguistics research allows us to conclude that some parts of the Brogue are remnants from English as it was generally spoken in the Early Modern English period, while other parts suggest origins in regional varieties of English dialects from that period. These latter conclusions are more speculative than the former.

## THE GRAMMATICAL ROOTS

Though the most distinctive aspects of the dialect may be its pronunciations, the story of the Brogue is best told by starting with a few grammatical notes. Grammar tends to be less variable than pronunciations among dialects. It also usually changes a little more slowly. Because of this, the grammatical features of the Brogue tend to trace back to those more widespread British patterns noted above. Generally, these patterns are noticeable now because the rest of English has changed whereas the Brogue has not. Perhaps the most notable example is how older Brogue speakers sometimes add an *a-* (pronounced "uh") to the start of some verbs that end in *-ing*, as in, "She's a-fishing today." This form derives from the Early Modern English standard for this type of sentence, which linguists call "progressive aspect," in which speakers would use the word "on" or "at" to signal this grammatical meaning. Thus, "She's at fishing today" or "She's on fishing today" simply becomes "She's a-fishing today" due to English's proclivity to reduce unstressed syllables to "uh." A common example of this syllable reduction can be heard in our pronunciation of *because* as "buh-cuz" rather than "bee-cuz." Ocracoke speakers, like most speakers of Southern English, can use two or three modal auxiliaries where mainstream English can only use one. Sentences like "I *might could* go to the party" or "you *might should* clean your room" are understood to carry special meanings. In these cases, I am not coming to the party, and you had better hightail it to your room and clean it or there will be consequences. It was during the Early Modern

English period that these words cemented their meanings and double modal usage dropped out of dialects in the southern half of England. Given the earlier arrival of British settlers and the later arrival of Scots-Irish settlers (from Northern Ireland), this feature may have been brought to the island twice.

Other distinctive grammatical features, such as the use of *weren't* where many dialects use *wasn't* and the dropping of the plural *-s* in specific contexts (e.g., "ten pound"), both explained in detail in chapter 14, were not widespread in Early Modern English. These features reflect either innovations on the island or some regional dialect influence, in the case of *weren't.* It is possible that the plural *-s* dropping reflects Irish English influence.

There are a few grammatical features that clearly reflect a Scots-Irish influence. Generally speaking, these are the features also heard in the mountains of North Carolina but not in the Piedmont region. One example is what linguists call "positive *anymore*." All dialects can use *anymore* with negative constructions, as in "We don't have wild ponies anymore," but only Scots-Irish influenced dialects, like the Brogue, can also use it in positive contexts, as in "We ride around in golf carts anymore" with a meaning of "nowadays." A second feature that shows the Scots-Irish influence is how speakers might use an *-s* on verbs with subjects that do not typically take it in other English varieties. In Standard American English, when a sentence subject is a group of people, it might be treated as a single collective, that is, as a singular noun requiring the *-s* be added to the verb, as in "Congress meet*s* this month." Brogue speakers may use this construction with subjects that are not usually treated as single collective nouns, such as in the sentences "People go*es* to Nags Head a lot" or "Some of them catch*es* crabs." The Brogue's distinctive grammatical features tell a complex story of influence from British dialects, Scots-Irish English, and Irish English, as well as some innovated items.

## DISTINCTIVE PRONUNCIATIONS

The pronunciations of the Brogue mirror the story of its grammar. The robust pronunciation of *-r* reflects the widespread norms of Early Modern English. Though it is now mostly restricted to the West Country of England, it was widespread throughout the Early Modern English period. The vowel pronunciations are a little trickier to pin down. The most iconic vowel of the Brogue is the *hoi toid* vowel. This pronunciation can be described roughly as pronouncing the so-called long-*i* sound as something like the sound most people use in words like *boy* or *enjoy*. Linguistically, what is happening is that the tongue starts in a different place in the mouth. When most Americans say the words *hide* or *time*, their tongue starts at the bottom of the mouth and if it moves, it moves up toward the top teeth. Southerners may say this vowel without much tongue movement, as in "hahd" or "tahm." O'Cockers start this vowel higher and further back in the mouth, resulting in their distinctive pronunciation. In the Early Modern English period, the most widespread pronunciation of this vowel likely started a little higher than the modern standard version, but was not backed like it is in the Brogue. Similar pronunciations of this vowel can still be heard in the West Country dialects of England, as well as many modern dialects of Australia. This is one of the reasons that O'Cockers are sometimes misidentified as Australians. While we cannot be certain of the connection, in part because vowel pronunciation is more fluid than grammar, this shared pronunciation could reveal a historical influence.

A second vowel that is distinctive in the speech of older O'Cockers is the "ow" vowel in words like *house* or *brown*. The more common way that Americans produce this vowel is with the tongue starting low in the mouth and then moving up and back through the pronunciation. Historically, the most common pronunciation of this vowel during the Early Modern English period would have been similar to the stereotypical Canadian pronunciation, as in "oot and aboot" instead of "out and about." Though we associate

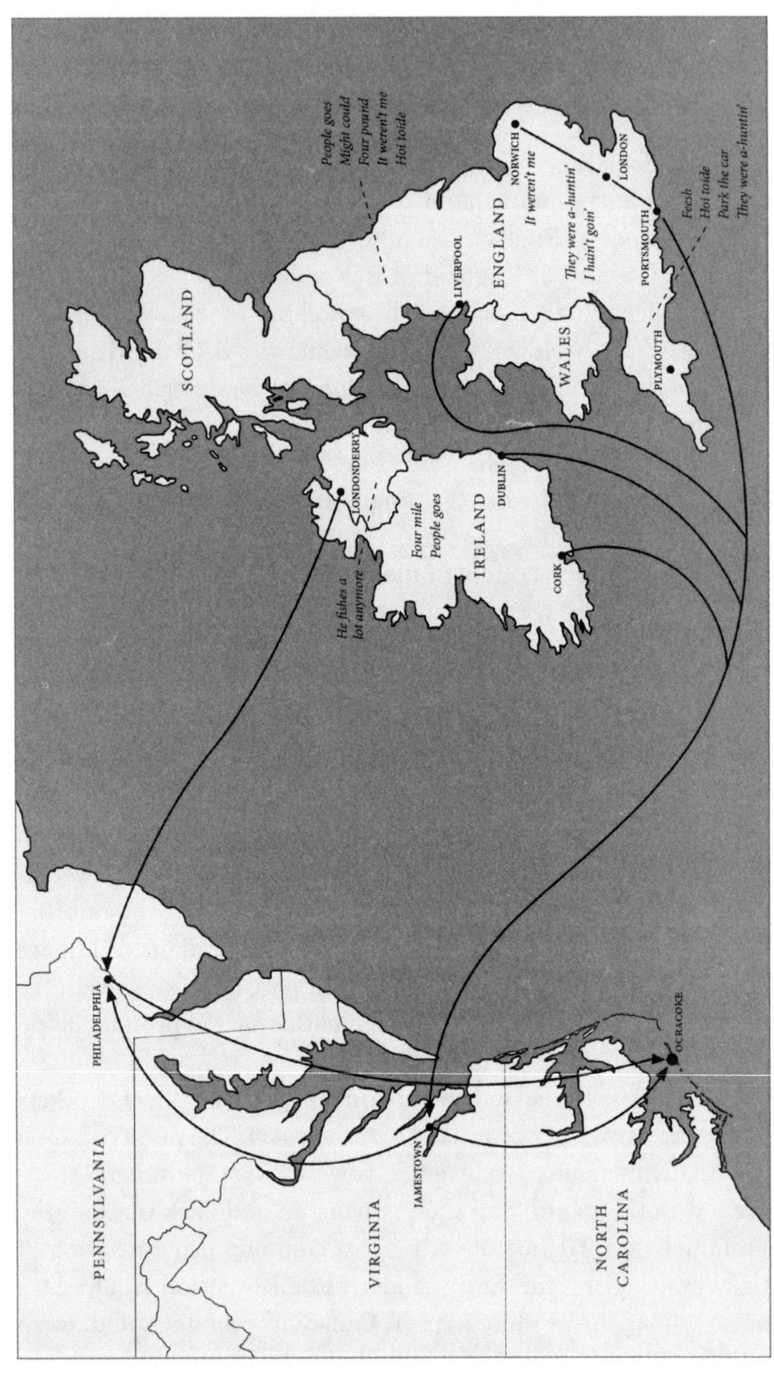


**FIGURE 6.2.** Historical sources for some of the features of Ocracoke English. Map drawn by Danica Cullinan.

it with Canada, this pronunciation can still be heard in New York City, New Orleans, and all along the Virginia Tidewater and Chesapeake Bay regions. This pronunciation involves the tongue starting more toward the middle of the mouth. O'Cockers do something quite different. They typically start in the lower to middle part of their mouths and then move their tongues forward rather than back, resulting in pronunciations like "hice" or "brine" for *house* and *brown*. This pronunciation can still be heard in other parts of the Tidewater and Chesapeake Bay regions. In fact, on Smith Island, Maryland, it is this vowel, not the "hoi toid" vowel, that locals are most known for. This feature most likely reflects a West Country influence. The fact that the Canadian-sounding variation also exists in this same geographical region demonstrates the importance that community founders can have on isolated dialects. Figure 6.2 summarizes the origins for where many of the features of the Brogue originated.

## EVIDENCE FROM WORDS

The vast majority of the words used on Ocracoke are shared with virtually all other English dialects. A handful are unique to the island, many of which were coined right there. Only a few unique words really offer any glimpse into the dialect's history. Chapter 3 examined the words *hammock* and *creek* and noted how they were widespread usages that have died out elsewhere. Chapter 4 reached a similar conclusion about the word *mommuck*. The same can be said of a word like *counterpane* to refer to a bedspread, a word used in Early Modern English and preserved only in isolated dialects like that on Ocracoke. Two words do offer a compelling look backward in time and into the two other main sources for the modern dialect. First, the word many people use to describe the dialect, *brogue*, is not a common word in English. The term likely derives from an Irish word for a specific type of untanned leather shoe called a *brog*. So iconic were these shoes to the Irish that the term became a shorthand for the person wearing the shoe and eventually everything associated with them, including their speech. Second, older O'Cockers used to use the terms *poke* or *poke sack* for a bag. This word likely came to the British Isles from French ("pouque") in the thirteenth century, but was preserved only in Irish ("póca") and Scottish Gaelic ("pòca"), where it meant "pocket." The usage on Ocracoke and in the mountains of North Carolina suggests it likely arrived with the Scots-Irish settlers.

## THE SIGNIFICANCE OF THE BROGUE'S ORIGIN

There may be something attractive about an origin story that traces a dialect back to a single source. Maybe we think of it as reflecting a sort of purity. Perhaps the suggestion that the Brogue is Elizabethan English is really a suggestion that it is valid. The pirate origin? That paints a romantic past full of intrigue. No dialect of English is an island unto itself, however. Giving up notions of dialect purity does not imply dialect contamination. In linguistics, there is no dividing languages into unadulterated and corrupt categories, as will be investigated more in the next chapter. Instead, there is a recognition that every language is a product of a historical dance whereby languages come into contact with each other and are inevitably changed. Even in isolation, no language is used the same way by all its speakers at any given time. Because of this, no language is immune to change. The metaphors that we use to talk about language are important. Diversity in a language does not mean it is sick, or polluted, or broken, or inadequate. Diversity is the norm.

If we abandon the myth of linguistic purity and focus instead on what is present rather than what is absent, we are left with a profoundly important conclusion. The Brogue is a mix of many different things. It contains Early Modern English dialects from the West Country, East Anglia, and other places in England. These are stitched together with Irish, Gaelic-influenced English, and Scots-Irish English. But beyond these historical inputs, the Brogue also is adorned with the innovations of a community bound together by its shared, forged—not inherited—culture. Words and phrases now a part of the dialect reflect the physical place and its flora and fauna, the local weather, foodways, ecology, economy, and persistence of a people living for centuries on a spit of sand dividing the sound from the ocean. The real story of the Brogue is that it and the people that speak it are *e pluribus unum*, out of many, one. The specific origins are important to the community's history, but the dialect tells us just as much about how the community has grown, developed, and endured. The history of the dialect is one of welcoming other voices, and that is a history worth celebrating. It is also a living history: as the dialect continues to change as it dances with other English and, more recently, Spanish dialects.

*Chapter 7*

# WHAT IS THE DIFFERENCE BETWEEN AN ACCENT, DIALECT, AND A LANGUAGE?

The previous chapters investigated where the Brogue did or did not come from. The primary finding was that it was an English dialect that had been influenced by Gaelic languages and other English dialects that had previously been influenced by Gaelic languages. And while it is doubtful that anyone would assume the Brogue to be non-English, this history does raise questions about the terms we use to describe variations in language, such as those in the title of this chapter.

## DESCRIBING LANGUAGE DIFFERENCES

People readily notice differences in ways of speaking, and they are not shy about sharing with others their observations about who speaks differently. You have probably heard statements like the following:

> She has a southern accent.
>
> That tennis player speaks with a strong Russian accent.
>
> I just love the Ocracoke Brogue!
>
> Northerners sound nasal when they talk.
>
> Many African Americans speak a distinctive dialect.

While folks know a southern accent when we hear one, we might not be able to pinpoint what it is that makes it southern. Because most people lack precise terminology to accurately describe dialect differences, they often talk about them with a small handful of vague terms. They might, for example, say that a dialect sounds slow, nasal, or drawled. These descriptions may seem straightforward, but linguists have demonstrated that they are not accurately applied by the general population. Dr. Dennis Preston, a well-known American dialectologist, notes that Americans commonly apply the term *nasal* not only to people who actually talk more "through their nose" than others but also to people who are highly non-nasal, but who sound different in other ways.

There are similar findings for descriptions of speech rate. While there is a general sense that Southern English is spoken more slowly than, for example, Northeastern varieties of English like that found in New York City, the reality is that there is more variation within the speakers of each region than there is across regions. Additionally, a number of factors go into perceptions of speech rate. Americans tend to make their judgments about speech rate not based on words per minute but instead based on the perception of various tongue movements of the speaker. Technically speaking, the southern "drawl" is really more about tongue movement during vowel pronunciation than measurably slow speech. For example, people with southern accents pronounce the vowel in *bait* almost like two vowels, so that the word can sound like *buy it*, the result of the tongue moving during the pronunciation of the vowel. This is perceived as being slower, even though when measured, it is not.

In fact, one of the most iconic features of "slow" Southern English, the long-*i* ("eye") vowel in words like *tide* and *time*, actually involves almost no tongue movement where other speakers have lots. In most American dialects, this vowel is composed of two vowels, "ah" plus "ee," pronounced quickly in succession, so that they blend into "eye." But in southern dialects, all we hear is the "ah" part, resulting in something more like "tahd" or "tahm." (The best way to grasp this is to try these pronunciations out for yourself while paying close attention to your tongue's movement or lack thereof.) A similar dialectal difference is heard in the classic Minnesota dialect. It is easy to hear the distinctiveness of how Minnesotans say their *o*'s a little differently from people from other English dialect regions, but few realize the sound is made by holding the tongue still during the pronunciation of the vowel. Practicing holding your tongue still during certain vowels can go a long way toward making you sound like a native Southerner or Minnesotan. Be warned, though, locals do not always react kindly to outsiders imitating their dialect. The point here is simply that while some speakers do talk faster or slower than others, dialects tend not, on the whole, to be spoken at markedly different paces than other dialects. Instead, other linguistic differences are interpreted as being related to speech rate.

Other descriptions of speech features tend to focus not on pronunciation details but on attributes associated with people who speak that dialect. For example, we might describe southern dialects as polite, uneducated, country, or rural. At first glance, these descriptions may seem to apply to the language variety, but really they are just judgments about the speaker. It is not the dialect that is polite, it is the person using the dialect. In many cases, these judgments say more about the person making the observation than the person being observed. The descriptions above are based on broad generalizations or stereotypes about the South. It certainly doesn't make sense to say "the South is all rural," "all Southerners are uneducated," or "all Southerners are polite," but that's largely what we are doing when we describe dialects in this way. That is, we are doing the thing that we are usually loathe to admit: we are unreflectively stereotyping people.

The ways we talk about language differences can be quite revealing. For example, lots of ways of speaking get described as "slang," "broken," "lazy," or "illogical," all of which imply harsh judgments about them. Not surprisingly, speakers of the dialects commonly described in these ways may be associated with negative characteristics, including being lazy or unintelligent. But the reality is that all dialects use slang; no dialect or language is broken; all dialects have an internal consistency; and no language variety can rightly be described as more or less logical than another (more on these points below). Importantly, it is generally seen as inappropriate to use labels like "lazy" to describe an entire demographic, but we rarely think twice about doing so indirectly by describing the language we associate with a particular demographic group.

## LANGUAGE AUTHORITIES

Sometimes, when people find out we are linguists, they ask us questions designed to validate some idea about why some group speaks the way they do. Some common examples include assertions like "Southerners talk slowly because it's so hot" or the converse, "In the North, they talk fast because they don't want to let the cold air into their mouth." (Neither of these is true.) Other times, we might be asked to confirm that people still speak Elizabethan English in the mountains (also not true). When people talk about languages, they often do so with a misplaced sense of expertise. While people would ask a chemist why a reaction occurs the way it does, they often tell linguists why speech varies as it does.

People's ability to notice and talk about language differences sometimes results in a self-consciousness or internalized insecurity about their own ways of speaking. For example, when we tell people we are linguists, it is not uncommon for them to respond, "Oh, well I must apologize for my strong accent" or "I'll have to watch my dialect." We also know that even when linguists are not around, people who are self-conscious about the way they speak are less likely to ask for help, contribute to a conversation, or feel comfortable in social settings with diverse groups of people. The implications of this are substantial. For example, linguistically insecure students who do not feel comfortable contributing in class are often thought to be uninterested in education. They also may not reach out for help when they struggle academically, and thus may fall behind their peers.

The point is really quite simple. People are good at noticing different ways of speaking, and this gives them a sense of authority that they would not feel in other scientific fields. Yet, when linguists look closely, we see that the general population is not always consistent or accurate in how they talk about these differences. Looking closely at what people say about languages and dialects reveals some interesting insights about their attitudes and perceptions of the people who speak them. Fundamentally, when people talk about a way of speaking, they are almost always commenting, at least indirectly, on people, not language itself. Because this is a book about language, in this chapter, we walk through some of the most common terms used to talk about language—terms you know well and may use but probably have never really thought deeply about. We believe that these terms and how they are used reveal some surprising, and important, things about language.

## ACCENT VERSUS DIALECT

Think for a moment about who comes to mind when you think about groups of people who speak a *dialect*. It is common for Americans to think about groups like African Americans, residents of the Appalachian Mountains, Southerners in general, or English speakers of Latino heritage. Then think of other groups that you consider to have *accents*. Maybe you think about Chicagoans, New Yorkers, or Californians. What is the difference between people who have *accents* and those who have *dialects*? Many times, the terms *accent* and *dialect* can be used interchangeably. For example, the phrases "In the mountains they have a distinctive accent" and "In the mountains they have a distinctive dialect" capture roughly the same sentiment. But there are times when the terms are not interchangeable: "That tennis player speaks with a strong Russian accent" and "I just love a French accent" cannot be restated as "That tennis player speaks with a strong Russian dialect" and "I just love a French dialect." The foreign-language examples highlight one key distinction between the terms: *Accent* refers to pronunciation, whether native ("a southern accent") or non-native (a "French accent"). *Dialect* is broader and encompasses not only pronunciations but also vocabulary words like *dingbatter* and *O'Cocker* and ways of putting words and sentences together. For example, you may have noticed that we sometimes write "on island" for "on the island." That's an example of a dialect feature related to sentence structure or grammar.

The difference between these terms is more than just linguistic; they can carry very different social connotations. Examining parallel sentences illustrates this difference. Someone who speaks with a distinctively southern voice may be described as having either a southern accent or a southern dialect. This works because Southern English is often a recognized way of speaking that is seen as nonstandard. Speakers from areas of the country where the dialect is not marked as nonstandard will be much more likely to have their speech be described with the term *accent* rather than *dialect*. For example, many Midwesterners are thought to have a distinguishable accent, but far fewer people talk about a midwestern dialect, because they assume the speech is standard. The current notion of standard American English is most closely aligned with the regional dialects found in and around parts of (roughly) Ohio, Indiana, and Michigan. The speech of these areas is so unremarkable to outsiders that many people from these regions mistakenly believe they do not have a dialect. They do—more on that below. The key difference for the present moment is that it is unlikely that someone would describe the speech of these areas by saying "Oh, I really like your dialect." Instead, they may say something like "Oh, I really like your accent." Conversely, speakers of African American English are likely to have their speech described as a *Black dialect* rather than a *Black accent*, or with any number of other judgmental labels, as noted above.

The linguistics of these two words can be summed up succinctly. *Accent* has two common usages: a description of foreign language influence on another language or the pronunciation distinctions of a dialect. All dialects have accent differences compared to other dialects, but dialects are more than just accents. They also vary by vocabulary, grammar, and language use conventions.

The social dimensions of these two words are a little trickier, but in general *accent* tends to be used to describe ways of speaking that are seen as "just different, not bad," whereas *dialect* tends to be used to describe ways of speaking that are often thought to be improper, broken, slangy, or just plain bad. It is easy to assume that the difference also entails information about being "further from the norm," but this is not always true. The Ocracoke Brogue, as noted in chapter 1, is the only American dialect routinely perceived as being non-American. It may be the "furthest from the norm" dialect in the United States, but it is often described as an accent by people who notice the difference but do not negatively judge the speakers.

In most common usages, the term *dialect* carries a negative connotation; that is, dialects are seen as deficient in some way when compared to ways of speaking that are not thought of as dialects. In other words, there is an implied criticism with the term *dialect* that might not be present with the term *accent*. While we probably do not think about this consciously when we use these terms to describe a way of speaking, the general pattern is quite strong: *dialect* gets reserved for the ways of speaking by groups who are considered marginal in mainstream society. The linguistic usage of *dialect* does not imply this judgment. When linguists use the term *dialect*, they mean it as a neutral label to describe a shared way of speaking among a regional or ethnic group. This definition is at the heart of the linguistic truism "everyone speaks a dialect."

## SLANG

It is not uncommon to hear people describe a dialect as *slang*. This is especially true for the dialect linguists call African American English, which popularly may be named a variety of things, including "Ebonics," "ghetto talk," or "street language." But African American English is more than slang. Remember, dialects are composed of vocabulary words, pronunciations, and grammar. *Slang* refers mostly to vocabulary of a very specific type—words that are used to signal in-group membership that are not easily understood by outsiders and, often, words that come and go quickly. Adults also tend to think about slang as something associated with youth, but age does not preclude one from using slang. Speakers of all dialects invent and use slang, but dialects that highly value language creativity, like African American English, may develop and use more slang than other dialects.

Speakers of the Ocracoke Brogue also value creativity in language use, and many of the words developed and used by islanders can be confounding to tourists . . . and even linguists. Part of the joy of slang (and insider vocabulary in general) is that it helps define who is a part of the in-group and who is not. Slang reflects an inventiveness with language that ought to be celebrated, but even with this positive view, it is not a good term for describing a dialect, since dialects consist of much more than fleeting word usages. A number of chapters in this book examine some of the unique vocabulary used on Ocracoke related to locality, ecology, topography, groups of people, weather, and movement around the island, but the dialect is more than just the sum of these words. It also has distinctive patterns related to pronunciation and grammar.

## DIALECT VERSUS LANGUAGE

As dialectologists, we are often asked how many dialects there are. This is a trickier question than you might think. In the case of English, we might start by thinking about dialects like British English, American English, Australian English, South African English, Singaporean English, and so on. Then, of course, each of these dialects consists of other dialects. American English, for example, has Southern English, Californian English, New York English, New England English. If you are a Southerner, you also know that there are differences among southern varieties, including ways of speaking in the Appalachian Mountains, Deep South, Coastal South, Mid-Atlantic, and so forth. These regional distinctions do not take into account important differences within said regions, such as urban versus rural dialects or dialects associated with ethnic groups, like Hispanicized English, African American English, or Lumbee English, each of which also has regional, social, and other dimensions of variation. Then, of course, within each of these sub-regional dialects, there is a tremendous amount of variation among speakers. As you can see, this widely held hierarchical understanding whereby languages are made up of a collection of dialects is a bit trickier than it might seem on the surface. At the very least, we see here that dialects are themselves made up of other sub-dialects. Furthermore, sometimes the differences between these sub-dialects can be even greater than differences between larger dialects. For example, for the past few decades at least, rural Southern English and urban Southern English are further apart than urban Southern English and urban Midwestern English. While we think about region as being the bigger cultural division, linguistically, it seems that rurality may be more important.

The presentation of dialects in the previous paragraph can be thought of as relying on the metaphor of a family tree: English is at the top and branches out to national varieties (i.e., American

English) that then branch further into broad dialect groups (Southern English) that branch into smaller ones (Appalachian English). But this metaphor doesn't capture the real story. A better way to think about the relationship among dialects is as a sort of pie that we can cut into "dialect pieces." We first slice the pie into six or eight "national Englishes" (British, American, Australian, and so on). We can then cut each of those slices into smaller slices like Southern US English and African American English. We can continue slicing these into even smaller pieces, until eventually we are left with tiny little dialect crumbs. In fact, no two speakers have identical dialects, so once those crumbs are too small to slice further, what we are left with is the individual speakers themselves. You are your own dialect crumb. Where this analogy falls apart a little bit is that people often have language abilities in more than one language: they may be part of an English pie at the same time as a Spanish pie. Or they might be a part of two slices of the English pie at the same time: Brogue speakers, for example, can often style-shift into a more mainstream dialect. Interestingly, the dialect used with outsiders is a blend of dialect pieces from midwestern dialects, southern dialects, and other ways of speaking. So, when we are asked how many dialects there are, linguists might just turn the question back on you by responding, "Well, that depends, how many pieces can you cut a pie into?" Because there is no scientific answer to this question, when we are asked about how many dialects there are in North Carolina, we often give a broad range, for example, "somewhere between five and 200," depending on how small you choose to cut the pieces of the language pie. We could be even more pedantic and suggest there are as many dialects as there are people. These answers may make it sound like linguists don't know much, but, in reality, it just means that a group's or a person's way of speaking is far more complex—and varied—than listeners give it credit for.

So far, all of the information in this section likely matches your intuitions about the terms *language* and *dialect*. However, it turns out that things are more complicated than we might think. The idea that languages are made up of dialects is basically right, but where exactly is the dividing line between language and dialect? A common method for deciding this is mutual intelligibility: If people can understand each other, they are speaking different dialects, not different languages. If they cannot understand each other, they are speaking different languages. This principle works well at the extremes. It is clear that Southern English and Midwestern English are usually mutually intelligible, and, thus, dialects of English. At the other extreme, English and Swahili are not at all mutually intelligible, so they are separate languages. But in reality, intelligibility exists along a continuum of "more" and "less" rather than as an absolute of "yes" or "no." There is no clear threshold of intelligibility that we use to separate dialects from languages. In other words, English, Spanish, and Russian are not so much different pies but slices of the same pie. And the place we decide to cut that pie is more arbitrary than we might believe at first. A few intriguing cases demonstrate just how inconsistent this distinction is.

Most people would classify Swedish, Danish, and Norwegian as distinct languages; but speakers of any of these languages can usually comprehend the spoken or written versions of the other two with little trouble. Contrast this with the dialects of German. For people who only speak Standard German, other German dialects —Low German, High Franconian, and some Upper German and Swiss German dialects—are actually pretty hard to understand. Based solely on the criterion of mutual intelligibility, we would have to consider all of these to be separate language groups. And there can be indeterminate cases in English, too. If you are a native speaker of American English, can you always understand British varieties like Scottish English or Irish English? Sharp borders between languages are not the norm. Instead, there is typically a continuum of shift from one language to another. But definite national borders do exist, and for much of the world it is these national borders, not linguistic criteria, that are used to separate ways of speaking into different languages. It has been quipped that a language is just a dialect with an army and a navy. This adage certainly is an inadequate way of determining what counts as one of the world's 7,000 or so languages, but it does highlight just how much our common definition of language is tied to national boundaries rather than any specific linguistic criteria.

Instead of fixating on demarcating borders of a language, linguists find it more useful to group ways of speaking into language families. Language families are defined by historical connections: they share a common historical ancestor. Linguists recognize 142 different language families. English is part of the Indo-European language family, and this family includes languages as diverse as Italian, Russian, Persian, and Hindi. Other large language families include Sino-Tibetan (Mandarin, Cantonese, Burmese, Bodo, etc.), Turkic (Turkish, Uzbek, Azerbaijani, Uyghur, etc.), Afro-Asiatic (Arabic, Hebrew, Amharic, etc.), and Niger-Congo (Swahili, Yoruba, Zulu, Xhosa, etc.). Some languages are not scientifically linked to other languages. These are known as language isolates, the best known of which is Basque. There are also a number of language isolates among Indigenous populations of Oceania, North Africa, South America, and the Pacific Northwest of North America. Additional research may find that some of these isolates may be grouped into small language families. These isolates include some of the most endangered languages in the world.

From a linguistic perspective, every language—even language isolates—consists of a variety of ways of speaking that language. There is no one who speaks merely English, Korean, or Basque. Instead, everyone speaks a version of English, Korean, or Basque specific to their regional, ethnic, and social backgrounds. To refine our linguistic truism from the end of a previous section, we might say that not only does "everyone speak a dialect," but it is impossible to speak a language without speaking a dialect of that language. This is another reason why the term *language* is difficult to pin down: it refers to a collective abstraction rather than a concrete entity. Because the distinction between a language and a dialect is more political than linguistic, linguists sometimes use the stuffy term *language variety* for any spoken language or dialect. Though it may seem pretentious at first, it is a good reminder that we all speak a variety—or many varieties—of language or languages.

It also helps remind us that mutual intelligibility is a matter of more or less rather than yes or no. In fact, English and Romance languages like French, Italian, and Spanish share enough vocabulary that it is sometimes possible—especially combined with clues like gestures and facial expressions—for speakers of different languages to communicate simple ideas across the linguistic barriers.

What is important about all this information? When we think about the Brogue, we recognize a unique way of speaking steeped in history and central to a local culture. This, in fact, is how we should view all dialects, as unique markers of a regional or cultural group's living heritage. The terms that we commonly use to talk about and classify language varieties tell us more about how society views the people who speak that way than it does about the way they speak. We tend to use the term *dialect* with some degree of negative connotation, but we really should not. From a linguistic perspective, every dialect has the same levels of grammatical complexity and reliance on patterns (for the Brogue, these patterns are described more in chapters 10 and 11), and all dialects allow their speakers to discuss complex topics. Any prejudice against a way of speaking is merely a prejudice against a person or group. Finally, the notion of a standard form of a language is really a theoretical construct. In reality, every language variety we hear and speak is a dialect of that language. All of these dialects are just as capable and organized as any other language variety. They each have a systematic grammar. Dialects reveal things about a speaker or community's past, but also about their imagined future. Dialects are a cultural resource as rich and important as dress, music, cooking, and art, and should be celebrated in the same ways. They also can be studied scientifically, which is what the next chapter investigates.

*Chapter 8*

# HOW DO YOU STUDY A DIALECT?

In January 2006, Walt and Jeff were traveling to a linguistics conference in Albuquerque. On the taxi ride from the airport to the hotel, the driver asked what brought us to New Mexico. When we told him we were there for the Linguistic Society of America conference, he probed a bit about our areas of research. After we told him we studied dialects, he responded, "That's the great thing about dialects. Anyone can study them as a hobby." Dumbfounded by the casual dismissal of our PhD training and years of research, we just laughed. But was he right? Can anyone study a dialect? Certainly anyone can observe language differences, and most people have a good sense of the social meanings or geographic distributions of many linguistic features; however, we—the authors of this book—want to believe there is something important about our training. But just in case any of our readers are looking to pick up a new hobby, this chapter outlines seven simple steps for studying dialects.

## STEP 1: PRECISELY IDENTIFY A DIALECT

Start by deciding what exactly you want to study. You may want to refer to chapter 7 of this book for guidelines on figuring out what exactly a dialect is, but it is essential to have a sense of the population of speakers you are interested in studying. As an example, if we wanted to study the traditional Ocracoke Brogue, we might exclude the youngest generation of islanders, residents who moved to the island after a certain age, and people who originally spoke a language other than English. Now, if we wanted to study the dialect variation of Ocracoke, all of these speakers make up an important part of the linguistic soundscape. Many times people think about a dialect as one thing. Linguists see a dialect as something loosely coherent but with substantial variation among speakers. Clearly defined dialect groups are rare, even on an island. Instead, linguists often look for transition zones (geographic, age, social, etc.) where there seems to be some sort of important linguistic difference among groups of people.

When we began studying the Brogue in the early 1990s, there were maybe 400 to 500 adult O'Cockers on the island. We interviewed seventy-eight of them, so perhaps 20 percent of them. For our follow-up study in the mid-2000s, we interviewed a slightly smaller number of speakers, but due to the decrease in the number of O'Cockers, perhaps a similar proportion. It is important to interview a large enough sample of your population that you can be reasonably confident in your assertions.

## STEP 2: OBSERVE THE DIALECT IN THE WILD

It may be tempting to assume you know enough about your dialect to jump into your study without first assessing the linguistic landscape. When people hear we study dialects, they often tell us something about how they perceive some group uses language. Observations about words and phrases tend to be relatively accurate, while observations about pronunciations and grammar are often less so. For example, when describing British dialects, many people make a blanket statement about how Received Pronunciation (RP) speakers drop their *r*'s. It is true that RP speakers drop their *r*'s in some contexts, but never, for example, at the start of a word. They are also prone to adding *r*'s where there are none in other dialects, such as in the phrase "vanillar ice cream." The point here is simply that our general interactions with people tend to exaggerate certain observations while completely missing others. If you spend some time carefully observing people using their dialect, you'll be better able to determine what aspects of it to study. At this stage, it is common to focus in on what stands out as different, but it is equally important to start to see what is not unique. For example, many dialects do not do anything nonstandard with their use of forms of the verb *be* (*am*, *is*, *are*, *was*, *were*, *been*), but it is important to note this usage as being standard even if it is the sort of observation that would have typically gone unnoticed by the nonlinguist. To really study a dialect, we need to know not just what is unique, but also what could be unique but in actuality is not.

## STEP 3: COLLECT DATA

There are many ways to collect dialect data, but the most common is the sociolinguistic interview. At first, the sociolinguistic interview might just seem like active conversation, but that is only one part of it. The first thing to consider is the observer's paradox, which states that people do not behave naturally when they are being observed. Because we need natural speech for our analyses, and because we cannot ethically record people without their consent, we try to do all we can to make people comfortable in the interview situation so that they minimize the monitoring they do of their speech. Some researchers have suggested that gathering narratives with intense emotions is one way to get people to speak more naturally. This approach holds the "danger of death" narrative as a key part of

FIGURE 8.1. Walt Wolfram and Natalie Schilling interview Rex O'Neal by his crab pots. Photograph courtesy of Herman Lankford; copyright NCSU Communications.

the sociolinguistic interview, in which the researchers ask the participants if they were ever in a situation where they thought they might die. Other researchers have found that these types of questions more often made participants shut down and withdraw from the interview. After all, who wants to relive traumatic experiences? There are a wide swath of topics people can talk about, so most sociolinguists are focused on getting people to talk rather than the topic of conversation. Figure 8.1 shows an interview taking place on the "home turf" of the interviewee, in an attempt to make him more comfortable. We can use just about any kind of conversation for our analysis, so we try to get our participants engaged in a conversation and forget that it is really an interview.

After you have made your interviewee comfortable, you can start to ask questions designed to elicit the features you are interested in studying. When doing a general dialect description, it is essential to elicit a variety of grammatical structures. For example, you would want to gather examples of how the speaker forms the past and present tenses of a variety of verbs. You would also want to investigate other verb constructions, such as the perfect aspect ("I have eaten") versus the progressive aspect ("I am eating"), and how they use modals (e.g., for example, *can*, *may*, *shall*, *would*) and other helping verbs. And with nouns, you need to note how they mark plural versus singular nouns, possessive versus non-possessive, and so on. There may be variation with other parts of speech, such as pronouns, adjectives, or prepositions. And remember, you cannot simply ask them directly about these structures because their own metalinguistic knowledge is untrustworthy. Instead, you might ask a question about a past occurrence, and then ask a follow-up question about a related event that happened before that past-tense occurrence. That way you can start to understand how the dialect marks different sequences of events in the past. Or perhaps you recognize there is something different about plural marking in the dialect, where some nouns are made plural with an *-s* and others are not. You might then slyly ask about various types of nouns, making sure your interviewee pluralizes them. For example, you might get them to pluralize human nouns, animal nouns, inanimate nouns, measure nouns, nouns with quantifiers or other modifiers, and nouns without. All this while trying to listen intently so that you can keep the conversation flowing as naturally as possible and continuing to think about the linguistic structures you are trying to elicit data for.

At the end of the interview, some linguists ask participants to read a passage and/or a list of words that target certain sounds. Introducing a script into the interaction is not without challenges, however. First, doing this only works if the language being studied has a writing system. Second, it assumes a level of participant literacy that might not be reasonable. Even with literacy, it is important to note that the writing will influence how a person says a word. For example, an Ocracoker might see "high tide" and forgo their usual pronunciation. In some cases, people will articulate overly standard pronunciations. For example, when seeing the word *often*, it is possible that a person will articulate the *t*-sound even though it is not a part of their dialect or the standard. The gold standard for language data is casual speech; but getting the right kinds of linguistic structures is challenging, so these reading passages and word lists can be useful supplemental data. As noted in step 1, it is critical to get these data from a large sample of your population.

## STEP 4: ANALYZE DATA AND FORM HYPOTHESES

Our analyses often begin with creating detailed transcripts. These help us search for linguistic features of interest. We might then go back and listen to every past-tense usage of *be* (*was* or *were*) and note which form is used and whether it was used in the negative (*weren't*) or affirmative (*were*). Maybe we are interested in the iconic vowel in *hoi toid*. In that case, we would use the transcripts to find every instance of the "long-i" vowel and then use computer software to analyze how the tongue moved during the vowel's production. We would also note the phonetic qualities of the sounds that come before and after the vowel, and perhaps, any additional contextual information (part of speech, stress, etc.) that may be important.

One curiosity of the Brogue is an unexpected usage of the word *to*. While Ocracokers use all the standard versions of *to*, they have one additional usage that stands out. The following includes some data documenting the uses of *to*.

| | |
|---|---|
| He's getting ready *to* get married | Part of infinitive verb phrase |
| That had *to* do with the fact that . . . | Part of infinitive verb phrase |
| You gotta take it all the way up *to* the mainland | Expressing location with respect to a point of reference |
| He went *to* Hatteras | Expressing motion in the direction of a specific point |

| | |
|---|---|
| He's *to* Hatteras | Saying where a person is located at this moment |
| Candy's *to* the post office | Saying where a person is located at this moment |

The first two examples are where *to* is part of an infinitive verb ("to get" and "to do"). The second two examples capture common prepositional usages of *to*. The last two are the ones that might stand out as different. These are used to say where a person is at a specific moment. Modern English tends to use *at* for these constructions. We may hypothesize that the Brogue uses *to* in the same places where other dialects use *to* but also where other dialects use *at*. Before we test this hypothesis, it is prudent to see if the rest of our data support our initial thought. We might then search our transcripts for every usage of *at*. Indeed, when we search our Ocracoke corpus, we find such standard English examples as, "I don't want any of that at all," "see, at one time, Portsmouth . . . ," and "look at that!" Here, we see *at* working as an intensifier (*at all*), as denoting a time (*at one time*) and meaning "in the direction of" (*at that*). So, all these usages are distinct from the special use of *to* that we noted earlier. Attempting to capture the variable's specific usage, we might suggest a hypothesis something like, "O'Cockers use *to* instead of *at* when they are describing the location of a person at a particular moment." As you can see, this can be a recursive procedure that requires the analyst to know a lot about how languages work.

## STEP 5: TEST HYPOTHESES

Our hypothesis is now ready to be tested. We might do this in a number of different ways. We could craft a "cloze sentence" in which we ask people to fill in a blank. For example, "Rex is _____ the store." We would want to include sentences where O'Cockers used *to* and *at* in our interviews to confirm that we are not just testing a single case but assessing the entire system. We might also test for any additional constraints. For example, does this work with past tense constructions such as "Yesterday, Rex was _____ the store"? Or with events in the future, in a sentence such as "Tomorrow, Rex will be ______ the store around noon"? We could also test whether the subject must be a human, or whether it could be an animal ("The dog was _____ the campground") or an inanimate object ("The ferry was _____ Hatteras"). We might test whether *to* can be used with any verbs other than *be*, such as in "She's waiting _____ the dock" or "I worked _____ the crab house." This gets tricky, as many similar constructions take *to* in standard English such as "She's walking *to* the dock." Again, notice that the use of *to* for *at* only occurs when it is related to the location of the person, a rule we arrived at after going through all of the possible constructions.

A second way to test our hypothesis is to do additional interviews with people targeting this form. Here we might get creative. For a feature like this one, we might create cardboard cutouts and construct scenarios where people need to generate responses that use these forms. For example, we may have a named human, a dog, and a boat. We could then use a map of the village to ask where various characters are with the hope of eliciting sentences like "The dog is *at*/*to* the campground." Again, we would want to test all the possibilities for use mentioned above.

A third way to test our hypothesis is to generate sample sentences as above but then insert either *to* or *at* in each sentence frame and randomize them so people do not see the two versions of the sentence next to each other. Linguists call this a grammatical acceptability task, because residents are asked if the construction is acceptable to their linguistic intuitions for the dialect. Additional follow up might try to capture who uses the feature by asking respondents to check boxes such as, "I would say this sentence" and "I hear people say sentences like this." For cases where respondents report they hear others use the feature, we may ask them to describe (or name) the people who use it. These processes are used to gather information about usage among one or more demographic categories of interest. For the specialized usage of *to* that we are examining here, it might be common for community members to say that they hear this construction from both older male and female islanders. If the data collected through this step do not conflict with the observations made earlier in the interviews, then it is time to refine the hypothesis into the most precise statement we can comfortably make about who uses the term.

## STEP 6: REFINE HYPOTHESES INTO ASSERTIONS

Taking in all the data noted above and drawing on our analysis of this feature in American English dialects, specifically in Ocracoke, we can make a strong assertion about the use of this feature on the island. Native islanders often use *to* for *at* when describing that a specific person or thing is at a specific place, regardless of the time being described. That is, this can be done if that spatial relationship took place in the past, is currently the case, or even if the occurrence is expected in the future. Technically, this feature is called "static locative *to*," where static location here simply means, as described above, a specific known place that does not change its location.

Additional research findings allow us to describe the social distribution of the feature. Speakers tend to be variable rather than categorical in their usage. That is, they use both the standard and nonstandard versions interchangeably. In her master's thesis, Janelle Vadnais found that this feature was on the decline in Ocracoke. In the older generations, the nonstandard *to* was the preferred form, occurring in 60–75 percent of eligible usages. For speakers born between 1953 and 1991, the rate dropped to around 40 percent, meaning that the standard form, *at*, had become more common than *to*. These rates are higher than neighboring communities on the mainland, perhaps suggesting that the island's isolation has helped preserve the usage longer than elsewhere. Vadnais found that the feature was used at similar rates among male and female speakers. One last wrinkle: while the demographic of Ocracoke during the period under investigation was overwhelmingly white, the form was also found in the speech of Muzel Bryant, the last remaining African American on the island. Though she was born in 1904, her usage rate (33 percent) was more similar to the younger generations than the older ones. This confirms a hypothesis based on other communities that static locative *to* was primarily ethnically coded as white and would have been a later adoption in the speech of any African Americans or African American communities who use the feature.

With all of this information, we may make a data-backed claim, such as "O'Cockers of both genders use static locative *to* in the same way as other dialects, but at more robust levels than nearby white dialects. Additionally, there is a gradual decline in usage, especially for speakers born after 1953."

## STEP 7: CELEBRATE THE DIALECT

Linguistic findings can often seem obvious to the casual observer, but the crystallized statement of how a dialect feature works often obscures the process that led to it. It most certainly obscures the community's role in providing data and testing hypotheses. Because of this, we always seek ways to use our findings to benefit the community that gave so generously of its time. On Ocracoke, we have tried to repay our debt in various ways. A number of these projects are described in other chapters of this book, including our work with the Ocracoke Preservation Society and the local school. Additionally, with community members, we compiled two oral history projects. This book is another celebration of the community. We have brought media crews from various news outlets to help spread the word about the unique linguistic and cultural heritage of the island.

Now it is your turn. Having uncovered some linguistic knowledge about this dialect feature, what can you do to celebrate the community? Maybe you can share your discovery with a friend. Or maybe you can show appreciation for the Brogue if you happen to hear it spoken on island. Appreciating the community as it is and was—as opposed to what you think it ought to be—goes a long way toward honoring the community's central role in our linguistic discovery. Linguistic analysis, in the end, is more complicated than it may appear on the surface. As the academic saying goes, anecdote is not the singular of data. While it is easy to make an observation about a dialect, few realize the sophisticated analyses and statistics that go into language description. Though we certainly would not discourage it, we suggest here that linguistic analysis involves much more effort than what one might associate with a traditional hobby. But that in no way should stand in the way of anyone's appreciation and celebration of language differences. If you are so inclined, we recommend leaving steps 1 through 6 to the linguists, and then joining us wholeheartedly in step 7.

*Chapter 9*

# WHY WOULD ANYONE STUDY DIALECTS?

In a world facing challenges like climate change, poverty, war, and hunger, language may seem like a relatively trivial matter. But it is not. Language is the backbone of culture, community, and identity. It is also among our most powerful and indispensable tools. We use language to teach, learn, console, love, harm, and create. To study language, you need to weave together strands of history, sociology, geography, anthropology, and psychology, intersecting with other disciplines. The ensuing tapestry is a portrait of all of us. To study the Brogue is to study the present and past citizens of Ocracoke and all of those who have shaped or been shaped by their time on the island. Studying dialects tells us a lot about what is means to be human. And it is our interactions as humans that inform the challenges facing our world. Maybe this feels like hyperbole, but in this chapter, we suggest it is reality.

## THE POWER OF LANGUAGE

Small language differences can be profoundly important. Politics is loaded with examples. Americans overwhelmingly oppose a "death tax" and support an "estate tax," even though the two terms reference the exact same program. The violence of war relies on othering the enemy; that is, a creation of an "us" and a "them." There are few things more commonly used for this process of dividing peoples than language. And once the battle has begun, language becomes the means for distinguishing friend from foe. Chapter 12 of the book of Judges from the Christian Old Testament recounts a war between the Ephraimites and the Gileadites that took place sometime between 1070 and 1370 BCE. In the account, the Ephraimites had just suffered a major defeat and were trying to return to their homeland across the Jordan River. The Gileadites set up checkpoints at the crossings and used language to identify the Ephraimites from other travelers. All travelers were asked to say the word *shibboleth*, a Hebrew word meaning "grain," before crossing the river. The Ephraimites' dialect lacked the *sh* sound, so they pronounced the word as "sibboleth," after which they were immediately killed—42,000 deaths because of a subtle dialectal difference.

While language can be used to identify foes, it can also be used to identify friends. Allied soldiers in the invasion of Normandy used the word *welcome* to identify American, British, and French friends, knowing German soldiers would pronounce the word "vel-come." In the Pacific theater, the word used to root out Japanese spies was *lollapalooza*, since most Japanese speakers replace *l*'s with *r*'s. Linguistic identifications are used worldwide for national security because language is one of the most authentic and revealing markers of cultural distinctiveness.

History abounds with examples that demonstrate how language is central to our—and our communities' and nations'—hopes and dreams. From renaming *sauerkraut* and *hamburgers* as *liberty cabbage* and *liberty sausage* during World War I to the 2003 renaming of *French fries* as *freedom fries* in the Congressional cafeterias as "a small but symbolic effort to show the strong displeasure many on Capitol Hill have with our so-called ally, France" (Rep. Robert Ney), language reveals all of our human hopes and desires.

The examples here describe times when language was used intentionally to identify and then include or exclude, but the majority of linguistic prejudice happens unconsciously. In the United States, inherited linguistic biases contribute to inequitable outcomes in housing, education, employment, and access to goods and services. A few examples highlight the insidious and pervasive nature of language prejudice. In their book *Dialects at School*, Jeffrey Reaser and colleagues detail linguistic bias in a variety of standardized tests including IQ tests, the SAT, and state achievement tests for reading, writing, math, and science. Even when the subject is not language, language differences impact measured student achievement. Dr. John Baugh has spent decades researching the connection between dialects and the perpetuation of (or increase in) housing segregation in American cities, many of which are more segregated now than at any point in our history. Finally, linguists like Drs. John Rickford and Sharese King have examined the ways linguistic bias on the parts of judges and juries has resulted in many miscarriages of justice in our criminal justice system. Education, housing, and justice are cornerstones of American society, and yet language prejudice continues to stand in the way of all Americans being treated as equal.

## "LANGUAGE IS CULTURE, AND CULTURE IS LANGUAGE"

In one sense, the scientific understanding of language is straightforward. As noted in chapter 7, all languages and dialects are systematic; that is, they follow a finite number of rules. They all have logical and illogical components (or, perhaps more accurately, consistencies and exceptions). They all have roughly the same ability to describe the world. They all vary at any given time and change over time. Accepting these scientific facts leads to an important conclusion: all prejudice about language is just prejudice against the people who speak that language. Because there has never been nor will there be a time when there are no social divisions in society, language will remain a vehicle to express our likes, fears, and hatreds of other peoples. It is precisely this last point that reveals the answer to the question at the start of this chapter: to study language is not just to study language, but to study people.

At the other end of the state, about as far away from Ocracoke as you can get in North Carolina, one of our Cherokee informants, Jean Bushyhead, captures succinctly why it is so critical to study languages and dialects, with the quotation that opens this section of this chapter: "Language is culture, and culture is language." In the Cherokee tradition, studying the language is the only way to understand the inherited cultural-historical past of the Cherokee people. It is the most important sign of a connection to one's tribe. While few communities hold their language as sacred as the Cherokee, studying the language of a community reveals its history, traditions, beliefs, and values. To a linguist, it seems impossible to understand a community without considering its linguistic history.

The main premise of this book is that understanding more about Ocracoke's historical and current linguistic status helps illuminate many aspects of islanders' past and present culture. And if we value the unique culture of a place, we should also value the languages and dialects of that place. By recognizing that language and culture are one and the same, our study of the dialect allows us a window to understand the local history, foodways, traditions, topography, ecology, economy, values, and norms. In fact, we go so far as to assert that you cannot understand a history or culture without considering the languages and dialects of the groups being studied. Understanding a community's norms around language reveals how residents understand the world and their place in it. In Ocracoke, this understanding starts with dividing insider and outsider—O'Cockers from dingbatters—but ending with an understanding of a community bound together by humor, playfulness, loyalty, and optimism.

## LANGUAGE IS SIMULTANEOUSLY INDIVIDUAL AND COLLECTIVE

It was long thought that true language was a uniquely human tool; that is, while other animals do communicate, only humans practiced language. That belief has been eroded in recent years, but our greater understanding of animal communication has not lessened the important role language plays in shaping our humanity. Instead, it is reasonable to posit that our language and literacy have only furthered the gap between humans and other animals as our world has modernized. Language has become ubiquitous, the backbone of commerce, travel, and entertainment. Our modern world also engages us in more linguistic diversity than perhaps at any other time in human history. In such a context, our language becomes a sort of personal marker that signals to others who we are and how we wish to be perceived.

All of this identity work is possible because of one of the most remarkable parts of our linguistic heritage: we are not taught how to speak; instead, we acquire our speech naturally, first by mimicking the sounds around us, but very quickly by experimenting with language in ways that we have never heard before. Very young children put their words together in novel ways. They create, they don't merely imitate. Because language acquisition happens without conscious thought or extensive external sculpting, it remains something intensely personal. There is a paradox about language in that is it simultaneously intensely personal and collective. Our voice tells others not just who we are, but how we relate to others. It tells them what we want to say, but also how we want to be understood. Our voices carry smiles, frowns, arrows, and bandages. All of this is possible because our voice is never just one thing but part of our malleable and diverse self, engaged in loosely choreographed dances with other complex humans.

It is this process of acquisition that makes language seem like an odd topic for scientific study; however, it is precisely the fact that language is so essential yet uncritically examined in the lives of people that makes it so worthy of scientific study. At the start of the twentieth century, Swiss linguist Ferdinand de Saussure put it this way, "In the lives of individuals and of society, language is a factor of greater importance than any other. For the study of language to remain solely the business of a handful of specialists would be a quite unacceptable state of affairs. In practice, the study of language is in some degree or other the concern of everyone." The implications of language difference touch every facet of modern life. Any thorough understanding of history, culture, or humanity must include study of language.

## LANGUAGE IS MORE THAN JUST OUR INHERITED PAST

Much of this chapter's discussion has focused on language as an indelible record of the past, or of the present moment. But language is also aspirational, a glimpse of our imagined future, who we wish to be. It is this intersection of past, present, and future that makes language so interesting to study. What does the language of Ocracoke say about its future? Chapter 24 looks at this question in more detail, but we end this chapter with some questions to consider as you continue reading this book. It is clear the Brogue is fading, but does that mean the community is losing its history and culture? Whose job is it to preserve the history of the Brogue? What might that look like? How will we know when the Brogue has disappeared? Does it disappear with the loss of the distinctive *hoi toid* pronunciation, or does it persist as long as dingbatters walk the island with that label? Can the local culture be as robust and distinctive without the Brogue? Will the next generation of O'Cockers lament the disappearance of the Brogue, or will they find new ways to connect to or express their cultural heritage?

Linguists do not study language merely to preserve something from the past or present. No one questions the importance of studying history or culture, because we understand the knowledge gained is essential to guiding the future of our species. This is also why linguists study language: we aim to understand the complex workings of humans in society, because this understanding is essential for combating remaining prejudices in society and can help create a more perfect future.

*Chapter 10*

# WHAT IS THE OCRACOKE ACCENT LIKE?

On his first visit to Ocracoke more than thirty years ago, Walt Wolfram was introduced to a group of men in the midst of an after-hours poker party in the Pony Island restaurant. The occasion was the celebration of an islander's retirement from the Coast Guard—a good reason for a party. Walt felt awkward, as an outsider in a group of men he had never met, but he was honored to be included in this locals-only event on just his second day on the island. Dave Esham, at the time the owner of the Pony Island Motel (now known as the Pony Island Inn), and the only islander Walt had met up to that point, introduced him to the group as the leader of a team from NC State who had come to study Ocracoke speech. Walt's discomfort intensified as he imagined the response his introduction as a professor doing research on language

FIGURE 10.1. David Esham and Rex O'Neal "saying a word" at the old poker house. Photograph by Ann Ehringhaus.

might evoke, when a friendly, curly-haired man by the name of Rex O'Neal stepped forward and said in a good-natured tone, "So you're studyin' speech. Well, it's hoi toid on the sound soid; last night the water fa'r, tonight the moon shine, no feesh, no feesh, whatcha 'posta the matter, Uncle Woods." Everyone laughed, and Walt felt relieved by the humor—though, to be honest, he had no idea what Rex had said. Figure 10.1 shows David Esham and Rex O'Neal at the place of Walt's Brogue baptism.

In retrospect, that episode launched the study of some of the major pronunciation features that characterize the Brogue, as well as one of the early studies of so-called performance speech in the field of linguistics (see chapter 14). As we wrote previously, it is the pronunciation of Ocracoke speech that draws the most attention of outsiders, so in this chapter, we look more closely at these distinctive pronunciations as well as how they are changing.

## SOUNDING NON-AMERICAN

As we noted in earlier chapters, many outsiders think that the Brogue sounds like a non-American dialect, and they often identify it as an English dialect from Australia, Ireland, or from somewhere in England, usually in the southwest of England where the speakers tend to use *r* after a vowel in words like *bear* or *prepare*. Other regions of England, where *r* after a vowel is absent, tend not to sound as Brogue-like to outsiders. As we reported in chapter 1, Chester Lynn, a Brogue-speaking islander who runs an antique shop from his home on Back Road, recounted how he fooled fellow travelers during a trip to Israel about his origins: "And some people [from] England . . . they thought that I was from London. And so, for a joke we went and told them that I was from outside of London, and they believed it for half the trip."

Chester still has one of the stronger Brogues on the island, and folks will sometimes visit his store just to hear him speak. He also loves to "say a word," one of the local expressions used to describe someone who likes to talk. Chester's experience matches the experiment we described previously in which famous British dialectologist Dr. Peter Trudgill played samples of Ocracoke speech to some of his students at the University of Essex. He reported that "they were unanimous in allocating an origin in England to the Ocracoke speaker, with most people opting for an origin in the West Country—that is, southwestern England." These judgments make sense. The strong pronunciation of the *r*-sound and the pronunciation of the words *tide* and *side* as "toid" and "soid" are reminiscent of pronunciations in the West Country, as well as Australian English (and even some other American English varieties). Furthermore, the production of the vowel in *sound* and *down* as "saind" and "dain" is not a production found in other American English varieties, contributing to the Brogue's non-American English identification. Finally, the peculiar sound of the vowel in *bought* and *caught* is more like the British and Australian production of the sound than any American English dialect. Together, these vowel nuances provide the basis for its classification as a dialect that is not American English.

To hear examples of these vowels, visit www.ocracokebrogue.com/chapter/10/QR10-1.mp3.

To hear these pronunciations in a classic island story told by two O'Cockers, Rex O'Neal and James Barrie Gaskill (from *Ocracoke Speaks*), visit www.ocracokebrogue.com/chapter/10/QR10-2.mp3.

Other Ocracoke sounds may strike listeners as more British than American as well. Older Ocracokers pronounce the neighboring island to the north, Hatteras, with a British-like *t*-sound in the middle, so that it comes out something like "Hah-tris," whereas most mainlanders would say "Hah-der-is," but these items are relatively restricted. It is really the vowels of Ocracoke speakers that have triggered its perceived likeness to British and Australian dialects. Sounding British or Australian is not a bad thing in American society, since even two and a half centuries after our independence from England, Americans still value British English as prestigious compared to American English varieties. This favorable perception of British dialects actually helps promote the positive stature of Ocracoke speech, especially in comparison to how southern dialects are often viewed in the United States. Such resemblances to British English are used as evidence of legitimacy in Ocracoke, as well as in other places that purport to have preserved older forms of English, such as the Appalachian Mountains. In a bit of an unexpected twist, most British folks actually favor southern varieties of English over northern ones because some of the southern features align more with British English. For example, the lowering of the vowel so that *mate* may sound more like "might" and *say* more like "sigh" is a feature of British English and Australian English as well as Southern American English. In fact, some of the pronunciation of vowel features in Rex's classic performance phrase of Ocracoke English, like "feesh" for *fish* and "far" for *fire*, are shared by a number of traditional southern vernaculars and are not unique to Ocracoke.

## VOWEL SOUNDS IN OCRACOKE

Leaving aside the strikingly different pronunciations noted above, the other vowels of Ocracoke tend to sound a bit more southern than northern. For example, older speakers would typically produce the vowels of *pin* and *pen* or *been* and *Ben* the same, following the pattern of pronouncing these vowels the same when they occur before nasal sounds like *n* or *m*. This, of course, is a common stereotype of southern speech, where speakers have to modify words like *stickpin* and *writing pen* to differentiate them. In one of our early interviews on Ocracoke, James Barrie Gaskill told us about a traditional island custom that he called "pony penning." As naive outsiders, we did not know if the animals were *pinned* or branded in some way to identify them, or enclosed in a *pen*, as in "cattle penning." The coalescence of short-*i* and short-*e* vowels before nasals was a trait shared by virtually all middle-aged and older O'Cockers and is still present to some extent in younger speakers. Each year, when we teach island eighth-graders about the dialects of North Carolina (see chapter 19), we ask the students in our classes to produce the words *pin* and *pen* to see if the merger of the vowels is still maintained. About half of the native Ocracoke students still produce the vowel in this traditionally southern way. Students not from Ocracoke favor distinguishing them, as do the majority of students who have Latino heritage but have grown up on the island.

To hear James Barrie Gaskill talk about island pony pennings, (from *Ocracoke Speaks*), visit www.ocracokebrogue.com/chapter/10/QR10-3.mp3.

Several other pronunciations in Rex O'Neal's performance are fairly widespread features of southern vernacular speech. For example, the pronunciations of *fire* and *tire* as more like "far" and "tar" are found throughout the Outer Banks, as well as in other southern communities and throughout the Appalachian Mountain region. Despite the widespread nature of this feature, we have collected several humorous stories about the confusion that might result from the misunderstanding of the pronunciation of "arn" for *iron* or from the failure to understand the pronunciation of *fire* as "far." In one case, a student at East Carolina University from the southern Outer Banks was unable to borrow an *iron* for an important event with a university leader because her classmates did not know what she was asking for. Whereas middle-aged and older O'Cockers might still use this form, few of the younger residents would now use this pronunciation.

To watch a vignette in which a Core Banker tells a story about confusion over her pronunciation of *iron* (from *The Carolina Brogue*), visit www.ocracokebrogue.com/chapter/10/QR10-4.mp4.

In a number of dialects, speakers will merge vowel sounds before the sound *l*, as in *pool*, *pull*, and *pole*, or *fool*, *full*, and *foal*, as well as *sell* and *sale* or *tell* and *tale*, so that someone might "tale a tale." Walt Wolfram was once embarrassed during an interview when he thought they said they had a *whale* in their front yard. The person pronounced *well* the same as *whale*, and Walt tried to follow up with conversation about how a *whale* from the ocean had managed to end up in their yard, confusing the person being interviewed. Lay people are not the only ones prone to confusion by the merger of different vowels.

While Walt did mishear *well* as "whale," whales occasionally are spotted from the island. To hear Dave Esham describe one memorable encounter (from *Ocracoke Speaks*), visit www.ocracokebrogue.com/chapter/10/QR10-5.mp3.

Another characteristic feature of traditional Ocracoke speech is the pronunciation of the vowel of *fish* like "feesh" and *dish* like "deesh." This can extend to other words that have a short-*i* vowel before a *sh* or *tch*, as in "keetchen" for *kitchen*, "deetch" for *ditch*, or "weesh" for *wish*. As with all pronunciation differences, there is a specifiable pattern that can be identified. Most O'Cockers think that this pronunciation is a classic feature of the Brogue, and it is sometimes included in the performance routines of Rex O'Neal, although, in reality, it is a trait used in a number of southern dialects. It is hard to tell why this trait is so strongly associated with the stereotypical Ocracoke accent; perhaps the frequency of the word *fish* on the island offers plenty of occasions to hear the word. This frequency, in turn, may have supported its strong association with Ocracoke English, even while it is shared with a number of other dialects. Older Ocracokers report that this pronunciation was commonly corrected in the school. Because of the attention the word has received over the years, some islanders have become quite adept at switching between *fish* and *feesh*, so many residents learned to use "fish" in school or with dingbatters but reserve "feesh" for everyday life.

Today, we can still hear pronunciations of "feesh" for *fish* in some of England's southern counties, such as Devon, Somerset, and Wiltshire, as well as more northern counties such as Lancashire. The fact that we can hear this sound on both sides of the Atlantic, like the pronunciation of the *oi* vowel of "toid" for *tide*, has to do with the historical connection between English and Irish settlers who probably brought it with them and then retained it through historical isolation. This pattern is also found in other isolated regions such as the Ozarks and Appalachia, which strengthens the historical explanation for the feature's presence. There are a lot more nuances about the vowels that sometimes sound very southern in their affiliation, like the pronunciation of *bed* with an extra syllable more like "be-ud," or the pronunciation of *boot* more in the front in the mouth, somewhat like "biut," but Rex's performance phrase demonstrates the distinctiveness of the traditional vowel system of Ocracoke.

## BEYOND VOWELS

Anyone who has visited Ocracoke during the hot, muggy part of the summer can understand why "skeeters," the local pronunciation of for *mosquitoes*, is heard so often on the island. So ubiquitous are the insects that novelty items feature them prominently, including a T-shirt that depicts an oversized skeeter proclaiming, "Send more tourists, the last batch was delicious." *Skeeters* is derived from two common traditional pronunciation changes. The first is the tendency to delete a syllable when it is unstressed at the beginning of the word, so that *tomato* may become "mater" and *potato* can become "tater." All dialects of American English do this to some extent, as in the use of *'bout* for *about* or *'cause* for *because*. Mainstream English tends to limit this process to a specific set of words, whereas Ocracoke, like Appalachian English and some other vernacular varieties of English, can extend it to nouns like *mosquito* and *tomato*, or even to verbs so that *remember* can sometimes be pronounced as "member." The second process found in "skeeters," "maters," and "winders" (for *windows*) involves the changing of the final *o*-sound to an *r*-sound. The rule here is that the change can only take place if the final syllable is unstressed. So, *fellow* becomes "feller," *yellow* becomes "yeller," and even *burrito* can become "burriter." However, when the last syllable is stressed, this change cannot occur, so *below* cannot become "beler" and *go* cannot become "ger." Intricate rules like these demonstrate how regular and predictable these pronunciations can be.

The closer we look at Ocracoke English, the more affinity we find with pronunciations in Appalachian English, which shares many features due to its Scots-Irish heritage. Another of the T-shirts that we saw early in our visits to Ocracoke read, "Young 'uns, hain't I been mommucked this day?" which demonstrates two additional features shared with dialects in the western mountains of North Carolina. The retention of the *h*-sound in "hain't" is preserved from the earlier pronunciations of *it* as "hit" and *ain't* as "hain't," since lost in other dialects of American English. Further, the loss of the *w*-sound in unstressed words like *one* (pronounced by most English speakers as "wuhn"), as in "young 'uns" for *young ones*, is also a trait of Scots-Irish dialects common in the Appalachian Mountains. For the record, the use of *mommuck* for "harass" or "agitate" is simply a preservation of an older term in English. *Mommuck* once meant "to tear into pieces or shred," and is found in a couple of Shakespeare plays. Islanders have simply extended the literal meaning, using it metaphorically to mean "harass" or "bother."

In some cases, dialect differences are not preservations of earlier forms but innovations that occur in the dialect. Some speakers of Ocracoke English add a *t*-sound to the end of some words, including *across* being pronounced as "acrosst," *dose* as "doast" (rhyming with "toast"), *once* as "oncet," *twice* as "twicet," and so forth. The term *doast*, derived from *dose*, has since had its meaning extended in Ocracoke, where is can now be used to mean a "cold" or "influenza." It may be used in a sentence like, "I caught a doast of something." It can also be used as a verb, as in "you better not doast me," which would mean something like "you better not get me sick." It has also been used for a large amount of something, as in "James Barrie caught a doast of crabs." While to our knowledge this term is found only on Ocracoke, the addition or retention of a *t*-sound after *s* is a common trait of Highland English, so it shares that aspect with the Scots-Irish dialects of North Carolina's mountains.

The final pronunciation feature of the Ocracoke Brogue that we investigate is its use of an *r*-sound after a vowel as in words like *bear*, *fear*, *cart*, or *fierce*. Across the sound in the Coastal Plain or in the Piedmont regions of North Carolina, the *r*-sound was lost in these phonetic contexts (e.g., "beah" for *bear* and "caht" for *cart*), especially among older inhabitants. This age difference suggests that dropping this *r*-sound was the dominant pronunciation throughout the inland South. In Ocracoke, however, the evidence suggests that islanders have always been robust pronouncers of these *r*-sounds. Nonetheless, there are a limited number of words that lose their *r*-sounds. Words like *yesterday* and *aggravate* may lose their *r*-sound because they occur in an unstressed syllable, yielding "yeste'day" and "agg'avate," which have managed to become classic markers of Ocracoke speech, as in, "Don't agg'avate me now, I'm busie*r* 'n a ho*r*net." In truth, these are quite limited contexts, but they may stand out because Ocracoke predominantly produces the *r*-sound in other contexts. The *r*-sound may also be dropped in an unaccented syllable at the end of a word, particularly after a *th* sound as in "brothuh" for *brother* or "togethuh" for *together*. Apart from the few patterned exceptions pointed out here, the Ocracoke Brogue falls in line with the Highland South and the *r*-producing areas of the North.

How can such a major difference between British English and Outer Banks English exist, given some of the affinities between them? To answer this question, we need to clear up some misconceptions about British English and other dialects that contributed to American English. First, not all dialects of British English are *r*-less. Some British dialects in the southwest are still *r*-full today, as are some scattered dialects in the midland area. Irish English also pronounces *r* in words such as *cart*, *bear*, and *fort*. Furthermore, contrary to some popular beliefs, *r*-lessness has not always been the predominant and prestigious pattern in England. In fact, around 1700, when Ocracoke was first being settled by Europeans, the limited *r*-less varieties were associated with uneducated, rustic dialects rather than the "King's English." It was not until the end of the 1700s that the *r*-sound began to drop out of elite speech, well after the first arrivals on Ocracoke and the Outer Banks. There was also an early mixture of some Scots-Irish and Irish settlers in Ocracoke that would have supported the pronunciation of the *r*-sound after a vowel.

The story of the *r*-sound in England and the United States teaches us an important lesson about language change and language prestige. While *r*-lessness became the prestige norm in England, in the southern states, and in New York City, the tide has shifted. Before World War II, *r*-lessness was the prestige norm in New York City and in the southern United States, where it was associated with aristocracy. After World War II, the absence of *r* became stigmatized in New York City, and associated with the dialects of those of the lower socioeconomic classes and rural areas of the South. The shifting status of *r* over the years shows us that it is not really how you pronounce something that counts, but who you are when you pronounce it. If you wait long enough, the "right people" can bestow status on just about any pronunciation. By the same token, the use of a language trait by the "wrong people" can stigmatize it regardless of its previous associations.

## PERSPECTIVES ON PRONUNCIATION

Our description of some of the features of pronunciation in traditional Ocracoke vernacular speech might seem a bit overwhelming to readers who do not study dialects as an occupation, but they are actually understated in this overview. The essential point, however, is that these patterns are governed by a complex set of rules that are exciting to uncover for phonetics nerds. The overall impression of Ocracoke English that emerges from our study is that it is distinctive, not so much because it has a few phonetic features that are unique to the barrier islands along the Mid-Atlantic coast, but because of the way that a set of phonetic traits are combined to create a unique dialect. For example, southern dialect traits like "fraysh" for *fresh* and "feesh" for *fish* occur side by side with the pronunciation of the *r*-sound in *farm* and *car* shared with northern dialects. When distinctive traits like "hoi toid" and "saind" for *sound* are added to the mixture, we get an idiosyncratic variety of English. Language is dynamic and always changing, but some of the ways Ocracoke is currently changing its speech differ from language change in other regions, even on the coastal barrier islands of North Carolina. We note later (chapter 24) that younger speakers in Ocracoke tend to adopt northern-like vowels rather than southern vowels. For example, when residents lack the iconic "hoi toid" pronunciation, they tend to adopt the pronunciation of "high tide" of the North or Midwest rather than the "hah tahd" pronunciation from the inland South. On Harkers Island, on the Core Sound to the south of Ocracoke, where the vast majority of visitors come from North Carolina rather than other states, the younger speakers tend to adopt the southern pronunciations when they abandon “toid.” Most of the new residents in Ocracoke who arrive from different states come from Northern or Midwestern states, as do most of the vacation tourists, bringing with them their pronunciations. Changes in pronunciation come from demographic shifts and the social meaning attached to specific ways of saying things. We hope that a growing appreciation of the heritage of the traditional and current Ocracoke accent will contribute to a corresponding respect for the role that the distinctive pronunciations on Ocracoke Island have had in the development of the Brogue and its subsequent change over time, including its current status as an eroding dialect.

*Chapter 11*

# IS THE BROGUE JUST BAD GRAMMAR?

When we first started studying the Ocracoke Brogue, the islanders were not quite sure what to make of our interest. The fact that language specialists were interested in their speech was understandable—that was a common theme among outsiders visiting the island—but our motivations were suspect. Did we come to Ocracoke to make fun of this distinctive dialect? Did we have some other ulterior motive? The reality, of course, is that linguists value all languages and dialects and study them in order to figure out how their structures are patterned. Linguists understand that all languages are systematic and patterned, and their goal is to uncover and describe these patterns. They make no value judgments about grammatical conventions—their objective is simply to find and describe the patterning. Linguistic analysis, in fact, uses the scientific method and is considered a science because of this method. It's the institutions and gatekeeping agents of society that have ascribed notions of what is good, bad, and ugly about language. Unfortunately, these agents unwittingly make judgments that fall in line with the self-supporting values of the ruling class rather than the facts about language.

Most islanders are well aware that outsiders recognize that the local speech is different. This recognition is especially acute for islanders who interact with tourists and other outsiders for a living. Outsiders strike different stances with respect to the islanders' unique dialect. Some of the interactions are quite noteworthy, ranging from outsiders who brazenly approach long-term residents and tell them to speak, as in the example of Candy Gaskill being told to "speak," as mentioned in chapter 1, or the example linked here, in which Vince O'Neal recalls making his first announcement on a Coast Guard vessel. Others disguise their intrigue by eliciting conversation that is more geared to listening to the speech of the islanders than to the content of the islanders' responses. If enough people keep telling you that you have a distinctive way of talking, eventually you will start believing it and accept it as part of your character and community.

To listen to Vince O'Neal tell the story of how his first announcement on his Coast Guard vessel was received, visit www.ocracokebrogue.com/chapter/11/QR11-1.mp4.

At the same time, native Ocracoke students have often been corrected in classrooms for using some of the traditional forms of the Brogue. Students reported that sentences such as "I weren't there last night" were corrected by teachers who said they did not use *was* or *weren't* correctly. Or, if a student were to say "It was more than four pound of fish," they might be told that they "left the *s* off" of *pound*. These are common structures used by Brogue speakers, so these teachers' responses imply, even if they do not state it explicitly, that the grammar of the Brogue is really nothing more than a collection of "grammatical errors."

Linguists take strong exception to this characterization, because applying the scientific method to language has proven that all languages and dialects have systematic patterns. This empirical fact applies to all dialects regardless of their deviation from the mainstream, standardized system of English that is endorsed by schools. We have argued this point repeatedly, if not always convincingly. There is great linguistic value mistakenly ascribed to the middle-class dialects used in schools, where the educational system pressures all students to conform to the language varieties of a small handful of students. In this chapter, we present evidence for our position that dialects operate with their own grammatical rules by investigating the two examples illustrated above, since they relate to grammatical rules of the Brogue. Similar investigations could be done for every grammatical difference found in the Brogue, because all such differences are patterned. "Grammatical mistakes," "bad English," "improper English," and other terms that disparagingly describe language are simply an inaccurate, biased description of the different rules that govern dialects that distinguish them from institutional mainstream norms and expectations. Curiously, there is often more tolerance for pronunciation and vocabulary differences, since these are long-recognized traits of different dialects in the United States, but grammar takes on most of the stigma associated with different dialects.

The grammatical structure of the Brogue may not be sanctioned in schools, but its features involve intricate systematic patterning in its own right. Chapter 8 walks readers through how a linguist might study the use of *to* for *at*, in sentences like "she's to the store," on Ocracoke. Recall that we discovered a pattern whereby this substitution can only happen for things that are temporarily in a place and not other usages where *at* is required. For example, O'Cockers would never say "look to that" instead of "look at that" or "I don't want that to all" instead of "I don't want that at all." While this pattern has a number of grammatical factors constraining it, the patterns we present below are more straightforward.

## *WAS* AND *WEREN'T* ON OCRACOKE

The use of *weren't* on Ocracoke where other dialects use *wasn't*, as in "I weren't there" or "It weren't in the house" is a local dialect feature that stands out. In the United States, this trait is found only among American English dialects in the Mid-Atlantic coastal region extending from the waterways of Virginia and Maryland in the north to the southern areas of coastal North Carolina. It is, however, a familiar, non-standardized pattern found in a number of British dialects, including some of the midland and southwestern regions of England.

In current standardized English, *was* is used to mark a singular form, as in *I was*, *she/he/it was*, with singular *you* being an exception because it was once used as a plural form. Recall from chapter 4 that historically in English *you* was plural and *thou* was singular form. So, historically, the distinction between *was* and *were* was purely based on singular versus plural subjects, as seen here:

| | |
|---|---|
| I was | We were |
| Thou was | You were |
| He/she/it was | They were |

Over time, *you* replaced the earlier singular *thou* form to indicate politeness when speaking to someone, leading to the exception that we have now, which is produced here:

| | |
|---|---|
| I was | We were |
| You were | You were |
| He/she/it was | They were |

Standardized English has maintained this inelegant system for a few hundred years. And while we can explain it via the documented history of the language, no one could argue that it is logical. Many times, dialects often change language in ways that make things more regular or clearer, especially when mainstream English has exceptions or irregularities. This is the basis for what the Brogue has done with *was* and *were*. Put simply, there is no linguistic need to distinguish between the two forms, so some islanders do not. Instead, thy use *was* across all subjects, as in the examples below.

| | |
|---|---|
| I was | We was |
| You was | You was |
| He/she/it was | They was |

While this change might seem like "bad English" at first, comparing this example set to the previous one leads to the conclusion that it is actually standardized English's irregular system that is less desirable. Linguists call the process of taking something that is irregular and making it regular either *regularization* or *leveling*. So, saying the Brogue has leveled to *was* means that O'Cockers use *was* as the conjugation for all grammatical subjects.

The intriguing thing about the past tense forms of *be* on Ocracoke is not just in the leveling to *was*, but in the repurposing of the form *were*. In the Ocracoke Brogue, whether you use *was* or *were* actually depends on whether you are forming an affirmative or negative sentence. In addition to leaving to *was* in the affirmative, O'Cockers also level to *weren't* in the negative, as is shown here.

| | |
|---|---|
| I weren't | We weren't |
| You weren't | You weren't |
| He/she/it weren't | They weren't |

Language is rather amazing in how it can shift and change structures, and dialects are one of the best examples of this creativity. This reconfiguration of the verb forms eliminates the irregular conjugation pattern of *was* and *were* while also increasing the clarity of the distinction between affirmative and negative sentences. This different grammatical use of *was* and *weren't* in the Ocracoke Brogue is highly patterned and systematic, just like the earlier use of these forms to differentiate singular and plural. This feature, restricted geographically to the coastal areas of North Carolina,

Virginia, and Maryland, is surprising in part because middle-aged and some younger speakers in some Outer Banks communities seem to use it along with older speakers, contrary to the expected pattern of dialect change for different generations of Ocracoke residents. We also found that islanders, especially women, were more likely to use *weren't* when talking among themselves than with outsiders; men seem less likely to adjust its use according to audience.

To hear Chester Lynn use this form in his speech, visit www.ocracokebrogue.com/chapter/11/QR11-2.mp3.

## PLURAL -*S* IN THE OCRACOKE BROGUE

Another grammatical structure often labeled as a grammatical error is the absence of a plural -*s* in phrases like "four pound of fish," "fourteen mile long," or "two acre of land." Again, we find this is not an error but part of an intricate pattern. There are two rules that govern this pattern. First, the omission of the -*s* plural occurs only with nouns of measurement. Words like *inch*, *foot*, *pound*, *acre*, and so forth are eligible to leave off the -*s*. Common nouns like *cat*, *apple*, *car*, or *hat* cannot omit the -*s* because they do not refer to a measurement, so we never hear sentences like "We have four cat/apple/car/hat."

The second rule of the pattern is that the measure noun that would usually have the -*s* must be preceded by a number word of some type, technically called a "quantifier." A quantifier just tells us "how many," and might be a precise amount (e.g., *four*) or imprecise amount (e.g., *many*).This means that *pound*, *acre*, *mile*, and so forth cannot omit the -*s* unless a quantifier precedes them. So, we hear *four pound* and *many mile*, but never hear "We caught pound of fish" or "We rode the bike for mile." Rules apply to all of the structures of the Brogue, and the job of linguists is to discover these rules and describe them.

To hear Chester drop the *-s* on measurement nouns, visit www.ocracokebrogue.com/chapter/11/QR11-3.mp3.

## WHY DO GRAMMATICAL PATTERNS MATTER?

It may sound strange, but every time we find a new pattern and describe it, we feel proud of our discovery. We also like to share our discoveries with others. We have now taught the rules described above to more than three decades of students on Ocracoke, and they are usually surprised to learn that all dialects are patterned and impressed by the complexity of the patterns. The students may not remember all the details of these or other rules we teach, but one thing is certain: students develop respect for how complex patterns can sometimes be, and therefore come to respect different dialects of English, including their own.

The two examples we presented above also highlight another lesson about dialects. Some patterns in dialects may be shared by other regional or social dialects, while there are a few that are restricted to particular regions. The omission of the *-s* on measurement nouns with quantifiers is common elsewhere in the rural American South and is well-documented in Irish English and in parts of England, particularly in the northern region. The pattern of negative *weren't* is restricted to coastal and island dialects in the Mid-Atlantic South and a few areas in England, so it is readily indicative that a person may be from the Outer Banks.

One subtle grammatical form we have found only on the island is the use of *-some* to intensify an adjective. If a person says "the meal was goodsome," it was very good and if they say it was "nastysome," try to avoid the dish the next time it is offered. When *some* is attached to a word, it no longer acts as a separate word but as part of the adjective. In other words, *goodsome* really counts as a single word, just like single words such as *awesome* and *wholesome*. Nothing can come between an adjective and the *-some* ending, so that a person cannot say, "The food was nasty sitting in the dish some."

A couple of other conditions also affect how *-some* is used. First of all, *-some* can only attach to words of two syllables or less. People can say *nastysome* or *prettysome* but they do not say *beautifulsome* or *ridiculoussome*. Also, *-some* generally comes at the end of the phrase; it does not often occur in the middle of the phrase, as in "He was an uglysome man."

In the following interview excerpt, Candy Gaskill explains how the use of *-some* attached to an adjective works.

> *-Some* can be used frequently. Can be used like, *good-some*, *bad-some*, like "boys, that's good-some to eat. Boys, that's bad-some to eat." You know that's not any good. And, as we spoke yesterday, you know, "Shoot, I feel badsome today." Especially, if you've been like Rex, like you've been out all night long you know and you've tied one on. And you gotta get up in the next morning, instead of a hangover, you'd just say, "Shoo, I feel badsome today."
>
> [noise/interviewer]
>
> Well, sometimes when you . . . sometimes it's been like used with *fast* and *slow*, you know, like, "Shoo, I wish that dingbatter would get out of my way 'cause he's slowsome" or "Shoo, that car's fastsome." I seen a Corvette in the parking lot and I said, "Shoo, I bet that car's fastsome." You know. So, it can be used in various ways, not only necessarily with food, or people, or what. I guess it just depends on the person and how they want to use and when they want to use it. So, or you can, you know, like with animals. You can say, "Shoo, that dog's doggysome." You know, that type of thing. You know, so it's just, *-some* seems to be I don't know why, it just seems to be an extra [oomph] added on to either *good*, or *bad*, or *stinky*, or *fast*, or *slow*. . . .
>
> Growing up, like if had played outside, and we had been running hard all day, we'd been swimming and doing this, that, and the other and everything. When we would get home, like our moms or our grandparents and whatever would say, "Shoo, y'all are goaty-some!" Which, meaning that we kind

> of smelled sweaty because we had been playing hard all day, we'd been swimming and usually we had 'tater rows either round our necks or in our arm slits, which are dirt. Pretty much was what it was, was just like plain dirt that you'd have in the cracks of your neck and cracks of your arms, and we just always called 'em 'tater rows.

To hear Candy Gaskill explain how *-some* works with adjectives in Ocracoke, visit www.ocracokebrogue.com/chapter/11/QR11-4.mp3.

At first glance, this unusual use of *-some* seems like a minor word difference, but further investigation shows that it is another example of the intricacy of the grammar of Ocracoke English. It might be hard to believe for the casual reader, but such nuanced details of language patterning are a delight to linguists. More importantly, they prove definitively that nothing could be further from the truth than the assessment that the Brogue—or any dialect—is little more than a collection of grammatical errors. Instead, every dialect is a collection of highly intricate patterns that characterize a community of speakers who use it as a primary form of communication.

One of the things we hope our teaching about dialects has done on Ocracoke is to convince islanders that their way of speaking is not simply "bad grammar" or a "collection of mistakes." It is a different grammar that follows a distinct set of patterns. They are not the same as mainstream, standardized English, but they are intricate, patterned, and deserve respect for what they represent about language. Chester Lynn happily expresses the change of attitude this understanding can bring about in the following statement:

> When Sam or me or somebody else would be talking to each other and we'd say, "All right, say, listen you. You ain't mommucking me no more. You mommucked me to death today!" And the teacher would try to interrupt us or try to afterwards when she'd hear us, she'd say, "Listen, that's

> bad English, and you should not say that." You know, and she would try to correct us in certain things we usually do when we get talking. And a lot of local people, when they get excited, they talk fast, you know. It's just a common thing with us. . . . And she would fuss at us and argue about us and say, "Listen you shouldn't do that. You shouldn't say that." You know. And it made everybody feel sort of bad because it was what you were taught. It was the way your parents or your grandparents talked, you know? And nobody wanted to feel ignorant or wanted to feel embarrassed, but it's the way your ancestors had been taught. And so that's the good part now with the Brogue is that people understand, that, you know, it was the family's descent and the family's legacy that went on. It wasn't that it was that bad English, it was just a different English.

To hear this passage from Chester Lynn (from *Ocracoke Still Speaks*), visit www.ocracokebrogue.com/chapter/11/QR11-5.mp3.

Chester sums it up perfectly, far clearer than a linguist usually would: it is not bad English; it is just different English. While there will always be social guidelines that deem some dialects or patterns to be better or worse, these evaluations have no linguistic basis. As the example with *was* and *weren't* demonstrates clearly, the distinction maintained in modern standardized English is not historically the pattern found in the language, nor is it logical or consistent. The version that the Brogue maintains is actually more linguistically consistent. In fact, when we look at dialects of English, linguists often find that the grammatical variations that outsiders are quick to demean are oftentimes more consistent or clearer than those found in so-called standard English.

*Chapter 12*

# DO MEN AND WOMEN ON OCRACOKE SPEAK DIFFERENTLY?

NATALIE SCHILLING, PHD

When outsiders think of East Coast US islands like Ocracoke, they likely think of activities and traditions like fishing, crabbing, clamming, and oystering, and of the men who kept their families economically afloat through maritime activities. In other words, when they think of an O'Cocker, they think of the traditional island waterman. Nowadays, of course, Ocracoke islanders make their livings in a variety of ways, but especially through activities related to Ocracoke's thriving tourism industry. But sometimes people forget that there's always been a segment of Ocracoke society who did not work the water—a group of people who kept the island community going in other, equally vital ways. And that is the women of Ocracoke.

## WOMEN'S TRADITIONS IN OCRACOKE

Over the centuries, Ocracoke women have participated in Ocracoke culture alongside men, and they have also developed rich cultural traditions of their own. For example, it was mostly women who cultivated Ocracoke's rich food culture, inventing and adapting recipes for such island staples as Ocracoke fig preserve and fig cake. Nowadays, Ocracoke's figs are so famous that there's an annual Fig Festival, complete with a Savory Fig Dinner showcasing lots of inventive dishes incorporating Ocracoke's famous fruit, and of course an Ocracoke fig cake bake-off.

Ocracoke women have also long been renowned for their skill, industry, and artistry in quilting. The well-known Ocracoke "cracker quilt" is a distinctive Ocracoke variant of a design passed down from colonial times, so called because the predominant design in its original form resembles a Christmas cracker, a tube filled with sweets first popularized in nineteenth-century England. And while you might think that traditional women's handicrafts like quilting, knitting, and sewing have gone by the wayside with the advent of online shopping and the replacement of in-person social activities with social media, Ocracoke women still get together for quilting parties, or quilting bees, just as they have for generations. The Ocracoke Needle and Thread Society meets weekly to piece together quilts that are raffled off to benefit the Ocracoke Preservation Society and the annual Ocrafolk Festival. Members of the society also take special care to ensure that the island tradition is passed down by giving quilting lessons to students in the Ocracoke School.

## DIALECT TRADITIONS, DIALECT INNOVATIONS—DIALECT LOSS?

Ocracoke's distinctive dishes are often a unique mix of elements from different source recipes. Island resident Margaret Garrish invented Ocracoke fig cake in the mid-twentieth century by substituting figs for dates in a traditional spice-cake recipe. Similarly, the Ocracoke quilt is a distinct take on a long-standing traditional pattern that now involves its own unique striping and coloration. In the same way, the Ocracoke dialect is its own distinctive blend and represents another expression of Ocracoke's unique culture and heritage. Just as women have been instrumental in giving Ocracoke culture its distinctive flavor, so too have they played their part in shaping Ocracoke's ways of speaking. Women and men sometimes use language very differently in Ocracoke, and these differences are an integral part of Ocracoke's colorful linguistic tapestry.

Linguistic studies across the United States and the world have shown that in many communities, as in Ocracoke, women and men have different patterns of dialect variation. This is particularly true in communities undergoing social and linguistic change. Very often, men hold onto linguistic traditions more strongly than women, who may be quicker than men to embrace dialect features from outside areas and let go of localized vocabulary, pronunciations, and grammatical patterns.

In our studies of dialect change across generations of Ocracoke residents, beginning in the mid-1990s, we have found that in many ways, the traditional Ocracoke Brogue has become less distinctive over the decades. This change is a product of tourism; as travel to and from the island became easier, the island was transformed from a primarily maritime community to one whose economy depends in large part on hosting tourists from outside dialect areas. Even the iconic "hoi toid" pronunciation for which islanders are known is now fading as Ocracokers adopt northern or midwestern pronunciations like *high tide* (this change is discussed in more detail in chapter 10). But the high tide washing over the Ocracoke dialect has not affected everyone in the community equally.

We studied usage levels for "hoi toid" versus "high tide" across three generations of our original study participants and found that, for the most part, older O'Cockers had a higher proportion of "hoi toid" (versus "high tide" or "hah tahd") pronunciations than middle-aged and younger speakers. This indicates that, in general, the "hoi toid" pronunciation is receding. But the picture was not as straightforward when we considered men's usage patterns separately from women's. Women's pronunciations followed the general pattern, with progressively lower usage levels for "hoi toid" in each progressively younger generation. However, one group of men went against the general trend—a group of middle-aged men who actually showed higher rather than lower usage levels for "hoi toid" than older island residents, who otherwise usually had the thickest Brogue. We came to refer to these men as the Poker Game Network, since they routinely got together for traditional island men's activities like fishing, crabbing, and playing cards. The men loved these iconic island activities, and they seemed to love the iconic dialect, too, showing their attachment to it by keeping certain features like "hoi toid" alive, even as they were receding around them.

Unfortunately, the Poker Game Network's increased usage levels for the "hoi toid" pronunciation and other features of the traditional Brogue wasn't enough to keep these features from fading among younger people; and younger generations, even in the 1990s, had lower rates of traditional features than middle-aged and older islanders. However, boys still used "hoi toid" more than girls, suggesting that traditional pronunciations like this had become associated more with masculine identity and with traditional male activities on the island like fishing and poker-playing. This idea was born out in a later study that we did of an Ocracoke men's group in the early 2000s, made up of men who were mainly the sons of Poker Game Network men. These guys still kept the "hoi toid" pronunciation alive, even though usage levels for this traditional feature were lower among other men their same age. They also used more sentence structure features of the traditional

Brogue, for example, "It weren't me," or "I weren't home," where *weren't* is used in place of *wasn't*—another classic O'Cocker feature (see chapter 11 for more).

## WHY DO OCRACOKE WOMEN SOMETIMES SOUND LESS BROGUE-Y?

Nowadays, there are still a few young men with stronger Brogues than other young people, including younger women and girls, just as there are still a few young men who engage in traditional men's maritime activities. It is hard to say how much of men's dialect retention and women's dialect loss has to do with associations between a thick Brogue and "men's work" and how much has to do with other factors. It may also be that women might strive to model more standard language for children, since they are still mostly the ones who raise them, and so maybe that is why they have been quicker to let go of features like "hoi toid" and "It weren't me." Or it may be that Ocracoke women adopt outside language features more quickly than men because, in some ways, they have had more contact with outsiders than men as the decades have passed. As the economy transitioned from fishing and related activities to tourism, it was women who first had day-to-day contact with mainlanders, since they worked in restaurants, hotels, and motels, while men who were giving up fishing moved into construction, hotel management, and other "behind the scenes" activities. O'Cocker Candy Gaskill, put it this way, when we asked her about the loss of the brogue back in the 1990s: "I think it's worse for the girls than it is for the boys, because the girls, they can't fish and they can't crab, you know, and take up a trade like that, so they eventually end up in one of the restaurants or motels. . . . They're on more of a day-to-day basis with the tourists and stuff, so I think they're losing [the Brogue] more than a lot of the boys are."

These gender-based differences were supported by some anonymous observations with people on and off the island. Walt Wolfram once asked an ancestral islander at the ferry station in Cedar Island why the current generation of women seemed to use the Brogue less than men. Her answer was poignant: "Because it doesn't sound lady-like." This statement supports the notion that the "hoi toid" pronunciation is now affiliated with masculinity. We also observe that only men are the "dialect performers" for outsiders, even though there are a few women whose Brogue is surely the equal of their male counterparts in the middle and older generations. Over time, the Brogue has come to serve as social capital primarily for men, connoting physical strength and familiarity with the traditional culture of Ocracoke. For women, it does not carry much social capital, and might even represent a period when they had less opportunity to participate in the Ocracoke economy and social life. In fact, when we teach our dialect awareness curriculum to eighth-graders in the school, we sometimes have a contest to see who can do the best imitation of Rex O'Neal's famous performance phrase featuring a number of Brogue-y features. It is common for the boys in the class attempt the phrase with gusto while the girls tend to be shyer about it, often laughing in the middle of their performance because it sounds so unusual for them to be using these features.

## WHAT COUNTS AS THE "REAL" BROGUE?

All of this is not to say that Ocracoke women do not speak a "true" Brogue. The Brogue, like any dialect, has lots of variation within it, and some varieties are more vernacular and different from "mainstream" ways of talking, while others are closer to mainstream standards. Women and men use language differently, different generations have their linguistic differences, and everyone uses language in different ways depending on the situations in which they find themselves. Ocracokers frequently tell us that they use fewer Brogue features when they are interacting with mainlanders than when they are talking with fellow islanders, and they also have lots of tales about misunderstandings when they inadvertently used Ocracoke features off island. O'Cocker Cathy Scarborough told a story about how she and her friend Melinda had dialect issues when they were away at university in the mainland city of Greenville, North Carolina. Interestingly, the confusion at the heart of this story feature a distinctive pronunciation of the "eye" vowel in the word *fire*, but it is not the traditional "hoi toid" pronunciation that causes the problem:

> Melinda and me, the story on us in Greenville was, we lived on the same hall. Of course they put one of us out in this corner and one in that corner, was how it ended up, and that wasn't exactly the quietest way to be, because we hollered the whole year long, back and forth, talk, talk, talk, and . . . they elected us to be the fire marshals for that floor, and what we were supposed to do if there was a fire in the dorm, or the fire alarm went off, was run around and knock on all the doors and say, "Fire! Fire!" You know, make sure everybody knew to get out. Well, we got laughing, because have you ever heard Melinda say *fire*? "Far! Far! Far!" And Daddy and everybody told her if she runs around hollers that wouldn't nobody know what in the world she was talking about anyway. You better elect somebody who can at least say the word!

Just as women are open to picking up dialect features from outside their local communities, so too are they adept at style shifting across situations, to make sure people around them understand. Letting go of a few features of a local dialect in certain situations does not mean you are giving up on your community. Quite the contrary, in the case of the women of Ocracoke. They preserve traditional foodways by promoting dishes like fig cakes, and they keep traditional women's crafts and social activities alive through maintaining the rich tradition of Ocracoke quilting. And even if a few *hoi toid*'s are lost along the way, the unique voices of Ocracoke live on, including in Ocracoke's vibrant storytelling tradition.

## WOMEN'S STORIES IN OCRACOKE

Dialect is not just about individual pronunciation and grammar features. It is also about ways of structuring conversations and painting pictures of community and personal life in vivid stories.

Men and women alike love to talk about Ocracoke's rich history and its present-day distinctiveness. Men have shared with us tales of danger on the water, humorous interactions with dingbatters, or off-islanders, and colorful characters from the past. Women share similar stories, and they also talk about women's distinctive experiences in the island community. Traditionally, the realm of women in Ocracoke was marriage, family, and children, with women historically depending on the island's hardworking men for their livelihood. Because of their position, women sometimes faced special hardships, through which they were buoyed up by family and community. Ellen Cloud once described for us how women got by when the family breadwinner died. We asked her whether there were paying jobs available for island widows, and she replied,

> No. And usually, once in a while, you'll find where they got money, but most of the time they didn't. They were allotted so many barrels of pork, so many barrels of flour, so much molasses for that year, and it was given to them in food or whatever. Not money . . .
>
> And usually, I've found that most of the women, they took in laundry, or, you know, cleaned house for somebody or did something like that to help support them. But most of the time, they remarried. I mean, it was almost a necessity to remarry if you have a big family. And the other thing I have found—and not just Ocracoke but in other genealogies I've done, too—a lot of times they marry, like, if the husband dies and the woman is left with children, she might marry the brother, the husband's brother. He might take on that responsibility of taking care of those kids and would marry her.

To hear Ellen Cloud's complete recounting of how inheritances worked on Ocracoke (from *Ocracoke Speaks*), visit www.ocracokebrogue.com/chapter/12/QR12-1.mp3.

We have also heard poignant stores about other types of challenges women in Ocracoke have faced to keep their families well and safe from harm. World War II was a particularly tough time in the island community, as it was throughout the world. Essie O'Neal (see fig. 12.1) told us of her memories from the war, including how she and the other women comforted children as artillery fire (luckily just for military training) rang out around them:

> But during the war, World War II, that was in '42, now. They had all kind of practice on this island. They had guns. They even had a cannon gun down there. And they used smoke screens. They used blackouts. And we had those green shades, and they were worn so much, you know, the dark green shades you pull down. You could see the light through the cracks. We had a blackout. Some kind of siren or something would go off, a horn or something, means you put your lights out. And we have to put the lights out, and there'd be babies in there a-cryin'—couldn't find our bottle, milk, or nothing. We'd sit down in that chair and hold that baby until it'd stop crying because it's afraid of the dark. And you could see the fire from them bullets through that —they were practicing—through them green shades. You could see that fire through them green shades, right. And you could hear them—those bombs off here in the ocean. They had blown up one of them ships. And the way the lights would jar, like that, sometimes if they were close. We'd go up that stairs, look out the window, over the ocean way and see them burning out there on the ocean, the ships. And it was scary.

To hear Essie O'Neal describe the blackouts during World War II (from *Ocracoke Still Speaks*), visit www.ocracokebrogue.com/chapter/12/QR12-2.mp3.

FIGURE 12.1. Essie O'Neal in her front yard. Photograph by Ann Ehringhaus.

There are also more lighthearted stories. Women and men alike have talked with us about favorite foods and recipes (those that are not too secret to share!), and they have told some funny food stories, too. Elizabeth Howard (see fig. 12.2) told us a tale about introducing Ocracoke seafood to friends at her off-island school, an interaction that caused a bit of confusion—or maybe bewilderment—just like in the earlier story about "Far Marshals" in the college dorm. Mrs. Howard's story also shows just how much O'Cockers love their unique community, culture, and dialect—and of course its foods:

> I had known some girls and boys, too, that went away to school, and they would not tell anybody they were from Ocracoke. . . . I guess that we were isolated, and maybe somebody had laughed at something they'd said, or I don't know why, but I've always told them I was from Ocracoke.

FIGURE 12.2. Island matriarch Elizabeth Howard. Photograph by Ann Ehringhaus.

Now, I've never told them anywhere else. And people did not know where Ocracoke was. They did not.

When I went to school in Angier [a bit south of Raleigh, North Carolina], my daddy sent a barrel full of oysters in the shell to me, and I gave them all away in that neighborhood. Well, of course, they didn't know how to open oysters, and nobody'd ever had an oyster knife. They had to use any kind of knife they had. They'd hit them with a hammer to break the shell. And they had never been to an island, as far as I was concerned. In fact, even up in Maryland, one time this lady found out that, she asked me, I think, to tell her where I was from, and I told her Ocracoke Island. And she said, "You live on an island?" And I said, "Yes, I do." And she sort of frowned, like, and she thought that was terrible: "Well, what do you eat?" And I said, "Well, honey, you name it, and we eat it." And I don't know anyplace that I have been—now I haven't been out of the USA—but I've been everywhere, I think, just about. I haven't been to Texas and the Western states. But I have never been anywhere where people eat any better than they do here on the island!

To hear Elizabeth Howard talk about introducing oysters to her mainland classmates (from *Ocracoke Speaks*), visit www.ocracokebrogue.com/chapter/12/QR12-3.mp3.

As you can tell, Ocracokers love to tell stories about misunderstandings between islanders and dingbatters. Some of these are set outside the island community. But Brogue-based miscommunications happen on the island, too, including as a result of marriage between islanders and non-islanders. The stories in this chapter also show how important Brogue vocabulary, pronunciations, and grammar features have historically been to both men and women islanders. People tell stories about distinctive pronunciations like "far" for *fire*; they sprinkle their tales with grammatical features like *a-cryin'*, and they use island words like *mommucked*, and interject island sayings like "He's an educated fool!"

In some ways, the traditional Brogue is fading away, as mainland features are being substituted for traditional Ocracoke ways of talking. And even if men hold onto the dialect a little longer than women, islanders of all types still maintain the aspects of Ocracoke culture and speech that have made it special for so long. The community is warm and welcoming, the stories are humorous and heartwarming, local arts and crafts are thriving, and the food is still delicious. Just as a date cake can become an island delicacy when figs are substituted for dates, so too is the language of Ocracoke enriched as new ingredients are brought in by a diverse array of new folks, whether tourists from the mainland United States, or newer residents whose heritage language is Spanish.

*Chapter 13*

# CAN DINGBATTERS UNDERSTAND THE BROGUE?

At first glance, the title of this chapter might seem absurd, but the number of stories O'Cockers tell us about outsiders claiming that they cannot understand them suggests that it is a question worth exploring. Further, consider that one of the best-known language books, *Men Are from Mars, Women Are from Venus*, centers on an intelligibility gap that is much smaller than the difference between the Brogue and other dialects of English. When it comes to outsiders understanding the Brogue, it is usually not a matter of "yes" or "no" but of "more" or "less." Digging a little deeper into this question reveals some interesting ideas to explore and highlights some of the most playful aspects of the dialect.

## WHERE DO PEOPLE THINK BROGUE SPEAKERS ARE FROM?

As we have noted throughout this book, the Brogue is unique among American dialects in that it is the only dialect regularly misidentified as being non-American, often mistaken as Australian, British, or Irish. Rex O'Neal recounts this phenomenon, "A lot of people will look at me, say, what are you? Is that an Irish-English accent? Where you guys from, anyway, Australia or what?" Residents face this scrutiny even more strongly when they travel, so much so that they sometimes turn it into a bit of a game. O'Cocker Chester Lynn is fond of telling the story, which we have recounted previously, of when he was on a guided trip to Israel and his accent piqued the interest of some of his fellow travelers. For the whole week, his fellow travelers believed he was from a small town outside of London!

Islanders have stories about the scrutiny their dialects garnered when they went away to college or joined the military. Resident Vince O'Neal recalls a time when he was in the Coast Guard and had to make an announcement on a boat: "The first time I ever reported on a Coast Guard boat and had to make [an announcement], everybody comes running out on the quarterdeck and said, 'Who in the world is this?' and 'Where are you from, son?' You kind of learn how to pronounce certain words so people can understand them." Kenny Ballance recalls the first time he brought college friends back to the island and he slipped back into his native way of talking:

> I invited some of my college roommates and classmates to come home with me one weekend. So, we came down, and we went out that night and got in with some of the local people here like Phil Styron and different ones that I grew up with. And so, when I got back to the house that night they said, "Kenny we just can't understand how that takes place." I said, "Well what are you talking about?" And they said, "Well when you're in Greenville going to college with us you talk fine, but

when you come down and you start mixing with the people you grow up with, we can't understand a word you say."

To watch a vignette in which Kenny Ballance recalls bringing college classmates back to Ocracoke (from *The Ocracoke Brogue*), visit www.ocracokebrogue.com/chapter/13/QR13-1.mp4.

As mentioned previously, even linguists have trouble identifying the Brogue as an American dialect. Recall the experiment of Dr. Peter Trudgill that we recounted in the opening chapter of this book, where his recordings of O'Cockers were universally judged to be speakers from the British Isles, most commonly from the southwestern area. Chapters 4, 5, and 6 examine the connections to British dialects more deeply, but most likely it is the distinctive pronunciation of the vowels in words like *high tide* as "hoi toid" combined with the robust pronunciations of the *r*-sound in words like *car* or *prepare* that lead people to these misguided conclusions.

## HOW OFTEN DO DINGBATTERS HEAR THE REAL BROGUE?

If you scoffed at this chapter's title question, you might reflect on just how much exposure you have had to the traditional island Brogue. Since the 1960s, when tourism really began to increase, islanders have gotten more skilled at style-shifting. Additionally, many younger folk from traditional island families acquired dialects of English that are quite different from the traditional Brogue. These facts make it difficult for visitors to be certain they even heard the Brogue while on island.

The style-shifting abilities of O'Cockers are impressive, and understandably so. When your livelihood depends on your ability to communicate effectively with tourists, or you just get sick of being asked "What did you say?," you might learn to change your speech in certain situations. Style-shifting was also reinforced at school when more and more teachers came from off island. We conclude chapter 11 with Chester Lynn's experience of being corrected by teachers in the school about his dialect. The tension between pride and shame—and inclusion and exclusion—is recounted by Barbara Garrity Blake:

> The people are extremely proud of where they're from, and I think the Brogue is sort of a badge of that. But then there's—there—the other side of that is there's a little bit of a shame factor too. And I was just talking to a woman from Marshallberg who is convinced that she didn't get a job that she just applied for because of her Brogue. You know, I don't know if that's true or not, but people are real conscious of that, you know. Do people make fun of us because we talk in—in this way?

The multiple pressures of tourism, in-migration, and education have certainly made it easier to understand islanders, but the lingering tensions between pride and shame have had a lingering effect, resulting in a range of language styles for islanders.

To hear Chester Lynn recall how the Brogue was treated in school (from *Ocracoke Still Speaks*), visit www.ocracokebrogue.com/chapter/13/QR13-2.mp3.

One example of an O'Cocker's linguistic range demonstrates just how dramatic the style-shifting of locals can be. During one interview, Rex O'Neal spoke in relatively flat and measured English, responding to questions from one of our graduate students. One bit of the transcript reads, "When I came back, the first four years after I came back, I opened myself up a little retail seafood business. In the summertime, I sold fish, cleaned and sold fish to restaurants, and also sold fish retail, me and three other guys together, opened up a little retail business and we sold fish retail." In this excerpt, there are relatively few distinctive features of the traditional Brogue. During the interview, a couple of Rex's brothers drove up in a pickup and they all began talking to each other. Rex immediately shifted his dialect. The rate of speech increased; his pitch accents took on a new, sing-songy lilt; his pronunciations shifted to be more like those of the traditional Brogue. The difference has to be heard to be appreciated, so before reading on, listen to the linked recordings.

To hear Rex O'Neal shift between different linguistic styles, visit www.ocracokebrogue.com/chapter/13/QR13-3.mp3.

If you had a hard time understanding Rex's conversation with his brothers, you are in good company. It took us many hours to create the imperfect transcript that accompanies the clip. The gist of the story is that a mandarin duck was causing some problems with one of Rex's traps. What is important here is not the story, but how different the speech of locals can be when they are talking among themselves. They have learned to accommodate to outsiders so well that you almost have to be lucky to hear much of the traditional Brogue. In fact, even the language Rex and his brothers were using might not have all the characteristics of the traditional Brogue. When asked what the old-timers sounded like, Rex voices the dialect of his elders by performing a traditional island saying, "It's high tide on the sound side, last night the water-fire, tonight the moonshine, no fish. What do you suppose the matter is, Uncle Woods?" This saying explains two bad nights of fishing, the first caused by water-fire, which is phosphorus in the water, and the second caused by a bright moon. In it, you can hear the traditional "hoi toid" vowels, the pronunciation of *fish* as "feesh," and the pronunciation of *fire* as "far." These contrast with the pronunciations Rex uses when talking to our graduate student and with his brothers.

To hear Rex O'Neal perform the dialect as he understood his elders to use it (from *The Carolina Brogue*), visit www.ocracokebrogue.com/chapter/13/QR13-4.mp4.

Many words and expressions that islanders use are unfamiliar to outsiders and can cause confusion. Roger Garrish tells a story of the Brogue being lost in translation just after his sister married a non-islander:

> And during the middle of the night my sister woke us all up laughing just as hard as she could laugh. And the next morning, we said, "What in the world did you, you know, what were the pair of you laughing at last night?" You know, "You woke the whole house up." My brother-in-law . . . and my momma that night when she had cooked for everybody and she was wore out and she said, "The crowd of ya has mommucked me to death. I'm going to bed." Well, my brother-in-law is an educated fool. And so anyway, he had never heard the word *mommucked.* So, he found a dictionary in the house and could not find the word. It drove him crazy. Because he thought that it was something offensive that, you know, and momma was upset about. And so, during the middle of the night he woke my sister up and said, "Sheila, what in the world did momma mean being 'mommucked?' Is she mad at us or something?" And my sister laughed. That's when she woke up the whole house.

Islanders know they speak a variety of English that can trip up outsiders, and while they are generally very linguistically accommodating, they seem to take delight in the moments where they have to explain something to the "educated fools" who visit the island. The website accompanying this book shares the full audio of two oral history projects we have done with the Ocracoke community. Many of these stories share additional humorous anecdotes in this vein.

To listen to Roger Garrish tell this story about his in-laws (from *Ocracoke Still Speaks*), visit www.ocracokebrogue.com/chapter/13/QR13-5.mp3.

There is something wonderful about overhearing islanders talking among themselves. Parts of the traditional Brogue come out, the pace and excitement of talk increases, and the intonation patterns seem to exude a sense of joy. It is almost as though such encounters cause the locals to smile, and that joy is reflected in the speech. The Brogue signals community, solidarity, kinship. It is perhaps these reasons, as much as accommodation, that visitors are not often exposed to the dialect. Despite being part of the draw of the island, it is a scarce commodity that islanders are protective of, but they are usually happy to share it with those who are genuinely interested in it.

## TALKING IN OPPOSITES

It is one thing, when listening to new dialects, to recognize that there are unfamiliar words and pronunciations. But it is a different thing altogether to be listening to a dialect and understand all the words and still have no idea what is being said. Islanders' love of language play can result in this exact situation. All users of English engage occasionally in what linguists call "semantic inversion." Phrases like "That party was sick!" or Michael Jackson's "I'm bad" capture this language feature; both phrases mean the opposite of the literal definition. No matter where you are from, if you are stuck inside on a rainy day, you understand the semantic inversion of an utterance like "Such a pretty day out there!" If speakers along the Outer Banks stopped there, we would not have much to say about this phenomenon. But along the Outer Banks, there is more to this usage than there tends to be inland.

Before digging in on just how far islanders can "talk in opposites" or engage in "backwards talk," it is worth noting that O'Cockers are not the only ones who do this. In fact, the usage has been documented more fully in Smith Island, MD, Tangier Island, VA, and Harkers Island, NC, island communities that share commonalities of history, commerce, culture, and dialect with Ocracoke. In fact, the illustrative examples shared below come from off island.

Dr. Natalie Schilling has studied this linguistic usage more than any other linguist has, and she has published a number of academic articles on the topic. Unless otherwise noted, all the examples in this section come from her work on Smith Island. While the examples that are familiar to outsiders involve simple opposites (e.g., saying it's nice out when it's really not), Dr. Schilling has documented examples where there is no obvious opposite, as in "He's barefoot!" meaning something like "Look at how proud he is of his new shoes." Or consider the following exchange, heard during a midsummer baseball game, where the cryptic "backwards" phrase "That's tomorrow!" isn't exactly the opposite of what is really meant:

> Speaker 1: When is your expectant time? [Said to a pregnant woman.]
>
> Speaker 2: January.
>
> Speaker 1: That's tomorrow! It'll fly by though.

Smith Islanders often build entire conversations with backwards talk in a form of communicative solidarity, as in this conversation involving a Smith Islander whose relative has become a pilot:

> Speaker 1: I took one flying lesson.
>
> Speaker 2: Well, I'd love to fly with you! [Meaning "I'm certainly not going to fly with you!"]
>
> Speaker 1: Who wants ye! [in response to Speaker 2's affectionate teasing]

Talking in opposites typically entails using adjectives and nouns with irony or exaggeration. For the skilled backwards talker, it is the extensions and not just the opposites that are most playful. Ann Rose of Harkers Island illustrates how this works by talking about the phrase "That crowd had the greatest time":

> It could be not necessarily positive. It coulda been that maybe they were fussing about something and feuding and hollering and screaming and whatever, but "greatest" means like intensity, you know. And "time" could be just an occurrence. So "that crowd had the greatest time," uh—they coulda been out there just been fussing and fuming or maybe out there fighting over some fish nets or something, you know.

Such playful verbal behavior sets apart islanders from non-islanders. It is a little like having a secret code. Marginalized groups sometimes employ opposite language, or "counterlanguage," to intentionally obscure meaning for those who are not a part of their group. In the case of backward talk, islanders describe some consequences when they use this way of speaking with those unaccustomed to it. Dr. Schilling reports an anecdote of some Smith Islanders who were in a gift shop in New York City, admiring the wares. One of the women in the group laughingly recounted, "Well, I seen this ring, it was beautiful. And I said, 'Well, that's ugly!' The man come up to me, he said, 'Well, everyone has their own opinions.' Well, I got tickled and walked away. This woman tried to explain to him, I said, 'Don't. Just let him keep wondering.'"

Counterlanguage can be used by islanders to distance themselves from mainland society. Some people catch on faster than others do. Houston Lewis of Harkers Island notes, "It took my wife 'bout twenty years to realize I was talking in opposites. I always, you know, talk in opposites. After a while, she learned it." With coy verbal routines, islanders assert—and embrace—their detachment by reversing who is an insider and who is an outsider. This reversal becomes a powerful symbolic behavior that places islanders in opposition to the "standard" uses of English—and proudly so. Now that we have let you in on some the workings of this secret code, perhaps it will not take you twenty years to learn it. But you are probably not going to be able to use it right—at least not according to those who use it natively. There is no denying that the Brogue, even in its current form, is about maintaining community insider status and keeping others at a comfortable distance. And these divisions are not necessarily good or bad; instead, the groups may be merely "us" and "them." But this grouping is powerful, and what dingbatters need to understand is that you can be loved and welcomed by community members, but you will never achieve insider status. While community insiders are happy to chat with you and will even style-shift to accommodate your dialect, it is unlikely you will ever truly understand everything they say. At the very least, you will not have the cultural background needed to understand the social meanings of all that is said.

To watch a vignette in which Outer Bankers talk about "talking in opposites" (from *The Carolina Brogue*), visit www.ocracokebrogue.com/chapter/13/QR13-6.mp4.

Returning to the chapter's title question, "Can dingbatters understand the Brogue?," the answer is something like, "Most of the time, adequately enough. Occasionally, not at all." Then again, this is how language always works. We do not communicate like computers, with inputs that produce consistent outputs. Conversations are negotiations, and when two people have more shared cultural information, they tend to arrive at mostly similar understandings of what is being said and what is being meant. As cultural and linguistic difference grows, assumed understanding becomes more problematic, even when we thought we understood someone perfectly well. Do not fret, however. Communicating across cultures and dialects can be a great opportunity to question more, learn more, and empathize more—all things we should do when we vacation in places with strong, close-knit communities.

*Chapter 14*

# WHAT ARE THE ARTISTIC AND LINGUISTIC PERFORMANCES ON OCRACOKE?

NATALIE SCHILLING, PHD

There is something about Ocracoke that inspires artistry. Between the natural beauty of the sea, windswept dunes, and twisted live oaks; the long, starlit winter nights; and the warmth, community, and creativity of its residents, the island is a special place for painting, photography, crafting, decoy carving, and performance. Ocracoke has long been home to top-notch musicians, and residents have enjoyed dance traditions from square dances with early

**FIGURE 14.1.** Mabel Gaskill and Ignatius Styron dance at Old Jake's. Photograph courtesy of the Chester Lynn Collection.

roots in the United States to the Latin American–inspired choreography of the Ballet Folklórico de Ocracoke. Figure 14.1 shows one of the early music and dance halls, Old Jake's. Island residents put on plays and musicals, and there are movies and books set in Ocracoke and other Outer Banks locations, too. These are not just the writings of residents or dedicated visitors, either. Megan McDonald (originally from Pittsburgh) has even set a book in the popular *Judy Moody and Stink* children's series on Ocracoke. *The Mad, Mad, Mad, Mad, Treasure Hunt* incorporates Ocracoke topography, history, and lore into an island mystery. There is also a long tradition of local creative writing and storytelling artistry. And while lots of performances are set onstage, everyday creativity with language abounds as well. In fact, one important lesson we learned in our dialect studies in Ocracoke is that it can be hard to draw the line between what counts as natural, everyday language and linguistic performance.

## A LONG MUSICAL TRADITION

O'Cockers have been making music practically since they first got to the island. Blackbeard and his fellow pirates likely sung sea chanteys during their revels in Ocracoke, while those who established permanent residence would have brought the musical traditions of England, Ireland, and Northern Ireland with them as well. There are strong language connections between the heavily Scots-Irish influenced Appalachian English dialect and the Ocracoke Brogue, and you can hear the musical connections, too. Bluegrass-style music is popular among island musicians, and this and other musical genres—and musical talent—have been passed down through the generations. Martin Garrish, one of Ocracoke's best twenty-first-century musicians, can trace his musical heritage in Ocracoke to his great-great-grandfather, the renowned William "Wid" Williams, while the O'Neal family can claim at least two well-known early fiddlers as ancestors, Thomas O'Neal and Ansley O'Neal.

There is a long tradition of island men getting together to make music in out of the way places. The song "Paddy's Holler" (from *hollow*, a low, wooded area) by Walter Howard is about one much-loved location for singing, fiddling, strumming, and dancing—and making meal wine, a local concoction made of fermented cornmeal, sugar, and fruit. In the 1930s, a group of island men, including well-known musician Maurice "Morris" Ballance, who played together became known as the Graveyard Band, for their habit of gathering in the woods near an old cemetery. Martin Garrish has resurrected the Graveyard Band, forming a modern group with this name as an homage to this important tradition. Garrish may be Ocracoke's most prolific current-day musician, playing not just with the Graveyard Band, but also leading the Ocracoke Rockers and playing with the Ocrafolk Opry. Other prominent deceased

FIGURE 14.2. Maurice Ballance (left) and Roy Parsons. Photograph courtesy of the Ocracoke Preservation Society.

Ocracoke musicians include the aforementioned Maurice Ballance and Roy Parsons (fig. 14.2), the latter of whom was well-known for his yodeling and went on to perform with Roy Rogers and the Ringling Brothers and Barnum and Bailey Circus. Edgar Howard also played with Roy Rogers, as well as Gene Autry, and appeared on *The Milton Berle Show*. In fact, he was once considered one of the world's greatest banjo players.

To hear Ikey O'Neal describe how to make meal wine (from *Ocracoke Still Speaks*), visit www.ocracokebrogue.com/chapter/14/QR14-1.mp3.

Musical groups, performers, and performances continue to thrive in Ocracoke. In addition to Martin Garrish's various groups, there is also the popular band Molasses Creek, featuring folk legend Gary Mitchell, and regular performance events, many sponsored

FIGURE 14.3. Dallas Mason plays with Martin Garrish and the Ocracoke Rockers. Photograph by Miggy O'Neal.

by Ocracoke Alive, a nonprofit dedicated to encouraging arts of all sorts. The band received national notoriety after being featured on Garrison Keillor's *A Prairie Home Companion*, and eventually had a number of top ten hits on the folk music charts. The annual Ocracoke Music Festival, held every year during the first weekend of June, draws people from far and wide, and the *Ocracoke Music Sampler* radio show, hosted by Gary Mitchell, brings in a wide virtual audience. Another popular addition to the Ocracoke performance scene is the Festival Latino de Ocracoke, featuring Latin American–inspired music, dances, food, and games, held annually since the mid-2010s. And Ocracoke performers are still going on to wider fame, just like they did in the old days. For example, (Preston) Jule Garrish, guitarist, songwriter, and Graveyard Band member, played and sang in the 2008 Warner Brothers film *Nights in Rodanthe*—along with much younger island resident

Katy Mitchell, then fresh out of Ocracoke High School. The Ocracoke Rockers are also passing the island's long musical tradition down through the generations; in the 2020s, they often have been joined on stage by Dallas Mason, the grandson of our longtime island friends Miggy and Rex O'Neal (fig. 14.3). Dallas is a musical prodigy already widely known for his skills as a drummer and guitarist—and as of this writing, he is only ten years old.

## THE WORDS BEHIND THE MUSIC

As linguists and dialectologists, we are particularly interested in lyrics. There are original Ocracoke songs about everything from fishing to love interests, and O'Cockers love to write about their island home—and their musical traditions.

Below are the lyrics of two original songs by Ocracokers: first, a song by Roy Parsons about how hard it can be to make a living from the water in Ocracoke, mixed in with a dose of humor, in typical Ocracoke style; second and, in a very different vein, a love song by Jule Garrish.

### LIFE OF A FISHERMAN

*Well,*
*Spots are selling for twelve cents*
*And flounder's twenty-four*
*Shrimp are selling for thirty-five*
*But still they ask for more*

*But here and on Hatteras Island*
*They work for what they get*
*They work all day in the violent hot sun*
*And all they get is wet*

*They sheave the reef for mullets*
*And drag the sound for shrimp*
*Pay their bills on Saturday night*
*And they haven't got a cent*

BEFORE I MET YOU

*I thought I had seen pretty girls in my time*
*But that was before I met you*
*I never saw one that I wanted for mine*
*But that was before I met you*

*I thought I was swinging the world by the tail*
*And I thought that I'd never be blue*
*I thought I'd been kissed and I thought I'd been loved*
*But that was before I met you*

To hear these songs by Roy Parsons and Jule Garrish, visit www.ocracokebrogue.com/chapter/14/QR14-2.mp4 and www.ocracokebrogue.com/chapter/14/QR14-3.mp4.

To see a posthumous tribute to Roy Parsons, visit www.ocracokebrogue.com/chapter/14/QR14-4.mp4.

A particularly poignant song about the value of keeping musical traditions alive in Ocracoke comes from Edgar Howard and can be found on the Smithsonian Folkways recording *Between the Sound and the Sea: Music of the North Carolina Outer Banks*, compiled by ethnomusicologist Karen G. Helms in the 1970s and featuring Ocracoke musicians like Lawton Howard, Elizabeth Howard, Jule Garrish, and Maurice Ballance, in addition to Edgar Howard. As you read the lyrics of "Let's Keep the Holler Alive" (written by Edgar Howard), you can just picture the old Graveyard Band playing among the live oaks of Paddy's Holler. And thankfully, you can also picture the young Ocracoke musicians of the 2020s keeping traditions alive—including Dallas Mason! As an added benefit for dialect buffs, the song contains many Ocracoke pronunciations too, including the distinctive “oy” for the *i*-sound in words like *alive*. There are also references to other island icons like meal wine and, of course, Edward Teach, aka Blackbeard.

LET’S KEEP THE HOLLER ALIVE

*Let’s all get on the ball*
*Or else there’ll be no holler at all*
*I remember well when I was a boy*
*Going up the holler just to spread cheer and joy*
*You could hear the fiddles playing any hour of*
*the day*
*Hear the banjos ringing as in Stephen Foster’s day*
*So let’s all swing with that jive*
*And let’s keep the holler alive!*

*Let’s keep the holler alive*
*You’ll move up the holler if you’re wise*
*All the big hotels are out on the beach*
*When you run through the holler you’re apt to*
*meet old Edward Teach*
*Most all of them up there are all doing fine*
*It’s no trouble at all to get a glass of that old*
*meal wine*
*It’s just plain paradise*
*So let’s keep the holler alive!*

To hear a performance of this song, visit www.ocracokebrogue.com/chapter/14/QR14-5.mp3.

## SAYING A WORD OR TWO

On the spoken side of things, Ocracoke also has a rich storytelling tradition. Donald Davis, a world-renowned professional storyteller who lives in Ocracoke, gives workshops on the practice, and there is lots of everyday talent as well. We have been treated to an array of engaging stories in our interviews with island residents for our dialect studies. We have heard tales on topics ranging from the weather to early island life to pranks folks play on one another. And of course there are ghost stories. Blackbeard was beheaded in 1718 off the coast of Ocracoke by Lieutenant Robert Maynard; it is said that on dark nights you can see a strange light moving in the water near Teach's Hole that may just be Blackbeard's ghost, still swimming in search of his lost head. It is also said that a flaming ship can be seen off the Ocracoke coast once a year during the September new moon, its ghostly passengers seeking revenge on the thieves who murdered them, robbed their corpses, and set their boat aflame in the early 1700s. And on land, we have spirits like the ghost of Mrs. Godfrey, said to have haunted the old Island Inn since she was murdered on the mainland in the World War II years. Philip Howard has gathered a bunch of ghostly and other historical stories in a book called *Digging Up Uncle Evans* (2008, Black Squall)—and he knows plenty of Ocracoke tales, being a descendent of William Howard, Blackbeard's quartermaster!

We have also talked with folks who have had personal encounters with family spirits. The following tale comes from Essie O'Neal and would have taken place in the early twentieth century:

> I had a little sister that she got sick. She had typhoid fever. And she didn't live very long. I think she lived about two weeks. . . . Well, we went, we didn't have any electric, we had kerosene lamps, so we burnt the lampshade. And it was getting dark and we needed to get a lampshade, so I went to the store to get the lampshade. And coming along back up the road, I heard something behind me, I don't know what it was. But I turned around and looked, and I didn't see nothing but a big white bunch of stuff. Something white. And so, I kept on going, and walking and walking, and I turned around and looked, and it was still behind me. Just a white, like a cloud or something—something like a cloud! And I never could find out what it was. But it scared me when

> I seen it was chasing me. And I didn't run, I didn't walk in that house, I run and busted right through that door, I was so scared. And my mother said, "What is wrong with you?" I said, "Do you see anything white back of me?" And she didn't know what I was talking about. And she said, "I didn't see nothing." I said, "It's just something white, I don't know what it was, something white." And she thought maybe, I don't know, I was dreaming or whatever. She said, "What's wrong with you?" But I couldn't get it off my mind, what it was. I could not get it off my mind! And it just stayed there. And the next day, I got up that morning, it was kinda late, and went through to the living room, and when I looked, the couch, there was a couch in that living room, the kind that didn't have no backs on them, I saw a great big white thing on that couch, and that's the first thing that I thought of was that white thing that was like a big cloud. My sister had died, and they had a sheet over her. And I screamed, and they all run to see what was wrong with me, and I said, "Mommy!" I said, "That's that thing that was going back of me last night!"

To hear Essie O'Neal tell this ghost story, visit www.ocracokebrogue.com/chapter/14/QR14-6.mp3.

To hear Rudy Austin tell another Ocracoke ghost story (from *Ocracoke Speaks*), visit www.ocracokebrogue.com/chapter/14/QR14-7.mp3.

Ghost stories are not just a thing of the past in Ocracoke. Supernatural tales remain an important part of the local culture. We close this section with a modern tale told by Chester Lynn:

> For some reason, someone just said, "Chester, you need to go. You need to be there for that service." I thought, well, I'm tired, and I still had my tuxedo on from the wedding. Well, I changed my clothes, took the tuxedo off, took a change of

clothes on the ferry, cause I knew if I got off the ferry, by the time I got to church the services would just be starting. So I did and went to the church and everything went so normal like it always did like a regular real life service. At the end of the service, people were gathered around the altar, praying. And one of the local girls that used to live here, she was playing the piano and they were singing praise choruses and singing. Well, all of a sudden something happened to her hands and in the music, and she, her hands didn't go all over the piano. They stayed in one spot but more than just piano music come from the church out of the piano. And after that happened, when that happened, everybody got quiet because it was so unreal. It was so strange, you know, and so beautiful and after that everybody got up and they looked in the pews because they'd always had tape players going, you know, to catch music and anything that happened. And there were three or four in the church, and none of them was going that night. The only night we know of where there definitely weren't one going at that time for that tape, you know, cause everyone thought, if there's a tape to that, we got it. And it weren't. Ant that was so sad because it only happened that one time and it was so unusual and it was so, so wonderful, so beautiful.

To hear Chester Lynn tell the story of the haunted piano (from *Ocracoke Still Speaks*), visit www.ocracokebrogue.com/chapter/14/QR14-8.mp3.

## PUTTIN' ON THE BROGUE

Finally, language itself is a subject of performance in Ocracoke. During one of our early interviews with O'Cocker Rex O'Neal, we were in the middle of talking with him about island life and history when he suddenly produced a phrase that did not seem to have anything to do with the topic at hand (quoted in chapter 10). But it did feature some of Ocracoke's most iconic pronunciations, which

Rex pronounced in an exaggerated way, including "hoi toid" for *high tide*, "feesh" for *fish*, and "far" for *fire*. Here's the phrase: "It's *hoi toid* [high tide] on the sound *soid* [side], last night the water *fa'r* [fire], tonight the moon shine, no *feesh* [fish], no feesh, whatcha 'posta the matter, Uncle Woods?" And here's what it means: It's high tide on the Pamlico Sound side of the island, last night there was phosphorous on the surface of the water and tonight there's a full moon, and, so now the fishing is poor. (Uncle Woods is a relative of Rex's.)

Rex's performance took us by surprise. As was discussed in more detail in chapter 13, we had thought our interview with him was relaxed and casual, since he was telling us all kinds of interesting stories, joking, and using what we thought was his regular, everyday Brogue, not formal speech put on for us outsiders. But when we heard the performance, with its heavy dialect, we thought, "Oh! Maybe that's the real Brogue!" A bit later, several of Rex's brothers drove up, and they and Rex had a long conversation. And Rex changed his way of talking yet again! This time, his dialect fell somewhere in between the friendly but somewhat more mainstream language he used with us and the exaggeratedly Brogue-y speech of his performance phrase. Examples of Rex switching between these three ways of speaking were linked in chapter 13.

So which way of talking was Rex's "real" dialect? We ended up realizing that we could not tell and that, really, it is a nonsensical question. We all change how we talk depending on who we are talking to and why. No one has just one way of speaking. When Rex shares information and stories with outsiders like us, he uses one way of talking, and when he talks with his brothers, he sounds different. And he has another way of talking when he wants to demonstrate the Brogue in its most distinctive form. None of these speech styles is more or less "natural" than any other; they are all natural for the context and purpose in which they are used. It is just that O'Cockers use more "performance style" than people with less noticeable language varieties do. They are proud of their distinctive Brogue, and outsiders often ask them to perform it.

Sometimes dingbatters go too far in their eagerness for Ocracoke dialect performance. As recounted in the opening chapter to this book, Candy Gaskill, told us how off-islanders sometimes treat residents like exotic creatures or trained pets who are supposed to perform on command: "I had a lady in here [the general store] last week I had a battle with. You might as well say a battle with, because she came up to the counter, and she said, 'Speak.' I said, 'Excuse me?' She said, 'Speak!' I was like, 'Do I get a biscuit?' She said, 'I wanna hear you talk.'" But for the most part, Ocracoke residents are happy to show off their unique dialect—as long as outsiders are respectful about it, and do not ask them to perform it out of context. O'Cockers are proud of all their distinct traditions. And a key part of what makes the island unique is its way of speaking. As Candy Gaskill also told us, the Ocracoke accent is special, "but it's a little more special than other people's accents," and the Brogue makes Ocracoke a "more special place than what it already is."

Yes, Ocracoke residents use their dialect in everyday conversation, but they also often use it to perform, whether in song, in storytelling, or in catchy phrases that highlight—and play with—language features. The Brogue itself is musical, and it is steeped in tradition and in history. That makes it a lot of fun!

*Chapter 15*

# WHAT IS THE WEATHER LIKE ON OCRACOKE?

NATALIE SCHILLING, PHD

Every time someone—resident or visitor—comes to or leaves the island, they have to think about whether or not the ferry is running, acknowledging how integral weather is to the island. In fact, there have been a few times our trips to the island were cut short or extended due to the weather. On a few occasions, we have managed to get off the island via the Hatteras ferry, only to find that the roads on Pea Island were flooded. But weather on Ocracoke affects more than just travel to and from the island, and so, with good reason, it is always on everyone's mind on the Outer Banks.

It is certainly true that talk about weather is commonplace in Ocracoke. Located on a thin and ever-shifting strip of sand that is twenty miles out to sea at its farthest point, Ocracoke is subject to all kinds of rough weather. It likely comes as no surprise that

Ocracokers are experts at handling rough weather when it comes their way. They build and maintain barriers, or *breakwaters*, along vulnerable coastline, they look out for one another when storms hit, and afterward they love to tell a yarn or two about it. Because weather is such an important part of life in Ocracoke, the Brogue is rich with specialized vocabulary, phrases, and sayings relating to it. And of course, just about everyone has a weather story—some scary, some funny, and many of them both at the same time. Ocracokers love a gripping tale with a funny ending, and it really helps to see the humorous side of what can be some pretty dicey situations.

## WHY THE FOCUS ON WEATHER?

Ocracokers' focus on the weather dates back to the earliest days of the island community. The first settlers were ship pilots, who stationed themselves on the island to guide ships through the treacherous Outer Banks island chain to mainland ports. The channel itself had a number of hazards, such as shoals and rocks, but rough weather could make the passage extremely treacherous. Shipwrecks were common in the early days, giving area waters the nickname "Graveyard of the Atlantic" (fig. 15.1). In fact, early residents made a good part of their living through *shipwrecking*—salvaging usable items from shipwrecks that had washed ashore. Homes today still contain relics—and some even have old ship timbers built into their walls and roofs. And islanders still tell stories about the old practice of shipwrecking—like this one by Blanche Howard Jolliff about a fellow islander who carted off some unusual "treasure" from the *Pioneer*, which wrecked on Ocracoke in October, 1889.

> This schooner went ashore here on the beach and it was called the *Pioneer*, and it had a general cargo, from what I understood it, sailing for New Bern [a mainland North Carolina town], and it wrecked on our beach. And it went all to pieces, the ship did, and all the cargo went all over the beach. And there were bolts of material and all kinds

**FIGURE 15.1.** Salvaging the *Nomis* shipwreck on Ocracoke, 1935. Photograph courtesy of the Ocracoke Preservation Society.

of shoes—women's, men's, and children's. And a piano, and food, cheeses, books, most anything you could mention—general cargo. And Mr. Tommy, he was always interested, you know, in things that went on before he was old enough to know about, and he always read a lot. So, he went out on the beach where everybody was salvaging this and that, and what he went home with was an armload of books. Of all the food and all the shoes and all the other things!

To hear Blanche Howard Jolliff tell the story of the shipwrecked *Pioneer* (from *Ocracoke Still Speaks*), visit www.ocracokebrogue.com/chapter/15/QR15-1.mp3.

To hear Chester Lynn describe how ship timbers were repurposed for house construction (from *Ocracoke Speaks*), visit www.ocracokebrogue.com/chapter/15/QR15-2.mp3.

The island way of making a living gradually shifted from piloting (and shipwrecking) to fishing, crabbing, shrimping, and oystering, but the focus on weather stayed just as strong. Working the water in a small boat can be dangerous, and knowledge of and respect for winds, waves, and tides is crucial. Just as every day brings sunrise and sunset, and every year brings its different seasons, so too do the waters cycle from *ebb tide*, or low tide, to *flood toid* or *king toid*, both words for extreme *hoi toids*. On some days, the water in the sound is smooth, even glassy, a condition O'Cockers call a *slick cam* (calm); on other days, the winds rise—it *breezes up* or it is a *hard blow* and it may be trickier to keep your balance on the boat. You may even find yourself getting *quamished*, or queasy, a term that derives from the Shakespearean word *qualmish*, meaning "prone to qualms or spells of sickness." Wind direction changes, too, and sometimes you skim along moving away from the wind, or *louard*, and other times you struggle forward into the wind, or *winard*. *Louard* comes from *leeward* (the calm side of the island or the side of the boat not being hit by wind) and *winard* from *windward* (the windy side of the island or the side of the boat being hit by wind), two other widespread maritime words. Other words are more localized, so while you might get *seasick* taking the ferry from Cape Cod to Martha's Vineyard or from Fort Myers to Key West, you probably will not feel *quamished* unless you are taking the ferry to Ocracoke or Hatteras.

Ocracoke watermen also have to know what conditions bring good fishing. Rex O'Neal's performance phrase, quoted a few other times in this book, links aspects of weather with fishing conditions. "Well, it's hoi toid on the sound soid; last night the water fa'r, tonight the moon shine, no feesh, no feesh, whatcha 'posta the matter, Uncle Woods." The saying refers to a specific set of conditions when fishing is likely to be poor: when it's high tide on the sound side, when it is especially bright at night ("last night the moon shine"), or when it is bright due to phosphorous glowing on the surface of the water ("water fire")—all of which add up to "no fish."

If you are a waterman whose livelihood comes from the sea, you also know a lot about types of fish; the sound and ocean waters of the Outer Banks abound with drum, flounder, speckled trout, and bluefish, and sport fishers try their hand at reeling in marlin, mahi-mahi, and wahoo. A more humble but useful fish is menhaden, also known in Ocracoke as *bunker*, *fatback*, and *alewives*, which can be used as bait or for their oil. Terms for crabs are abundant, too; to take a few examples, *jimmies* are male crabs, *sooks* are females, and *peelers* are crabs that are molting or shedding their shells in preparation for growing a new, larger one.

## HARD BLOWS, SNOW DRIFTS, HURRICANES—AND PIGS!

Nowadays, the Ocracoke economy has shifted again, from commercial fishing to tourism. But the weather hasn't lost its central importance. You need good weather to bring in tourists, and it can be unpleasant to have to brave conditions when it is *airish*, chilly and breezy, or when you are facing a *hard blow*, a strong wind. In fact, any traveler to Ocracoke realizes that bad weather is a major cause for canceling ferry service and making the road to the north unnavigable because the sand has blown onto Highway 12. Ocracoke has had more than its share of dangerous and destructive storms, including hurricanes and *nor'easters*, another term the island shares with communities up and down the US Eastern Seaboard, to refer to storms with winds from the northeast. These storms are common, and islanders are pretty used to them. They also sometimes have to contend with rarer weather occurrences. Dale Mutro told us, in vivid detail, of spotting a series of *waterspouts* by the ferry dock nestled inside Ocracoke harbor:

> And I remember one time, I was working at Texaco gas station, in the summertime, and I was standing there to the door, and I looked and I said, "My God! Is this a—" I mean, you see the classic tornado-type thing, you know, where you'd see it coming out of the sky, curving kinda thing. And it was a waterspout, it was like, back of the island up here, and it was going toward the southwest, and it doesn't, you know,

> it doesn't have to be with a thunderstorm either. It's like you can have certain atmospheric conditions where it's just, you know, conducive to, you know, waterspout development. I mean, you can have halfway sunny days, and— We went down here to the base dock, what we call the base dock, down here by the ferry dock, and we watched them over the sound one day, just, you know, popping out of the sky.

To hear Dale Mutro talk about waterspouts (from *Ocracoke Still Speaks*), visit www.ocracokebrogue.com/chapter/15/QR15-3.mp3.

And there is sometimes even snow and ice, despite the Outer Banks' southerly location and watery surroundings. The island can even be iced in and cut off from supplies. Clinton Gaskill told us how, in the very early twentieth century, his father once took a trek on the ice in search of food—only to be sent right back to where he started: "In 1917, 1918, the whole sound frozed over. My daddy was to Harbor Island, a place called Harbor Island Clubhouse. He runned out of grub. He had to walk from the Harbor Island to Core Banks. And he told me, I hear him say it, he walked all around so many air holes, he said, that was just so afraid that he was gonna hit one of them. He says he made it through there because the Coast Guard to Portsmouth sent him across the inlet to go home!"

To hear Clinton Gaskill tell the story of when the Pamlico Sound froze over (from *Ocracoke Still Speaks*), visit www.ocracokebrogue.com/chapter/15/QR15-4.mp3.

At the same time, islanders are used to weathering a few days of storm-related isolation—actually more so than mainlanders, according to island resident Bubbie Boos:

> It snowed here a couple years back a bit. Had a nice big blizzard in '83, '86, something like that. I remember stepping out of my father's and mother's house and going up to my

chest in a snowdrift. But it usually—we've had about three major snows that I can member. Remember the sound freezing over, the creek freezing over. . . .

That was a bad blizzard we had back in '80-something. But, you know, we were back out functioning the next day. I mean, we don't know nothing about snow hardly, but yet we respond and make it through better than people that deal with it their whole life. You see it on the news every day. They're freaking and panicking. You can't buy a loaf of bread or gallon of milk in any store. I mean, hello, at the worst you're going to stay snowed in a couple of days at the most. I mean, especially places that's prepared for it. There's people out plowing.

To hear Bubbie Boos talk about how the island responds to snowfalls (from *Ocracoke Still Speaks*), visit www.ocracokebrogue.com/chapter/15/QR15-5.mp3.

Then, of course, there are the worst storms of all: hurricanes. We have recorded stories from island residents about hurricanes dating back to 1933 and 1944 and as recent as Dorian in 2019. Dorian brought a record-setting storm surge and closed the island for months—or at least closed it to outsiders, since O'Cockers and other year-round residents typically stay put rather than evacuate in even the wildest weather, banding together to help one another prepare for, endure, and rebuild after the worst of the weather has passed. (You can read more about Hurricane Dorian in the following chapter.) Sometimes storm preparations pay off, and sometimes they have unexpected consequences, as we see in the following two stories about the memorable 1944 hurricane. The first one is from Blanche Howard Jolliff, who told us how her father's measures saved his boat:

When we heard the hurricane was coming, the '44 hurricane, he ran out and secured his boat. He always had a big stake in the lake where he tied it to, and then he would put out an

> anchor. But this particular time he put out two more anchors so that she more or less stayed in the same position. So, his was the only boat in the lake that didn't go ashore. There were a lot of trawlers, a lot of trawlers here, shrimp boats and so forth, and most of those did go on the shore, too. One of them even took a store down!

To hear the full story Blanche Howard Jolliff tells about the storm of '44 (from *Ocracoke Still Speaks*), visit www.ocracokebrogue.com/chapter/15/QR15-6.mp3.

In the second story, from O'Cocker Essie O'Neal, Rex's mother, the family house is saved, but there is a bit of a wrinkle. In classic Ocracoke style, Miss Essie sees the lighter side of what was actually a very dangerous and most likely quite frightening event. (And for context, Miss Essie had eleven children, all boys!)

> That was the storm. This was another thing we're talking about. I had a new maple bedroom set. And I had just got it in the house, three or four days, when the storm come—the '44 storm. We had a pretty day, just like this. No wind, pretty sunshine. And the day that came over that day and said there's a bad storm heading right straight for us. And we didn't believe it: "They ain't no storm," you know. "They ain't no storm come." Said, "Yes, it's heading right straight for Cape Hatteras." And it was a pretty calm day. And that night, after it got to dark good, went out on the porch with Harry and we went out on the porch and the stars was shining. He says, "I don't think there's no storm." He said, "It don't look like a storm." And everything was calm. But let me tell you, when we woke up the next morning, I thought the roof was gonna come off my house. I never heard such a hard wind. It was a hundred miles, blowing a hundred mile. I never heard such a hard wind. And he said, "You better get up and get all them kids ready, get them dressed, we'll have to leave here." And I was working fast as I could to get 'em all and put 'em to

FIGURE 15.2. The storm of '44 carried the mailboat *Aleta* and the *Miss Willis* from Silver Lake (left side of picture) to dry ground. Photograph courtesy of the Ocracoke Preservation Society.

the table, hurry, get them breakfast and everything. Harry looked, and the tide was a-rolling right in the yard. Come up so fast, it was a-rolling in the yard. And we got them, and that's when we left. And when we left out of that gate, I tell you, it was about four foot of water in the gate when we left. And we had to leave here in a boat. We had a half-grown pig. And he didn't want him to drowned, you know. He had a old, big wooden trunk-big old-timey trunks. So, he put him in the trunk and put the trunk on the porch. I said, "When that pig floats around in that trunk, he'll think he's in a boat." And we went on Mickey's—Mickey that lives over there, closer to that graveyard down there, that cemetery. That's where we spent that storm out. Tide run off at Amy Lake. Harry said, "I'm going up to the house, if we got a house." We didn't even think we had a house. And I said, "Can we go?," and he said, "No, better stay here, wait till I go." So, when he come back, he had a sad news to say. He said, "Well, I'll tell you, I saw the house was standing." He said, "But the door was wide open, had blowed open," he said, "and the first thing I met was the pig coming out of the living room."

I went into the bedroom, and, honey, he had with his hooves cut that maple bedstead all to pieces. I had to throw it out; it wasn't no good anymore. He'd ruined that bedstead. I told him, I said, "Don't ever get another pig! 'Cause these young'uns is enough for to take care of, without taking care of a pig!"

To hear Essie O'Neal's story of the storm of '44 (from *Ocracoke Speaks*), visit www.ocracokebrogue.com/chapter/15/QR15-7.mp3.

## GETTING CREATIVE WITH THE WEATHER

As you can see, islanders have a lot to say about the weather, which leads to creativity in describing it. They tell engaging stories that put us on the edge of our seats—and make us laugh, and they come up with colorful words and phrases. There are also weather-related signage and weather-themed souvenirs for sale in island gift shops. Shoppers walking up to Village Craftsmen, a shop run by generations of one of the oldest island families, the Howards, are greeted with a series of high-water marks indicating flood levels from various hurricanes—with Dorian well above the rest. And once inside, you can buy a wine glass also marked with high-water levels. Just be careful—you may feel quamished if you drink a Dorian-level pour. And then there are place-names that are weather- and water-related; for example, *Water Fired Road* is surely a nod to the well-known "hoi toid on the sound soid" saying.

Finally, islanders take weather terms and expand their meanings in creative ways, in a process linguists call metaphorical extension. We are all familiar with the extension of the word "eye," literally a body part, to refer to the eye of a potato, the eye of a needle, and, yes, the eye of a hurricane. In Ocracoke, there are even more weather- and maritime-related metaphors. The word *scuttle* originally referred to a small hatch in a boat or ship but is now commonly used to refer to a small space in a house as well—perfect for riding out a storm. And *scud*, originally a nautical term meaning "to run in front of a gale with little or no sail set" is now used to refer to automobile or boat trips, as in "Let's take a scud around the island." Ocracokers might also say they feel *miserable'n the wind* even when there is no sign of a storm, to indicate that they feel agitated, uneasy, or unsettled. It is not clear whether this phrase is a shortened form of "miserable in the wind" or "miserabler than the wind," but either way the meaning is the same—you are feeling just as bad as if you were caught out in a hard blow.

When it comes to weather in Ocracoke, islanders do more than just talk about it; they often do something about it. They study it. They prepare for it. They help each other overcome it. And they adapt to changing conditions as they arise. In some ways, you might even say that their natural surroundings are just as much a part of the long-standing Ocracoke community as the people themselves. Ocracoke and its weather are at heart still wild and untamed, and that is where their beauty and bounty lie.

*Chapter 16*

# WHAT IS THE WORST STORM IN OCRACOKE'S HISTORY?

As noted in the previous chapter, when you live on an isolated island, the weather is always on your mind. Tides and winds can shut down the ferry system, nor'easters can reshape or destroy the dunes (and block the roads!), rain showers can flood the roads and carry sand onto them, and waterspouts can even pick up small fish from the Atlantic and drop them in town with seawater rain. Even with all these other weather-related events, in Ocracoke, hurricanes are the natural phenomena with the most potential to transform the island and island life. The danger is right there in the term *barrier island*: Ocracoke sits near the Gulf Stream and is potentially the first place a storm might touch land, when it is at its strongest. And North Carolina is one of the states most likely to be battered by a hurricane. This chapter is not about language. It is also not about all the major storms that the island has withstood. It is about the spirit of the community, which is brought into sharp focus by the natural disasters that have impacted the island's past and present.

## HURRICANES IN OCRACOKE'S HISTORY

Every O'Cocker can recite a list of storms so severe that they have entered island lore. The early storms are known primarily by their dates, and include the storms of 1846, 1899, 1933, and 1944. A few were so bad they were given their own monikers; for example, the island's oldest residents all refer to the storm of 1899 as "the ole August storm." This was the storm that had brought the highest flooding island residents had seen up till then, destroying all but a few of the village's houses. It even washed away two churches, two schools, and a boatyard. One of the most curious stories of this storm involves two porpoises getting lodged in a crook of an oak tree, only being freed when a large branch broke off in the storm.

For most current residents, it is the storm of '44, also called the Great Atlantic Hurricane, that serves as the touchstone for how bad a hurricane can be on the island. Younger residents have all heard the stories of Silver Lake being cleared of every boat and the mail-boat *Aleta* being deposited by the storm in the yard of an enlisted Navy man stationed on the island. Other boats crashed into houses, ended up on the electric lines, or were otherwise lost. The Coast Guard even lost two ships to the storm. The winds knocked over the water tower and damaged or destroyed many structures. But we can point to at least one moment of humor amid the destruction: this was the storm that, as we recount in the previous chapter, resulted in a pig taking refuge in a trunk in Essie O'Neal's house.

To hear Charlie Williams's recollection of the storm of '44, which emptied Silver Lake of every boat [from *Ocracoke Speaks*], visit www.ocracokebrogue.com/chapter/16/QR16-1.mp3.

In more recent years, named storms have had significant if not quite as devastating impacts on the island. Islanders can recite the names Hazel, Gloria, Emily, Bertha, Isabel, Alex, Irene, and Matthew and recount their stories in detail even years on. Storms like Isabel, Alex, and Emily all brought winds in excess of 100 miles per hour to the island, but with modern construction, it is the water, not the wind, that poses the biggest threat to the village. Hurricane Dorian, in 2019, proved this, and it has now become the new touchstone by which all future hurricanes will be compared.

## A PORTRAIT OF DORIAN

On August 24, 2019, a tropical depression in the Atlantic became organized and strong enough to be classified as a tropical storm, Dorian. Three days later, the tropical storm brought heavy rain to Barbados and then made landfall on Saint Lucia, in the Caribbean Sea. The prevailing wisdom tracked the storm to the northwest, where the mountains of the Dominican Republic and Puerto Rico, along with dry air in that region, would likely cause the storm to dissipate. But Dorian tracked more northerly than anticipated and instead passed by the US Virgin Islands, where on August 28 it intensified to a small Category 1 hurricane, bringing hurricane-force winds to Saint Croix and Saint Thomas.

North of the Virgin Islands, the storm encountered very warm water and intensified to a Category 2 storm over the next twenty-four hours. Then things sped up. The storm intensified quickly, becoming a Category 4 hurricane on August 31 and reaching Category 5 status the following day, when it made landfall on Great Abaco in the Bahamas. Dorian's sustained winds of 185 miles per hour and gusts of over 220 miles per hour tied the record for the strongest winds observed for a landfalling Atlantic hurricane. The storm brought with it a devastating surge of water twenty-three feet above sea level. The storm left some 70,000 Bahamians homeless and caused a record $3.4 billion in damages to the nation. The official death toll in the Bahamas is seventy-four, but five years later, an additional 282 people remain missing. The storm may even cause the extinction of the Bahama nuthatch; the trees the bird relies on were so thoroughly destroyed that it is doubtful they will recover before the species disappears.

After ravaging the Bahamas, the storm's intensity fluctuated over the next few days, eventually dropping to a Category 2 hurricane on September 6, where it made landfall just north of Ocracoke, at Cape Hatteras, with sustained winds of around 100 miles per hour. The storm continued its track northeast, paralleling the US coastline and eventually making landfall in Nova Scotia and again in Newfoundland before dissipating off the coast of Greenland on September 10.

## DORIAN ON OCRACOKE

Despite the news from the Bahamas, by the time Dorian was churning off the Carolina coast, it seemed like any number of other storms. The preemptive state of emergency declaration by the governor and the county's emergency evacuation order did little to persuade most islanders to leave. Though this may seem unwise to outsiders, Ocracokers have ridden out countless comparable storms. Time is of the essence when trying to save property after floodwaters recede, and being trapped off-island after a storm can result in dangerous mold and mildew growing in wet insulation. Residents generally feel the most prudent decision is to stay on the island so they can begin cleanup immediately. There was nothing reckless about the fact that most of the community remained on the island as Dorian approached.

Dorian's outer bands brought rain and wind to Ocracoke overnight, but initially it did not seem remarkable compared to other recent storms. By early morning, however, it was clear to the islanders that they were experiencing a storm unlike any since at least 1933 and perhaps 1899. At about 7:30 a.m., a 7.4-foot storm surge rushed through the village, the water rising faster and higher than any resident had ever seen. Residents' accounts of this moment are chilling. Trudy Austin was in her house with her sister when she saw the water come flooding in. She decided that they should try to move a cottage behind her house that was on higher ground. She had to break open the upper part of her door, as the water level was by then too high to open it the normal way. She quickly bundled her eyeglasses, medication, and cellphone in a bag and left for the cottage. She recalls,

> We didn't know when [the rising water] was going to stop. It was just so rapid and so quick and it was getting higher and higher. So, we were floating going over there to that cottage. . . . We were floating. My sister had my arm; I had her arm. I had enough thought to grab my glasses, my cellphone, and charger real quick in the house, and my medication real quick. And I had a bag extended [above my head] and the water was here going around the corner. I'll never forget an actual wave come over my head 'cause it was just cold, even though it was in September, and just washed over our heads. And actually, water got into the bag and my cellphone, of course, didn't work after that. You're trying to tell people you're alive, you know, and so that's just something strange that will always stick with me, how that wave went over my head.

To hear Trudy Austin's account of the floodwaters, visit www.ocracokebrogue.com/chapter/16/QR16-2.mp3.

The storm's surge came fast. As Nat Schramel, owner of the Flying Melon, recalled in an interview with *Yahoo! News*, "In two minutes, I watched it go from no water to more water than I've ever seen in my life. There was this dramatic surge. And then I watched this slow, gradual rise getting closer and closer." The surge came from the sound side of the island and was ultimately about twice as high as had been predicted. It was a foot higher than the flooding during the storm of '44, and it remained throughout the village for nearly two hours. Elsewhere, parts of the Pamlico Sound appeared

FIGURE 16.1. Ocracoke residents Albert O'Neal and Brian Kissel take to the streets in a boat to check on residents. Photograph by Connie Leinbach/*Ocracoke Observer*.

to dry up as the wind pushed the water into the back side of the barrier island. Once the eye passed to the north, the winds shifted, and the water started to recede. Immediately, islanders took to the streets in their boats, checking on residents and rescuing those trapped in their homes, some of whom had gone into their attics to avoid the floodwaters. One elderly man was medevaced out by the Coast Guard. The island was without power and unable to operate its water treatment facilities for a number of days. The fire station occupies the highest ground in the village and was dry, so it became a meeting place for residents and quickly became the local command center. Eventually, it would also become the island's kitchen and serve as a storeroom for donated goods. Stunningly, no one died, a tribute to how islanders care for each other. Residents went quickly to those who they knew needed help and rescued them safely. Figure 16.1 shows a moment from such a rescue.

## AFTER THE FLOODWATERS

Post-Dorian Ocracoke was a different place. Residents sprang into action, but many describe being awestruck by what they saw around town. Every resident can describe the piles of debris that lined the streets. Ocracoke resident Jason Wells notes that it was more than just losing things:

> And of course, you know, another part of this that really affected me and the community of Ocracoke more so than your run-of-the-mill town is that at least half of the population of Ocracoke I've known all my life. So, when I go down the street and see all of someone's belongings out in front of their house, it's not just some guy that I kind of sort of know. It's someone I went to school with them. Or I went to school with their kids. Or I went to school with their parents. Or you know, just the relationships on Ocracoke are so different.

To hear Jason Wells describe the impact of the storm on the community, visit www.ocracokebrogue.com/chapter/16/QR16-3.mp3.

According to Tom Phal, Ocracoke's county commissioner at the time of the storm, over a third of the buildings on Ocracoke were severely damaged, and 88 of 105 businesses suffered significant damage. More than fifty homes were demolished. Virtually every vehicle on the island was flooded and totaled. Houses were gutted, and in some instances, torn down. Residents began the hard labor of saving what they could. Piles of debris grew in the streets as residents removed anything inundated by the sea: insulation, furniture, carpeting, and so on. Salt water is especially hard on electronics; it ruined many air conditioners and, in some cases, houses' wiring. As the piles grew, the reality of the destruction took hold.

North Carolina governor Roy Cooper visited Ocracoke the day after Dorian passed. Though the island would remain officially closed to visitors for nearly three months, volunteer groups such as the American Red Cross, the Salvation Army, the North Carolina Baptists on Mission, Samaritan's Purse, and the United Methodists Committee on Relief were allowed on island and began arriving within days of the storm. They helped with the cleanup, and some groups remained for months, assisting with the rebuilding. The Outer Banks Community Foundation created an Ocracoke Disaster Relief Fund and raised more than $1.2 million from over 6,000 donors. Individuals and groups from all over sent contributions to community organizations, churches, and the school. The support the island received from the mainland was remarkable, but the story of the islanders' responses is even more incredible. The relief effort was run out of the Ocracoke Volunteer Fire Department building, which opened in 2016 on a piece of land that was built up substantially to be higher than other island locations (see fig. 16.2).

Ocracoke is the sort of place where good-natured ribbing and teasing is commonplace. But when tested, it is also the sort of place that comes together like nowhere else. The story of Ocracoke after Dorian is remarkable but can be summed up succinctly: Everyone did all they could to help absolutely anyone who needed anything at all. In practice, this spirit manifested in many ways, but perhaps most clearly in the Ocracoke Strong Kitchen.

There's an old adage that goes, "When you have more than you need, build a bigger table—not a higher fence." Even in a time of crisis—not abundance—the Ocracoke community opted to "build a bigger table." In fact, the Ocracoke Strong Kitchen "built a table" big enough for the entire community. Ocracoke Strong Kitchen was organized in the days after Dorian by O'Cocker Jason Wells, co-owner of Jason's Restaurant. The initiative began when Wells organized a few other islanders to grill some donated chicken for the community and relief workers. One meal led to another, and soon Ocracoke Strong Kitchen was providing multiple meals a day to all residents and volunteers. For months, Wells and his core group cooked for the island every Monday, Thursday, and Saturday.

FIGURE 16.2. The Ocracoke Volunteer Fire Department building, built on high ground, stayed dry during the storm and became the headquarters of the relief efforts. Photograph by Connie Leinbach/*Ocracoke Observer*.

Members of Hope Mennonite Church of Pantego cooked on Tuesdays. Wednesdays were covered by the Ocracoke Latino Ladies. Chrislyn Wedderien and the Little Washington Community took care of Fridays. For Wells, cooking was the thing he knew how to do to best help his community: "I suck at carpentry. I can't help people with that, but this is something I can do. It makes people happy, which makes me happy." Wells recalled in an interview with the *Ocracoke Observer*, "And it was not only was it great for the community, but it also provided something for us to do, a purpose, you know. Instead of sitting in the house and feeling sorry for myself. . . . It gave me a purpose and it gave me something to do and obviously I love to cook and I love my community, so it provided all of those things." For his part in organizing the Ocracoke Strong Kitchen, Wells was awarded the Governor's Medallion Award for Volunteer Service.

To hear Jason Wells talk about his work with the Ocracoke Strong Kitchen, visit www.ocracokebrogue.com/chapter/16/QR16-4.mp3.

Other stories from the recovery capture similar accounts of strength and resiliency. In some cases, residents ended up better off than they had been before the storm. One such example is Chester Lynn, whose house on Back Road was flooded and needed to be completely gutted. Community members and volunteers from the Methodist Men redid the entire interior of the home, making it handicapped accessible, allowing Chester—who requires a walker or two canes to walk—to move around his home better than he had for years.

Uplifting stories of the community's resiliency must be balanced with the reality of what islanders lost. There is no way to quantify the losses of irreplaceable family heirlooms, but other things can be measured. The mountain of debris that amassed in the parking lot of Lifeguard Beach—dubbed "Mt. Trashmore" by some and "a mountain of memories" by others—and was eventually hauled away by boat, weighed more than 6,000 tons, or roughly 13,000 pounds per resident. Such loss is hard to fathom, but so were the floodwaters that eclipsed all previously recorded measurements.

## OCRACOKE POST-DORIAN

If Dorian was the worst storm since 1933 or even 1899, it might be tempting to contextualize it as a once-in-a-century storm, the likes of which the island will not experience for some time. But the reality is scarier. The Village Craftsmen, an artists' gallery on Howard Street, has a marker of hurricane flood lines since 1985. For over a decade, Alex (2004), stood as the high-water mark, until in 2016, when the floods from Matthew surged six inches higher. Dorian eclipsed this record by more than two feet. Philip Howard, owner of the Village Craftsmen, wondered in an interview with the

*Coastal Review*, "Was Dorian a once-in-a-lifetime event or is it the new normal?" This question cannot be answered yet. In the five years since Dorian, the community has clearly decided to embrace the hope that Dorian was the exception, not the new normal. It may be the optimism inherited from surviving at the edge of the world for so long, or perhaps it is simply that the love of the place is stronger than the fear of the future. Either way, the community has once again become a vibrant place, marked by many of the things that have always been part of the fabric of Ocracoke.

To the casual observer, Ocracoke appears to be back to the community it always was. There are no longer piles of debris. Houses and businesses have been repaired or rebuilt. Businesses are again packed with dingbatters. The careful observer will notice many houses—and, indeed, the Methodist Church—have been raised substantially. It is also easy to overlook that many traditional homes have been razed, replaced by bigger homes of a different style. Understandably, it was the oldest homes of long-time island families, which tended to be built on the ground rather than on pylons, that were most likely to be destroyed by the flooding. With this change, the careful observer should notice the island community really does appear quite different. They would also notice that the old school has been replaced with a new structure. The "Ocracoke strong" signs that persisted around town for the first few years are also now gone.

The community does not seem to dwell much on the storm these days. Tourists ask about it, and most islanders know how to respond sufficiently but without revisiting old traumas. That is not to say such trauma does not exist. There are still active support groups on the island for residents still struggling with the storm's impact.

When we ask residents about the impact of Dorian on the community, a number of residents tell us they think the storm and the recovery brought the community closer. Others suggest that the storm just exposed what was always there: an island community maintained only by its residents' willingness to do anything they could to help their neighbor. Perhaps Dorian was a terrible baptism for the non-O'Cockers, with the positive outcome of them understanding just a little more deeply what it means to be a neighbor on an isolated barrier island. By preserving islanders' stories and memories of the storm and the community's recovery, we hope to help everyone understand just a little better the remarkable community spirit of Ocracoke.

*Chapter 17*

# WHAT DID THE OLD-TIMERS SOUND LIKE?

When people talk about the Brogue in Ocracoke, they usually have in mind the oldest generation of people. When asked to identify Brogue speakers, students in the school also tend to refer to their grandparents or a few well-known, older personalities who can perform the dialect at will for outsiders. Even linguists tend to cite O'Cockers who speak the most vivid versions of the Brogue when they are trying to illustrate the features of the traditional dialect, falling prey to "exotic language syndrome"—the tendency to seize upon the most unusual features in describing the uniqueness of a dialect while ignoring its many similarities with other dialects.

At the same time, some of the more distinctive traits are found in the older speakers on Ocracoke and less so or not at all in the speech of middle-aged or younger speakers. We need to realize, however, that all dialect variants, including those of the oldest, the middle-aged, and the younger speakers on Ocracoke are of equal interest in the study of dialects. Furthermore, Ocracoke speech has always existed on a continuum where different speakers show some—but not all—of the features described by linguists who try to be comprehensive in their coverage.

## ESSIE O'NEAL: A CASE STUDY

We can illustrate the speech of older Ocracokers several decades ago with a couple of examples we recorded early in our 1990s study. When we arrived on Ocracoke, we were immediately aware of the family of Harry and Essie O'Neal, one of the well-known families of the island. Harry and Essie O'Neal had eleven boys, which naturally stands out on an island the size of Ocracoke. Further, one of them was Rex O'Neal, who has been featured regularly on television and website programs about the Ocracoke dialect. In fact, linguists refer to him as a "dialect performer" because he can—and does—produce a rendition of the dialect spontaneously when talking to outsiders. The first time Walt Wolfram was introduced to Rex O'Neal at a poker game his first week in 1992, Rex uttered his now famous "It's hoi toid on the sound soid" routine we discuss in some previous chapters. The large family of O'Neal boys and their families are still well-known to everyone on the island, although some have moved off the island.

The father, Harry O'Neal, was born in 1901; he was an excellent carpenter as well as a jack-of-all-trades. Of course, he also fished. His wife Essie was born in 1915. With eleven rambunctious boys to care for, she exhibited incredible amounts of energy and was a character in her own right. Harry died in 1977, so we were not able to interview him; but we interviewed Essie in the mid-1990s, before she passed away in 1999. She was a graphic storyteller, and the day that her daughter-in-law Miggy O'Neal and Walt Wolfram interviewed her, she told stories without interruption for well over an hour. She had a knack for vividly recounting incidents in her life, from the great hurricane in 1944 to funny stories about drunk pigs that found the remnants of homemade meal wine. Below is her account of the hurricane of 1944, which is presented, but not analyzed, in chapter 15. In the transcript below, occurrences of vernacular grammatical differences are italicized, while instances of three vowels that are noteworthy appear in boldface. The story is linked again here so the reader can hear the vowel differences.

To hear the illustrative passage from Essie O'Neal, visit www.ocracokebrogue.com/chapter/17/QR17-1.mp3.

> That was the st**o**rm. This was another thing we're t**a**lking ab**ou**t. I had a new maple bedroom set. And I had just got it in the h**ou**se, three or f**ou**r days, when the st**o**rm *come* —the '44 st**o**rm. We had a pretty day, just l**i**ke this. No wind, pretty sunsh**i**ne. And the day that came over that day and said there's a bad st**o**rm heading r**i**ght straight for us. And we didn't believe it: "*They ain't no st**o**rm*," you know. "*They ain't no st**o**rm come*." Said, "Yes, it's heading r**i**ght straight for Cape Hatteras." And it was a pretty calm day. And that n**i**ght, after it got to *dark good*, went **ou**t on the porch with Harry and we went **ou**t on the p**o**rch and *the stars was* sh**i**ning. He says, "I don't think there's no st**o**rm." He said, "It don't look l**i**ke a st**o**rm." And everything was calm. But let me tell you, when we woke up the next morning, I th**ou**ght the roof was gonna come off my h**ou**se. I never heard such a hard wind. It was a hundred miles, blowing a *hundred mile*. I never heard such a hard wind. And he said, "You better get up and get all them kids ready, get them dressed, we'll have to leave here." And I was working fast as I could to get 'em all and put 'em *to the table*, hurry, get them breakfast and everything. Harry looked, and the t**i**de was *a-rolling* r**i**ght in the yard. Come up so fast, it was *a-rolling* in the yard. And we got them, and that's when we left. And when we left **ou**t of that gate, I tell you, it was about *f**our** foot* of water in the gate when we left. And we had to leave here in a boat. We had a half-grown pig.

> And he didn't want him to dr**ow**ned, you know. He had a old, big wooden trunk-big old-timey trunks. So, he put him in the trunk and put the trunk on the p**o**rch. I said, "When that pig floats ar**ou**nd in that trunk, he'll think he's in a boat." And we went on Mickey's—Mickey that lives over there, closer to that graveyard d**ow**n there, that cemetery. That's where we spent that st**o**rm **ou**t. Tide *run* off at Amy Lake. Harry said, "I'm going up to the h**ou**se, if we got a h**ou**se." We didn't even think we had a h**ou**se. And I said, "Can we go?," and he said, "No, better stay here, wait till I go." So, when he *come* back, he had a sad news to say. He said, "Well, I'll tell you, I saw the h**ou**se was standing." He said, "But the door was w**i**de open, had *blowed* open," he said, "and the first thing I met was the pig coming **ou**t of the living room."

The boldface vowels are critical in identifying the uniqueness of Ocracoke speech. They are (1) the vowel in *high tide* that is pronounced as "hoi toid"; (2) the vowel of *sound* and *house*, which tends to sound more like "saind" and "hais"; and (3) the *ou/au* vowel in *talking*, *storm*, and *porch*, which is different from other American English dialects in small, technical ways that tend to be overlooked by many North Americans. As we talk about in more detail in chapter 11, the island articulation sounds more British than American.

To hear how the *ou/au* vowel is produced in differentdialects, visit www.ocracokebrogue.com/chapter/17/QR17-2.mp3.

In the marked transcript, the prominence of the phonetic features that characterize the Ocracoke dialect should be apparent. While grammatical features tend to occur infrequently, the potential for the pronunciation of three distinctive vowels occurs more than five times as much as all of the possible grammatical features of the dialect. This may be one of the reasons that phonetic differences tend to be associated with the Ocracoke Brogue rather than grammatical ones. A limited number of vowels can occur with great frequency, since each word in English has at least one vowel.

Essie O'Neal is a modest user of the iconic "hoi toid" vowel, using a weakened version in *shine*, *wide*, and other words, but not the robust "hoi toid" present in her son Rex's performance dialect. The pronunciation of the *ow* vowel in *brown* and *sound* on Ocracoke can be distinct, so that *sound* sounds more like "saind" and *brown* sounds like "brain." Despite being less stereotyped than the *hoi toid* vowel variant, this pronunciation is actually more distinctive to the Ocracoke Brogue (and other islands along the Mid-Atlantic coast) than the vowel of "hoi toid." Essie reveals a modest version of this pronunciation of *ow* in words such as *house* and *around*, but it is not as distinctive as it is in some islanders. Although this vowel pronunciation is certainly a marked trait of Ocracoke to linguists, for some reason it has not become a stereotype of Ocracoke in the way the "hoi toid" vowel has. In fact, Rex O'Neal does not even pronounce *sound* as "saind" in his classic performance production of "It's hoi toid on the sound soid." We honestly do not know why this is the case, since this pronunciation can sometimes be quite noticeable to outsiders and linguists. The last vowel we bolded was the vowel in words such as *caught*, *bought*, and *talk*. Essie adopts the British-like pronunciation, though it is not something routinely noticed by people other than specialists in phonetics. We also think that this may be one of the subtle reasons Ocracoke speech is the only dialect in America that outsiders think is not an American dialect.

The grammatical structures that Essie uses are fairly typical of linguistic structures found in a number of other regional vernacular dialects of English, including different irregular verbs such as "blowed" for *blown*, "come" for *came*, "run" for *ran*, of "heist" for *hoist*. Her negative constructions also show traditional island patterns, such as, "They ain't no storm come," along with the absence of *-s* with nouns of weights and measures (*hundred mile*, *four foot*) and the *a*-prefixing in *a-rollin'*, often associated with Appalachian English. Essie also puts her children "to the table" rather than *at the table*, a common Ocracoke use of *to* for *at* in "static locative," as discussed in chapter 8. Finally, the use of *dark good* for "very dark" is similar to the use of *-some* as an intensifier added to a word, as we described in chapter 11.

To hear three more stories from Essie O'Neal (from *Ocracoke Still Speaks*), visit www.ocracokebrogue.com/chapter/17/QR17-3.mp3 (*top*), www.ocracokebrogue.com/chapter/17/QR17-4.mp3 (*middle*), and www.ocracokebrogue.com/chapter/17/QR17-5.mp3 (*bottom*).

## OTHER OLD-TIMERS

A prototypical older Ocracoke male is Robert "Washie" Spencer, also a member of an ancestral family in the area for several centuries. He was born in 1921 and lived as a single person on the island of Ocracoke all of his life. As with Essie O'Neal above, he also recounts the Hurricane of 1944, which was one of the most severe hurricane to hit Ocracoke before Hurricane Dorian in 2019 (see chapters 15 and 16). The transcript is marked the same way as Essie O'Neal's transcript; grammar features are italicized and the same three vowels appear in boldface.

> The last real bad one they had—c**ou**rse, they had some since then—the last real bad one they had was 1944. Dad was here in the Coast Guard. Dad said there never was a prettier day. There was a feller there was named Acock Br**ow**n. You might have heard of him, he was *a man owned* a paper printing company. He was d**ow**n at Beaufort and then he went up to Manteo. Well-known. Very smart man. Very smart man. He told them he got attached to the Navy somehow or other, intelligence or something, I think. Dad

said he *come* ar**ou**nd and told them all, "We're gonna have a bad hurricane." Everything was beautiful. Beautiful. Everybody looked at him like he was crazy. But that day it *come* in—of c**ou**rse, I was in the Pacific, I was in the Philippines, but we had a typhoon ab**ou**t the same time. I got c**au**ght in that, typhoons are w**or**se. Anyway, Dad was done in the service and **I**ris and Jane Russell and some more of the fell**er**s around here, they had what they c**a**ll a beach boat. They go **out** to sea with, row your net **out**, catch fish, you know, pull your net ashore. My w**i**fe's grandmother, her name was Miss Midgett, they called her, her name was Elizabeth. They had to move some of those people from the water to carry 'em to the l**i**ghth**ou**se. She wasn't home. And a bunch of women and a hog or two in that boat. And when they went back d**own** where we lived, our home there by Albert Styron's st**o**re **o**n the end, he said it was up to here. Tiptoe with her. He took her in a boat with *them people* in it and the h**i**ghest part of the l**i**ghth**ou**se then. And he said they went over to the h**i**ghest part of the l**i**ghth**ou**se then, with *them people* and that hog in there, and *them people* went r**i**ght over top of that h**i**gh l**i**ghth**ou**se then and the mother's washing machine and all that turned bottom up in the kitchen, crashed through the window, turned bottom up in the kitchen. And the boats *come* ashore ab**ou**t where the c**o**ffee shop—no, I don't think the c**o**ffee shop is there now —by the post **o**ffice.

To hear the illustrative passage from Washie Spencer (from *Ocracoke Speaks*), visit www.ocracokebrogue.com/chapter/17/QR17-6.mp3.

Washie Spencer uses some of the same kinds of irregular verb formations that Essie O'Neal uses ("come" for *came*), and the southern vernacular construction "he was a man owned a paper printing company" without the relative pronoun *that* or *who* (e.g., "he was a man *who* owned . . ."). He also uses the object form "them" for

FIGURE 17.1. Blanche Howard Jolliff. Photograph by Ann Ehringhaus.

the demonstrative *these* (i.e., "them people"), a common structure in many vernacular dialects. He uses an inventory of structures that overlaps with Essie's, but the two speakers are not uniform in their use of structures. In fact, there is considerable variation from speaker to speaker within the older generation.

A couple of other speakers are presented in the following linked audio excerpts to provide further samples that demonstrate some of the similarities and variations among speakers in the older generation. Elizabeth Parsons was born in 1935 and died in 2016 at eighty-one years of age. She ran a gift shop for thirty years and became a folk artist in her later years. She tells a story about dead body that washed up on Ocracoke following a storm. (Richard) Clinton Gaskill was a respected member of the Ocracoke community, considered one of the true "old salts" of Ocracoke Island. He was born in 1905 and died in 1999 at ninety-three years of age.

He was a commercial fisherman and hunting guide, and an archetype of the male O'Cocker of his generation. He tells the story of how island men would pen horses and sheep every Fourth of July. Finally, Blanche Howard Jolliff, born 1919 and died in 2018, tells a story about how her mother used to domesticate some goslings as pets (see fig. 17.1). This collection of voices shows both the similarities and the differences in the speech of O'Cockers from the early twentieth century.

To hear Elizabeth Parsons tell the story of a dead body washing up on Ocracoke (from *Ocracoke Speaks*), visit www.ocracokebrogue.com/chapter/17/QR17-7.mp3.

To hear Clinton Gaskill describe the annual pony penning (from *Ocracoke Speaks*), visit www.ocracokebrogue.com/chapter/17/QR17-8.mp3.

To hear Blanche Howard Jolliff talk about raising goslings (from *Ocracoke Still Speaks*), visit www.ocracokebrogue.com/chapter/17/QR17-9.mp3.

Additional samples of older speakers are found on the two oral history CDs the Preservation Society and the Language and Life Project compiled, *Ocracoke Speaks* (2001) and *Ocracoke Still Speaks* (2011), though CDs are now an antiquated way for storing oral histories. These oral history projects are included in their entirety on the website that accompanies this book.

Despite the earlier, physical isolation of the island, the older residents had varied life experiences and interacted with different social groupings within the island while knowing everyone, and some lived away from the island for periods of time as well. For example, a number of men joined the Coast Guard or moved to Philadelphia to work in the shipyards for extended periods, and they were no doubt affected by these experiences socially and linguistically. Others, including many older women, stayed on the island raising their children, but some also had off-island interactions and stays at different points in their lives. These are the kinds of experiences that would lead to diversity within the language community. People sometimes forget that Ocracoke has always had plenty of linguistic diversity among its residents. In fact, linguists who study small communities are often surprised by the linguistic range of diversity that exists in some very small language communities, and even within families. The language of these communities is often much more varied than we imagine, challenging the assumption that these isolated island communities are typically uniform in language.

## VOCABULARY AMONG OLD-TIMERS

Throughout this volume, we have highlighted many words and sayings common to the island. Unless otherwise noted, most of these remain in use by or at least familiar to the younger generations. But there are a number of old-timers' words and sayings that are now being lost among the youngest generations, and some of these offer insights into changes on the island.

Despite Ocracoke's having the first established post office on the Outer Banks (1840), there has never been home delivery of mail on the island. Since the 1960s, islanders have received their mail via post office boxes at the community post office, with the current location (across from Howard's Pub) opening in 1997. During the years between 1840 and the 1964, the mail arrived by boat at the post office dock, with the *Aleta* being the most well-known of the mail boats. In this period, residents would congregate daily at the post office dock, and as the mail was unloaded, the postmaster would call out the names of people receiving letters or packages. Residents referred to this practice as "calling the mail over." The phrase could be used in other ways, such as asking, "Has the mail been called over yet?" As Chester Lynn recalls, if you were not there to collect your own mail, "someone would carry it to you. The mail weren't like it is today. If you weren't there, your neighbor would carry it to you and it weren't a big deal."

Below we list some other words and phrases that old-timers used and that are becoming less and less familiar to the current generations. Many of these were found in other southern varieties of English, but some are unique to Ocracoke. This list is not at all exhaustive, and includes mostly words not discussed elsewhere in this book. Sample sentences are offered only for items where the usage might not be clear.

**begombed** or **begaumed** (adj.): To be soiled with a sticky or greasy residue. "Ellen's shirt was begombed with paint."

**cat** (n.): An island version of baseball where it's possible to put out a baserunner by hitting them with the ball, as in dodgeball. The game was usually played with sticks for bats and homemade balls, such as balled up aluminum foil.

**catawampus**, **catterwampus**, or **cattywampus** (adj.): In a diagonal position, crooked, not square. "The boxes were piled up all catawampus." (**Whopperjawed** is used in the same way).

**counterpane** (n.): Bedspread.

**face 'n' eyes** (n.): Face, often with derision. "Get out of here! I don't want to see your face 'n' eyes again today."

**fatback** (n.): Menhaden. An oily fish.

**fetch up** (v.): Appear, show up. "He finally fetched up again after his vacation."

**fladget** (n.): A small piece. "We got a fladget of cake." **See smidget**.

**for to** (prep.): In order to. "She came for to visit."

**goaty** (adj.): Foul-smelling. "Y'all are smelling goaty! Go bathe."

**guano** (n.): fertilizer from sea birds. "We got us some good guano for our garden." (Also pronounced as "guanner.")

**lay a cussin' on** (verb phrase): To swear at someone. "She really laid a cussin' on him last night."

**lighter wood** (n.): Kindling to start a fire.

**meehonkey** (n.): An island game that meshed hide-and-seek and Marco Polo. Children would hide across the village and adjoining areas and to allow the seeker an opportunity to find the other players; those hiding would occasionally call out "meehonkey" (likely imitating the sound of a goose).

To hear James Barrie Gaskill describe how meehonkey was played (from *Ocracoke Speaks*), visit www.ocracokebrogue.com/chapter/17/QR17-10.mp3.

**pizer** (n.): A porch on a house. From the Italian *piazza.*

**Russian rat** (n.): A nutria (a large member of the rodent family).

**smidget** (n.): A small piece or slice of (usually) food. "Cut me a smidget of that fig cake."

**turn out** (v.): dismiss. "The principal turned out school because of the cold."

**wampus cat** (n.): A fictitious animal used to scare or tease children. Also used on Ocracoke for people who are especially noteworthy in some say, such as being especially silly or heavy. "There's no one else like him! He's a real wampus cat."

**whipstitch** (n.): Every now and then, sporadically. "We only see them every whipstitch."

**whit** (n.): A considerable amount of time. "He's been off island a whit now."

**whoop and holler** (n.): Hide and seek, played much like meehonkey.

This is simply a small, selective list of some of the older forms still used or remembered by the older generation that are rare or unfamiliar to the younger generations.

*Chapter 18*

# HOW IS THE BROGUE CHANGING?

One of the reasons we started studying the Ocracoke Brogue several decades ago was because it appeared to be changing so rapidly that it seemed essential to document it before it vanished. After more than three centuries, one of the most distinctive dialects of American English was vanishing fast under the waves of new residents and tourists. Even outsiders knew Ocracoke for its distinct sounds, and throughout North Carolina folks still refer to it as *Hoi Toider* speech, but we wondered just how long this iconic dialect would remain.

In the previous chapter, we discussed how the Brogue is usually associated with the oldest speakers in the community, the folks who have been least affected by the inundation of *dingbatters*. Also, older speakers were more likely to marry fellow islanders, a situation that often resulted in their children speaking more like their parents and the peers of other island children. Middle-aged and younger islanders are more likely to have spent some time off the island and to have interacted more with outsiders, and may even be the product of a "mixed marriage." On Ocracoke, a "mixed marriage" is one where one of the partners is a native O'Cocker and the other is from off (i.e., anywhere other than Ocracoke).

The vast majority of summer inhabitants are visitors to Ocracoke, and a decreasing number of residents are born into families where both parents are "ancestral islanders." In mixed marriages, the traditional dialect is vulnerable to shift by the children, who often end up speaking a non-Brogue dialect. The number of native Ocracoke residents where even one branch of the family goes back to the 1700s is decreasing with every generation. In a recent local count, between 300 and 350 out of a population of about 900 year-round residents were ancestral islanders—or *O'Cockers*. Of course, during the tourist season, the population swells by several thousand with day-trippers and vacationers, and there may be as many as 10,000–12,000 people on the island during a summer day. During the vacation season, a visitor may wonder where all the O'Cockers are among the lines of people waiting at a restaurant. Some may work behind the scenes in the tourist industry, while others are too busy to sit down for a leisurely meal and a laid-back chat. And a few islanders can escape to selected private spots at the Fish Camp in Oyster Creek. Some residents even opt to leave the island entirely during the summer months. Between the visitors and transplants, even on the quietest days, O'Cockers are vastly outnumbered by outsiders, so it is understandable that the traditional vernacular dialect is under pressure. In the current circumstances, there is little doubt that the Brogue is changing.

To hear Bubbie Boos reflect on recent changes to the island (from *Ocracoke Still Speaks*), visit www.ocracokebrogue.com/chapter/18/QR18-1.mp3.

## DIALECT EROSION

It is quite apparent to outsiders and to community members themselves that the traditional dialect of Ocracoke is eroding. If a visitor

**FIGURE 18.1.** James Barrie Gaskill and his son, Morty, in the early stages of our research and again fifteen years later. Photographs by Ann Ehringhaus and Neal Hutcheson.

talks to an older, middle-aged, or younger islander, the dramatic change in dialect over the generations can be witnessed firsthand, though there is a lot more to this change than meets the ear. When we consider some of the social dynamics in the community along with population change and economic factors, description can become more complicated, and even confusing. Nonetheless, the gradual dissipation of the dialect seems to be obvious, with most people assuming it is a simple matter of direct, progressive erosion due to the population demographics in a popular tourist site.

When we collect language samples in a community like Ocracoke, we like to include speech from the oldest, middle, and younger generations, and that is how we originally selected our pool of speakers in Ocracoke in the 1990s. We have samples of speech that range from early teenagers to folks in their nineties. That way we can get a good idea of how language change is taking place over generations, assuming that different ages represent the different periods of the island's linguistic history. We even refer to this as the difference between "apparent time" and "real time." In a real-time study, we would have to commit to tracing the dialect over decades; apparent time is a shortcut to assess how language change over time takes place without spending the rest of your career in the community. People can, of course, make changes in their speech over a lifetime, but these language changes tend to be modest once speakers reach adulthood. Thus, when we interview a speaker who is eighty-five years old, we are making an assumption that we are hearing what the community's dialect was like around sixty-five years ago. In addition to our extensive, earlier study, we have conducted a couple of subsequent studies of Ocracoke, one where we interviewed some of the same speakers fifteen years after our original study, to see if individuals were changing their speech over their lifetime. Figure 18.1 shows the subjects of a real-time study, a father and son, at two different moments in their lives. The body of apparent-time and real-time studies of the Brogue make it one of the most thoroughly documented dialects in the country. We will discuss our real-time study later in this chapter, but simply note here that the middle-aged speakers from our original study did not change their speech much as they aged, supporting the use of apparent-time methodology in this community.

The kind of dialect recession found in Ocracoke is not the only model that leads to the erosion and the loss of a dialect. For example, on Smith Island in the Chesapeake Bay in Maryland, a community with a dialect that sounds a lot like the Ocracoke Brogue has existed since the early 1600s. That dialect is also headed for extinction, but it is actually getting stronger as it does so. The demographic and economic situation on Smith Island, however, is quite different from that on Ocracoke. The population of Smith Island, stable for many years, has recently declined from around 800 to slightly over 200. While there are economic factors contributing to the decline, the larger impetus is that the island itself is losing land to the rising Chesapeake Bay; in fact, Smith Island is expected to be immersed in the bay by the end of this century. With few vacation homes and little tourist industry, the island remains relatively secluded, despite the occasional mid-afternoon stop by a group of tourists on a tour boat during the vacation season. Furthermore, as more residents leave the island in search of steady work, the dedicated members of the younger generation have intensified the dialect as a part of their isolated, resilient identity. Given the continuation of the island's disappearance into the bay, we can predict that the island will eventually be without inhabitants by the end of this century. When this happens, the dialect will also die. This is a very different kind of situation from that on Ocracoke, but it underscores how ecological conditions, population demographics, and identity have an important role in determining how a dialect might erode.

## THE SOCIAL SIDE OF DIALECT RECESSION

As we noted above, the way in which dialects shift is more than a simple matter of population demographics and economics. There are also social factors and attitudes within the community that affect the rate and direction of the change. Different social affiliations may result in nuanced differences in ways of speaking among groups of some islanders; in fact, these groups can be instrumental in determining how a dialect will change over time. There are also different kinds of interpersonal contacts that people have with insiders and outsiders that can affect language shifts, as language differences carry social meaning.

To hear Rex O'Neal tell a humorous story about how different early tourism was on Ocracoke (from *Ocracoke Still Speaks*), visit www.ocracokebrogue.com/chapter/18/QR18-2.mp3.

One of the groups that existed when we first came to Ocracoke was referred to as the Poker Game Network. This consisted of a group of middle-aged men who got together a couple of nights a week ostensibly to play poker. This group's legacy is encoded in one of the island's street names, Poker Player Road. They also tended to hang together in other social activities. In the process, they acquired a rugged island male persona sometimes characterized as an "old salt." The group was male-exclusive, and wives and partners were typically excluded from meetings at poker houses. There is currently a house in Oyster Creek that displays the sign "Poker House" on the exterior as a tribute to this heritage. The current house was constructed over the original shed built for playing poker and hanging out by the long-term owner of the Pony Island Motel (now the Pony Island Inn), Dave Esham. The original building had a comfortable poker table, television, bar, and other amenities. A couple of the main participants in the Poker Game Network had gone to college and returned to the island following their education and some experience at mainland occupations. While it is reasonable to assume that these off-island experiences eroded their Brogues, the opposite was true. On their return, they seemed to embrace their island identity even more intensely than they had before they left.

In a follow-up study, fifteen years after we conducted our original study, we interviewed some of the same speakers who were middle-aged during our earlier study, as well as some of the younger speakers who were by then in their later twenties and thirties. The Poker

Game Network was no longer functioning, but we tried to find a group of younger men who might be comparable to the original Poker Game Network—that is, a group of middle-aged men who shared parallel attitudes about their island status. Some of these men congregated at the Pelican, then a side bar associated with a now-closed restaurant. Although the group of men we identified was quite different from the Poker Game Network, they similarly embraced a rugged male persona that was committed to the island and proud of their island heritage. They further planned to live on the island, earning a living (or, at least, part of their living) through marine-related activities, such as fishing tours, guiding trips to Portsmouth, marine-based activities for tourists (parasailing excursions, renting kayaks, etc.), working on the ferry, and fishing. This group of men did have stronger Brogues than similarly aged men who were not a part of this group, but their dialects were not as strong as the men in the Poker Game Network. This finding demonstrates that even among those committed to traditional island ways of life, including traditional ways of speaking, there was significant erosion of the dialect between generations.

Another factor that we considered in the community was gender. Chapter 12 detailed the differentiated roles for men and women in Ocracoke, with women traditionally staying home on the island and they were not typically involved in the fishing industry (see fig. 18.2). Further, women tended to stay on the island raising the children, while the men sometimes traveled with the Coast Guard or worked on shipyards in Philadelphia and Norfolk. Before World War II, men served as the primary breadwinners, mostly through fishing and other marine-based activities, while women were confined to the domestic domain. Following the war, particularly in 1950s and 1960s, the tourism industry developed rapidly on the island, with the inauguration of a regular state-run ferry service and the paving of some roads. Women started working in the new industry, serving visitors in hotels and restaurants, running specialty shops, and through other tourism-related occupations. In the process, women came into increasing contact with speakers of outside dialects some years ahead of their male

FIGURE 18.2. A group of island men using traditional fishing methods. Photograph courtesy of the Chester Lynn Collection.

cohorts. At the same time, men were finding it increasingly difficult to earn a living through their traditional male occupations related to the water. The economy was transformed from marine-based to tourist-based as some men began relinquishing their traditionally male occupations in order to participate in the tourist economy.

With this background information in mind, consider some of the language dynamics that might have been affected by different social groups in Ocracoke. We conducted an extensive investigation of the pronunciation of *tide* as "toid" for different age groups, social groups, and different genders. We choose this vowel sound because it is the most symbolic vowel representing Ocracoke speech—the first sound often associated with Ocracoke speech. We observed each case of this in the interviews we conducted and noted whether it was pronounced with the local pronunciation (e.g., "toid"), a standard variation (e.g., "tide"), or an inland southern pronuncia-tion (e.g., "tahd"). In some cases, we used sophisticated computer tools to verify our judgments acoustically. This exercise would give us a percentage of cases where the local "soid" vowel was used instead of the "side" vowel. For example, one speaker might use this pronunciation 25 percent of the time and another, 75 percent of the time. Then we averaged the figures for different groups of people, such as the Poker Game Network men versus non-Poker Game Network men, women, and so forth, and compared the groups. The data were then subjected to rigorous statistical examination to determine how significant the changes we observed really were. The results demonstrate how language change takes on social meaning in the community, and how it intersects with population demographics and economics.

We will spare you the statistical outputs from the multivariate analyses and instead offer a broad overview of the findings. For older women and men, we did not find a significant difference in the use of the *tide/toid* vowel based on gender, though older women used a little more of *toid* vowel than men. The pattern for middle-aged speakers was a bit more nuanced. One of the results showed that the middle-aged, Poker Game Network men actually produced more of the *toid* vowel than the oldest generation, indicating that there was probably some social reason for doing this. Remember that the Poker Game Network was a group of men who highly valued the image of the rugged fisher, a primarily masculine persona. Middle-aged women, however, used less of the *toid* vowel, though they outdid middle-aged, non-poker-playing men. We also did a small study of a few gay men among ancestral islanders and found that they tended to have less incidence of the *toid* vowel than other men and women. These facts tend to underscore the interpretation that, although the *toid* vowel was once gender-neutral, it was taking on an association with a rugged masculine identity. This was further confirmed by the younger generation, where the younger men used it significantly more than the younger women. In our follow-up study, fifteen years after the initial recordings were made, we found the Pelican Group of young men (i.e., a group of men who regularly congregated at the Pelican bar) used it more than other younger speakers, suggesting that a strong island identity remained the best predictor of who maintained the local pronunciation.

Comparing speakers whom we were able to record in both studies, we found that the group of people who show the most shift in their speech over real time were the younger males, not the females, particularly men who hung out at the Pelican. In fact, as with the Poker Game Network men, some young men who went to college on the mainland would return to the island and recapture some of the flavor of the Brogue. That is, they were less Brogue-y in their youth and more Brogue-y in adulthood, after they had made the choice to return to Ocracoke. We did not find the same trend among women who returned; they were instead quite consistent across the two studies.

If nothing else, we have shown that there is a somewhat more complicated explanation of how the Brogue is eroding, nuanced by gender ideologies and attitudes about the island assumed by different groups of people. The obvious story of a dialect eroding due to tourism is more complicated than it seems at first. In Ocracoke, as in all communities, the social meanings of various linguistic features are essential to understand in order to describe accurately the complex ways in which the dialect changes. For sure, the dialect has changed and eroded in its linguistic shape, but the way in which it receded indicates how different values and attitudes by the people of the island are reflected and maintained in the midst of language use.

In this chapter, we discuss only the changes we measured for one specific vowel, but the same trends can be found when looking at other dialect features. Nearly all the pronunciation and grammatical features discussed in chapters 10 and 11 show similar recession to what we observed for the pronunciation of *tide* as "toid." In fact, some of the non-iconic features of the dialect have receded even faster, perhaps stamped out in schools or simply lost since they do not carry social prestige. Vocabulary changes do not map so neatly onto the recession trends we observed. Words do change over time, but they can have greater staying power than distinctive pronunciations or grammatical differences. Some words, like *fladget*, meaning "a little piece," seem to have been lost among younger speakers, but others, like *buck*, meaning "a good friend" remain robust. Terms for outsiders shifted in the 1970s, when *dingbatter* entered the island's lexicon via the television show *All in the Family*, as discussed in chapter 2. In the mid-2000s, we thought we were witnessing a generational shift when the youngest islanders starting using *touron* instead, but that term has yet to unseat *dingbatter* as the term of choice to refer to outsiders.

## WHAT DIALECTS ARE REPLACING THE BROGUE?

There is one final observation about dialect change to be noted. As some of the traditional pronunciations change, they tend to be replaced by more northern-like rather than southern-like vowels. For example, when residents stop using the "toid" pronunciation, they do not adopt the southern pronunciation where the glide is weakened, sounding like "tahd" rather than *tide*. Other vowels are not so exclusively northern, and some Ocracokers pronounce *pin* and *pen* with the same vowel while others do not. This is unusual for rural areas of North Carolina, which remain fairly consistent in the pronunciation of the words *pin* and *pen* with the same vowel. This suggests that the new norm for younger Ocracokers is not as southern as their mainland cohorts.

Why might native Ocracokers start adopting northern vowels? On one summer trip, we had our students go to every motel parking lot in Ocracoke and tally the states the cars had come from. Well over three-quarters of the cars were from states to the north, such as Virginia, Pennsylvania, Ohio, New Jersey, and other northern or midwestern regions. Rarely did they find cars with plates from South Carolina, Georgia, Alabama, and other southern states. So, it is likely that the dialects of new residents and visitors are influencing which pronunciations emerge to replace the traditional, local pronunciations. In terms of vocabulary, however, there are still plenty of southernisms, even if the pronunciation is clearly sounding less southern. Ocracoke's remains a distinct dialect among those of North Carolina, but in a much different way because of its recent history.

## ENDANGERED DIALECTS

In the biological sciences, the classification of a species as "endangered" is a widely recognized concept and often a politically charged fact. Thanks to the combined efforts of scientists and citizens, legislative action now protects a wide range of animals and plants on the brink of extinction. At the same time, the dramatic decline of the world's languages goes largely unnoticed, except by a small group of linguists and anthropologists—and by native language speakers. By comparison with biological endangerment, the state of the world's languages is much more severe. There are between 6,000 and 7,000 languages in the world, and linguists who document them predict that up to 90 percent of these languages will be extinct by the end of the twenty-first century. By comparison, 25 percent of mammals and 14 percent of birds carry the endangered label.

Is the extinction of a language or dialect really comparable to the loss of a biological species? Should we worry about language demise as much as the death of a bird species? After all, people do not stop speaking when a language or dialect is no longer used; they shift to another variety. Further, some folks may argue that the world would be much better off if there were only one language used by everyone. This may be true on a simplistic, pragmatic level, but there are other considerations. It would be more efficient and economical if all humans were the same size and wore the same style of clothing, but such homogeneity would not leave room for the expression of individual and group identity.

A window of scientific opportunity closes every time a language dies. The more languages we have, the more we can learn about how language works in the human mind and in society. In biology, the observation of many different kinds of birds flying can teach us more about the aerodynamics of flight than the observation of a single species of one size, weight, and skeletal structure. When a language goes extinct, an essential and unique part of human culture and history dies with it. Imagine what it would be like to be the last person to speak a language, with no one to talk to in your native tongue—the language of life experience, of artistic, emotional, and spiritual expression. The language in which you dream. The scenario might seem unimaginable for English at this point in history, but it was not always this way. English was once a minority language in danger of being overwhelmed by other languages, just like so many other languages now threatened by extinction.

Linguists readily understand the threat to the majority of the world's languages and work fervently to document and preserve them. But what about dialects? Linguists are not nearly as concerned about the demise of different dialects. When we think about it, that seems to be an inconsistent stance. For one, the difference between a language and dialect is not nearly as clear as some people assume. And the distinction is often highly political, as described in chapter 7. For example, Swedish and Norwegian are mutually comprehensible and would be considered dialects of the same language if it were not for the national boundary between the countries. By the same token, Mandarin and Cantonese are not mutually intelligible, but they are grouped together under the politics of Chinese nationalism. In some contexts, native English speakers find it nearly impossible to understand certain forms of English: for instance, when the Ocracoke men play poker together, the off-island wives find their rapid-fire conversational style unintelligible, but no one considers it a different language.

To watch a vignette in which a television correspondent struggles to understand two O'Cockers talking to each other, visit www.ocracokebrogue.com/chapter/18/QR18-3.mp4.

Even though the Brogue is "just" a dialect of English, it remains culturally and linguistically important. For dialects like the Brogue, there is a symbolic association and identity just as strong as that for different languages. Losing something so distinct does impoverish the linguistic landscape of North Carolina, and it also represents the loss of an important cultural legacy among O'Cockers. But despite the community voicing its stance on the importance of the dialect, it is impossible to force younger generations to use it, so the dialect's traditional forms are now merely a whisper of what they once were.

We have personally fought for the inclusion of Ocracoke as an "endangered dialect" for a couple of decades now and given papers at different conferences advocating this position. Admittedly, some linguists studying language recession and endangerment have been resistant to our position. We have argued that, for scientific reasons, it is just as important to study language diversity within a language because these studies show how much variation can be shown within a unified system. Even if we are not interested in the scientific study of language, there are cultural and historical reasons for considering dialects significant artifacts of a cultural group. For almost four centuries, European-descended people have been living on the Outer Banks of North Carolina, and one of their cultural icons has been the way that they speak. It is not accidental that they have often been referred to as *Hoi Toiders* or *Brogue speakers*—a label symbolizing a distinct linguistic, historical, and cultural group of people. The dialect is one of the first things that comes to mind when people think of Ocracoke and the Outer Banks, and its cultural and historical significance needs to be recognized. Though it is beyond linguists to try to resist the shift that is now taking place given the demographic, economic, and social changes within the community, it should at least be preserved and documented as a critical part of this island's history and culture.

*Chapter 19*

# DO THEY TEACH THE BROGUE AT SCHOOL?

Like the island itself, there are a few unique qualities that distinguish Ocracoke School from other schools in North Carolina. Though in recent years the school population has increased, it is still the smallest K-12 school in North Carolina, with a current student population of around 165. It is also the only public school in North Carolina without a cafeteria. The latter is simply a matter of community compactness: nearly all the students go home for lunch. Ocracoke School is also home to the nation's longest continuously running dialect education program—a collaboration between the school and linguists at North Carolina State University that dates back to 1993.

When Walt Wolfram came to NC State in 1992, he already had an established history of actively giving back to the communities in which he conducted research. Ocracoke was the first North Carolina community in which he did intensive research, and long before his research project was finished, he was already seeking ways to thank the community for welcoming him. In addition to working with the community to build a local dictionary, he later created a television documentary about the island's Brogue, which became part of the Ocracoke Preservation Society's "dialect room" exhibit. But even before these efforts, talking to students in Ocracoke School about the island's linguistic heritage was one of the first ways he demonstrated appreciation for the community's sharing of their time and stories. Out of this early experience grew what was to become the longest-running dialect education program in the world, now over thirty years.

## WHY DO STUDENTS NEED TO LEARN ABOUT THEIR DIALECT?

Much of the time, our awareness of language difference has more to do with how other groups sound different or distinctive. Even in communities with dialects that are universally noticed as distinctive, there is often only limited understanding of all the things that make a dialect different. Regardless of your dialect background, your way of speaking is a little like the air around us—or water to a fish—you don't really know it is special until you are made aware of it. You can speak a dialect your whole life without ever learning about the nuances of your dialect's patterns or the cultural and historical forces that shaped it. In fact, because language is acquired rather than learned, people generally have little understanding of the inner workings of a language they may use flawlessly. A helpful analogy is that you can drive a car even if you have no idea how everything under the hood actually works. By focusing on what makes a dialect work, we can build students' knowledge about the dialect, which, when combined with information about the history and cultural importance of the dialect, can make students see the dialect as more valuable.

Merrian Midgett, one of the first students to experience our educational program in the school, reflected on the importance of learning about the linguistics of the Brogue and noted, "If we didn't know [the Brogue] was unique, we would take it for granted." O'Cockers have been told for the past seventy-five or so years that they "sound different." This can make you start to feel ashamed of your dialect and seek to change or hide the way you speak. Gail Hamilton—the first teacher we partnered with at Ocracoke School—recalled that her students always felt a little inadequacy about the way they talked. The early work of the educational program, Hamilton said, "made such a big difference in the perspective my students had of their conversations . . . because they realize they're unique and it's something they're proud of. It's 'Brogue pride' now. And so, they're no longer embarrassed. They're not. They're proud of what their heritage has given them."

Instead of abandoning the dialect, recent generations of O'Cockers have often embraced switching among different styles (or registers) of speech when interacting with tourists. But the ability to style shift does not mean that there is not some residual insecurity associated with using traditional ways of speaking. As part of the collaboration with the school, Walt and his linguistics students hoped to help dispel any lingering notions that the Brogue was "bad English" and to celebrate it as the unique cultural artifact that it is. As linguists, we aim to celebrate all ways of speaking, and so, beginning in the early 1990s, Walt embarked on a partnership with Ocracoke School to teach every O'Cocker a little bit about what the air around them is, and what makes it so special. The first collaboration with Ocracoke School took place during the spring of 1993, only a few months after Walt and his students had begun conducting interviews on the island. Reusing some educational materials from previous projects and infusing them with information about the historical and current development of the dialect, local vocabulary of note, and information about the cultural significance of the dialect, Walt and his students then taught a one-week

FIGURE 19.1. Jeff Reaser, seen here as a graduate student, teaches a group of island eighth-graders about their dialect. Photograph by Walt Wolfram.

course on the Ocracoke Brogue during their spring break. Thanks to shared enthusiasm for the dialect unit from the school, teacher, and students, Walt continued to return with students every year with the goal of ensuring the locals did not take the dialect for granted—or worse, be ashamed of it. Jeff became a part of these efforts in 2000 (see fig. 19.1).

The collaboration proved fruitful. In the early years of the program, Walt and his students would often teach about dialects in Ms. Gail Hamilton's English language-arts class. Though Ms. Hamilton fit some stereotypes of the strict grammar teacher, as a native islander, she always welcomed information about the local dialect. Some people think that there is a tension between learning about dialects and teaching standard English. In fact, many studies have demonstrated that learning about dialects can actually improve students' standardized test scores on reading and writing exams. Even absent these benefits, the value of learning to value one's history and culture—of which language is an essential component—is immense. This unique history is something Ms. Hamilton tried to get her students to appreciate: "Being unique is something to cherish, not to chunk." Katie O'Neal, a current teacher at Ocracoke School and former student and teacher in the dialect program notes, "The Brogue is a product of Ocracoke culture. Celebrating it is acknowledging our history and honoring our roots."

From the beginning, the curriculum had a few consistent goals. First, it sought to teach students that all speakers of a language speak a dialect (see chapter 7). Second, it taught them that all dialects were patterned, rather than merely haphazard or "bad English." Finally, it taught them that dialects were connected to the past, but that they were always in the process of changing. To accomplish this, Walt and his students created worksheets that led the Ocracoke students to discover things about their language. For example, a now classic activity Walt created involved using students' linguistic intuitions to discover the three rules that govern the *a*-prefixing pattern (e.g., *He's a-huntin' and a-fishin'*). The rules are simple but subtle. You can only attach an *a*-prefix to words ending in *-ing* if:

1. the *-ing* word is a verb, as in "he's a-fishing" (contrast with an adjective "he's charming" or noun "teaching is hard work," neither of which can take an *a*-prefix);
2. the *-ing* word does not have a preposition immediately before it ("they destroy the beauty of the island a-littering" is fine, whereas "they destroy the beauty of the island by *a*-littering" is not);
3. the *-ing* word has its primary stress on its first syllable ("they were a-following the trail" is fine, whereas "they were a-discovering the trail" is not, as the stress is on the *cov* rather than the *dis* syllable).

Speakers who use this feature conform to these rules even when they are unable to explain them, so even students who have family members who used this form have no idea about how the pattern works.

Early on, the curriculum focused mostly on the local Brogue's features, its history, and its cultural significance. As the collaboration continued, the curriculum grew. In 1996, *The Ocracoke Brogue*, the first documentary of the Language and Life Project (LLP) at North Carolina State University, produced by students Phyllis Blanton and Karen Waters, became a highlight of the week. Seeing their community on-screen in a linguistics documentary made the students feel validated about their dialect. To get them to understand more intimately how the dialect was changing, students were tasked with interviewing community old-timers. As the LLP expanded its research, information and media about the Lumbee Indians and Mountain Talk (the dialect spoken in the Appalachian Mountain region) were added, expanding the scope of content well beyond the island.

The curriculum project took a big step toward formalization in 2005. Two things spurred this transition. First was the release of the LLP documentary *Voices of North Carolina*, a sixty-minute video produced by Neal Hutcheson that included vignettes that supported discussion of not only the dialects of the coast and mountains, but also those of the Lumbee, Cherokee, and African Americans. It also documented the changing dialects in North Carolina's urban settings and the emergent role of Spanish in North Carolina. For the first time, we were able to present a broader picture of the richness of North Carolina's linguistic diversity.

The second impetus for formalizing the curriculum was a statewide curriculum on language that Jeff Reaser developed as part of his doctoral dissertation. This program was designed to help teachers meet the state's eighth-grade social studies curriculum, and most critically, to be teachable by any classroom teacher, even those without a background in linguistics. At this point, we could have left the curriculum for the teachers at Ocracoke School to teach, but by now the collaboration had become an opportunity for us to mentor our graduate students. Walt and Jeff have returned to Ocracoke with a new batch of grad students every spring break to teach the new eighth-graders, missing only 2021, due to the

COVID pandemic (we made up for it by teaching both the eighth and ninth grade classes in 2022).

It is noteworthy that the curriculum was endorsed by the state's Department of Public Instruction in 2007, the first curriculum of its type adopted in the United States. This success was only possible because a small school on a small island recognized the cultural importance of its fading Brogue some thirty years ago. The ensuing partnership is now the longest-running partnership between a school and linguists anywhere in the world. Katie O'Neal, a current teacher in the school from a well-known island family, participated in teaching the program when she was a student in education at NC State. She noted in a 2017 *Ocracoke Observer* article, "It was so interesting seeing the Brogue from a different perspective and realizing its importance more than I ever had before. It also made me so appreciative of everything that Walt Wolfram and Jeffrey Reaser, along with their students, do for the island. I hope this program will continue on for another twenty-five years and get local kids more interested in their heritage."

## THE COMMUNITY'S RESPONSE

From our perspective, the collaboration has been incredibly successful. We routinely have students "come out of their shells" during our week—especially children of local families and, more recently, children of Latino heritage. Our impressions are that, in general, students are engaged, interested, and even enthusiastic about the program. Though of course, maybe they are just always that way, or perhaps whenever there is a guest in the room. But the feedback we get from students is encouraging. Our informal observations lead us to believe that the experience is memorable and meaningful. Three decades later, we remain highly grateful for this unique opportunity.

We have also had the opportunity to discuss the impact of the program with some of the students and teachers who have been involved with it. When asked for their reflections on the program, many, like Chad O'Neal, an eighth-grade student in 1995, note that it is "interesting to learn about our origins . . . heritage, and history." Anita Fletcher's son experienced the program in 2022, and reflecting on her son's experience she noted, "It's very important. [The Brogue] is a part of who you are and where you grew up and your family." Merrian Midgett describes the importance as teaching students "their roots and giv[ing] them a sense of community."

When they were told the program on Ocracoke is the oldest and longest-running of its kind, Chad O'Neal said, "It's an honor the community doesn't take lightly," and Merrian Midgett remarked, "It makes me happy that Ocracoke is known for something other than Blackbeard!"

Perhaps the two O'Cockers most familiar with the program are Katie O'Neal and Gwen Austin. Ms. Austin has been the teacher in whose class we have taught most frequently, and as such, she has seen the program develop over the years and watched as a generation of island children have been taught it. One thing that she notes is how important the program is not just for children of long-standing island families, but for those of newly arrived families:

> The community has changed so much, many have no clue about our rich past and especially the native Brogue. Many just come to Ocracoke without knowing a thing about our rich history. As we grow, I think we *HAVE* to educate our youth and our changing community. As this Brogue and our traditional way of life disappear, I think it is so important for *ALL* the kids to learn about where they are living and what this island used to sound like before the infusion of so many folks from other places moved in and tourism became our way of life.

She describes learning about the dialect as learning about the "heart of our community. We must teach our past and explain how, as we grow, we are losing so much of what we used to be. We are so unique, and I am so glad that NC State feels that we are too."

Katie O'Neal's experiences with the curriculum are unique, as she was a student in the eighth-grade class we taught in 2011.

FIGURE 19.2. Katie O'Neal, seen here as an NCSU undergraduate, participated in the curriculum as an eighth-grader before returning to teach the curriculum with us. Photograph by Walt Wolfram.

Eventually Katie made her way to NC State, where she majored in education (see fig. 19.2). Over spring break in 2017, she joined us and our graduate students to teach the curriculum. She is the only person to experience the curriculum as both student and teacher. Now, as the special education teacher for Ocracoke School, she is able to reflect on the impacts the curriculum had on her, her peers, and her students.

Ms. O'Neal recounts her own experience of learning about the dialect and how it made her understand and appreciate her father's Brogue: "As a kid, I noticed the way [my dad] talked differently (especially with native O'Cockers) but was not aware that it was a *dialect* until this program." After learning about the history of the Brogue, she realized how important it was to being an O'Cocker. She notes, "The Brogue is a part of our cultural identity." This appreciation, she thinks, is especially important to native families but extends to all Ocracoke residents: "It's important for all students—even if they just moved here—to learn about the Brogue. I believe it gives students more reason to appreciate their community. And gives those who have family ties here—a deeper understanding of themselves and their families." This sentiment was also shared by Ms. Hamilton, the first teacher we worked with. She laughed as she recalled how the non-native island schoolchildren would attempt to imitate the Brogue after we had taught them about how special it was: "In fact, [non-native island children] would practice with the O'Cockers to see if they could pick up the Brogue. It was hilarious. It was funny. And they realized how unique and important it was, and so they embraced it too. They didn't quite pull it off, but they tried. . . . It was funny. It was fun too. And it united the students—those who moved here and those from here."

Thinking about the long-standing partnership, and the fact that it has been recognized for its uniqueness around the world, Ms. O'Neal reflects with pride, "Yes, it's something that's been culturally recognized on an international scale. Visitors and off-islander friends know about Ocracoke because of our beaches, but also now because of the Brogue."

Teaching the program in Ocracoke School is always one of our favorite weeks of the year. And it seems as though it is a highlight for students, too. Ms. Austin notes, "Each year the eighth grade looks forward to this class. The older kids even get a little jealous when they see the NC State team come in. I love it because the kids get exposure to a 'university' class; it makes them feel so special." We definitely aim to make the week memorable, through engaging activities, multimedia content, educational games and contests, including a summative game of Dialect Jeopardy, and "dialect buttons," which we use to celebrate language diversity in North Carolina at venues across the state, including the North Carolina State Fair. Ms. Austin describes the impact on the students: "The students tell me each year they remember all the college kids that you all bring. The buttons, the cool videos, which they find funny how everyone sounds. They find it hard to believe the entire island sounded that way. They almost don't believe it." These sentiments reinforce our own impressions that the students see this collaboration as something important and memorable. Indeed, when we are around the village, it is not uncommon for a former student to come up to us and tell us about when they got to experience the dialect curriculum.

Returning to the question that serves as the title of this chapter, “Is the Brogue taught at school?,” the answer is both yes and no. For nearly three decades now, every eighth-grade student at Ocracoke School has learned about the dialect. But that education about the language is concentrated in a week that might spill over here and there as students make connections to other content they are taught. Outside of that week, the vast majority of language instruction at Ocracoke School is not dissimilar from that found in schools elsewhere in the state. That is, it tends to focus mostly on building fluency—especially textual fluency (i.e., reading and writing)—in the English used in school and professional contexts. Though our program does not seek to undermine the primacy of standard English, it does raise the question of why that variety is considered standard, and what that means for individuals and communities with very different dialects. Knowledge of the history and patterned nature of dialects is critical to being a more empowered language user, and we hope that our work has empowered at least some children who may have otherwise felt some shame about their dialects. Ms. Austin thinks we have been successful in this regard. She notes, “The true native children, which now are so few, enjoy seeing their family and have pride in knowing they are part of that elite group.”

We believe that our partnership with Ocracoke School has added one more element to the list of traits that make the school and community unique. We can say with near certainty that, percentage-wise, the population of Ocracoke is more knowledgeable about its local dialect than any other English-speaking community in the world. Walt often captures this distinction with the quip, “More people on Ocracoke know what an isogloss is than in any other place in the world.” (An isogloss is the boundary between two dialects.) Neither this information nor our program will preserve the Brogue, but given the importance of the dialect to the community’s history, we intend on continuing this partnership as long as we are invited back, and hope to educate the next generation of islanders about this unique cultural resource and history.

*Chapter 20*

# ARE THERE AFRICAN AMERICANS ON THE OUTER BANKS?

It may not be apparent to the casual beachgoer, but African Americans have played an important role in the development of the Outer Banks. Unfortunately, this story has not been told very often. Much like the prehistoric Native American Indian populations who inhabited the coastal islands and the currently emerging Latino population, African Americans have been largely invisible, despite the fact that between 1800 to 1860, they comprised almost 50 percent of the populations of the sixteen tidewater counties.

## HISTORICAL OVERVIEW OF AFRICAN AMERICANS ON THE OUTER BANKS

The coastal region has never been an exclusively white enclave, and some long-standing African American families and communities have been a significant part of the coastal tradition. For example, in the mainland portion of Hyde County, the county Ocracoke is located in, the African American population has made up approximately one-third of the county's residents since its establishment in the first decade of the 1700s. Hyde County's current Black population (1,501 out of 4,897 total residents in the 2020 census) remains quite stable.

From the early 1700s up through the Civil War, the Outer Banks had significant populations of enslaved Africans who arrived via Virginia and Maryland. Records indicate that they made up between a quarter to a third of the population in coastal communities. For example, in the first federal census (1790), thirty-one enslaved people were living on Ocracoke, almost 20 percent of the total population of 157. The enslaved population on the island increased until the Civil War, when more than 150 enslaved people lived on Ocracoke. The neighboring island of Portsmouth, now vacated, had an additional 100 enslaved people, and mainland Hyde County, across the Pamlico Sound, had a population of over 200 enslaved people. Historian Philip Howard notes in an Ocracoke Newsletter article, "Slavery on Ocracoke," that "from the earliest days free men of color and slaves also worked as pilots, lighterers, and stevedores," and many of them became skilled watermen in fishing, ferrying, and piloting. (Lighterers were those who transferred cargo off and then back on large ships so they could safely pass over the shallow sandbar at the mouth of the inlet.) In their occupations, the African Americans who resided there were people of the water, much like the Anglo population.

David Cecelski's book about African Americans on the coast of North Carolina, *The Waterman's Song: Slavery and Freedom in Maritime North Carolina*, documents the development of "a maritime section of the Underground Railroad" that flourished along the coastal waterways of North Carolina between the 1800s and the

Civil War. The combination of skillful African American watermen and a conspiring network of freedmen created a maritime route to freedom through the complex geography of rivers, estuaries, pocosins, and tidal marshes along the coast. By the mid-1800s, this escape route became such a common passageway to freedom that one Wilmington correspondent lamented that it was "an everyday appearance for our negro slaves to take passage [aboard a ship] and go North" (quoted in Cecelski, p. 174).

During the Civil War, the Union army considered it essential to control the waterways, so in 1862 over 11,000 Union troops overwhelmed and defeated the Confederate forces on Roanoke Island. Following their occupation, and in commemoration of the attack leader, General Ambrose Burnside, the Union army built Fort Burnside on the north end of the island. As described by David Stick in the book *The Outer Banks of North Carolina*, they then set to build an official Freedmen's Colony to "establish a colony of negroes upon Roanoke Island . . . to settle colored people on the unoccupied lands, and to give them agricultural and mechanical tools to begin with, and to train and educate them for a free and independent community." The Civil War changed the lives of many African Americans on the Outer Banks and altered the demographics of particular coastal locations, but the ratio of African Americans to whites for the overall population did not change appreciably. The enslaved populations generally left island communities such as Hatteras, Ocracoke, Portsmouth, and Harkers Island, but Roanoke Island's Freedmen's Colony became a large enclave for ex-slaves and freed African Americans. Within a few years, this village grew to approximately 600 houses and almost 4,000 people. However, an order to restore the land to the original owners was issued in 1866, ending the experimental community and scattering the majority of the Black residents. The colony was abandoned in 1867, but about fifty African American families continued to live on the island, eventually buying small plots of land, and some of their descendants remain there today.

From 2006 to 2007, the Language and Life Project (LLP) created and curated, with the Outer Banks History Center in Manteo, an exhibit celebrating the African American community of Roanoke titled *Freedom's Voice: Celebrating the Black Experience on the Outer Banks*. The exhibit included images and artifacts of the current and historical Black communities, a documentary on the community for visitors, interactive audiovisuals, and audio clips on themes such as education, community activities, religion, and so forth, taken from recorded oral history interviews conducted by LLP staff. The exhibition brought together history, culture, and language, highlighting African Americans' involvement in the historical Freedmen's Colony as well as previously overlooked contributions of African Americans in this region.

To watch part of the documentary included in the *Freedom's Voice* exhibit, visit www.ocracokebrogue.com/chapter/20/QR20-1.mp4.

## LINGUISTIC OVERVIEW OF AFRICAN AMERICANS ON THE OUTER BANKS

Naturally, the LLP is vitally interested in the dialects of different African American communities on the Outer Banks, and we have interviewed almost 100 African American and fifty Anglo speakers in mainland Hyde County. We have also interviewed about forty African American speakers who are descendants of Freedmen's Colony and live in Manteo. In Ocracoke, we were also privileged to interview the island's last African American resident, Muzel Bryant. The next chapter is devoted entirely to Muzel and her family, who lived on the island continuously since 1865—obviously a unique situation.

Mainland Hyde County, similar in some ways to Ocracoke in its historical isolation, contrasts with Ocracoke in that is not at all a tourist destination. In fact, its primary connections to tourism are Lake Mattamuskeet, which draws bird watchers, and the Swan Quarter Ferry, which carries tourists to Ocracoke after they have driven through the rest of the county. Few families have moved to mainland Hyde County after the initial settlement by

Anglos and enslaved African Americans during the first decades of the 1700s. For example, the 2020 census reported a population of 4,589, including the permanent residents of Ocracoke Island, while the initial census in 1790 reported 4,120. That is not a lot of new residents over almost two and a half centuries. The area remains rural: 85 percent wetlands with a density of about four people per square mile.

Our interviewees in mainland Hyde County ranged from teenagers to centenarians, so we could look at differences among people of different age brackets. In the following samples, we present the interview transcripts of a typical older African American speaker in his nineties and his great granddaughter, who lived in the same house in mainland Hyde County growing up. For comparison, we have an example of an older white Brogue speaker from Ocracoke and a younger white speaker from mainland Hyde County. A couple of grammatical uses to note in the transcripts are italicized.

**Older African American (b. 1910), Hyde County**

Aah, but if I'da stayed out there where he left me, he *might woulda* chopped me in the head or something, can't never tell. So, that made his daddy mad cause I beat him. He was taking up for the boy but *he weren't* taking up for me.

**European American (b. 1944), Outer Banks**

Well, like say we started on that end and started running 'em back this way, and then they used to come up along—see *there weren't* all this—this was swamp here, we used to hunt. On every one of these houses.

**Younger African American (b. 1975), Hyde County**

. . . a light *be following* you 'cause there's so ma—that, so many *peoples* got killed that a light *be following* you. And then they have, they have told this story about, like, if this woman *be on the road thumbing* and you stop and you give her a ride and then you think *she honestly in the car with* you and then when you turn over she's not in the car with you.

**Younger European American (b. 1979), Hyde County**

*I weren't* about to get my tail *whupped* just for him talkin' junk, so. If I'da had rear view mirrors I'da never jumped it 'cause the cop was right behind me when I did it. I had no idea he was behind me, because if he hadda, I'da never jumped the curve.

To listen to these speech samples comparing older and younger Anglo and African American Hyde County residents, visit www.ocracokebrogue.com/chapter/20/QR20-2.mp3.

We played longer versions of these recorded excerpts to a group of people from Raleigh, North Carolina, and asked them simply to identify whether each of the speakers sounded white or Black. The results were fascinating! Both the older white and the older Black speaker were identified as being white by over 90 percent of the listeners. At the same time, more than 90 percent of the listeners identified the younger African American speaker as Black and the Anglo speaker as white. Remember that the great grandfather and his great granddaughter were raised in the same house in Hyde County and lived there all of their lives. For a linguist, this is very insightful, because it indicates that older African American speech and white speech seemed to be more similar than current-day African American speech and white speech. The older African American speaker uses the leveled *weren't* form for all of the negative sentences (this pattern is described in detail in chapter 11) as in, "He weren't takin' up for me," just like the white speaker's use in the sentence "There weren't all this—this was swamp here." And if you listen closely to his speech, you can hear the older African American speaker use a lot of the pronunciations of words found among older speakers in Ocracoke, including the infamous *oi* vowel for *time*.

On the other hand, the younger African American speaker does not use this general negative *weren't* form at all, while the white speaker has maintained it. The younger African American speaker also uses the iconic *be* to denote a habitual activity, as in, "So many peoples got killed that a light *be following* you. And . . . if this woman *be on the road thumbing*." Additionally, she also does not use the *be* form in the sentence "You think *she honestly in the car* with you," another classic trait of current African American English. The older African American speaker never uses the so-called habitual *be* and rarely uses the absence of *be* in a construction like *she honestly in the car*.

A lot more analysis could be added here that is found in Drs. Walt Wolfram and Erik Thomas's book, *The Development of African American English*, but it is very technical and intended for a professionally trained linguist. It is sufficient here to note that our research on African American English in the isolated situations on the coast of North Carolina has shown that earlier African American English in this area was more like the localized dialect spoken by Anglos, though still not identical. To a much lesser extent, the same trend was revealed in the study of African American speech on Roanoke Island, though this region was not nearly as isolated as the uniquely situated wetlands of Hyde County. The African American speakers in Roanoke likely had earlier and more intense contact with other language groups, resulting in earlier language shift away from local Anglo norms. While Roanoke Island was connected to the mainland by bridge in the 1920s, there was little infrastructure connecting Hyde County with other inland areas other than logging roads until later. For a long time, the shoulder of the major highway into Hyde County had a sign that read, "The Road Less Traveled"—and apart from the one highway leading to the ferry, it was totally true.

It is intriguing that the coast of North Carolina, where African Americans are rarely seen in most tourist areas these days, constitutes one of the most meaningful places to research language related to the history of African American English—and it is one of the major reasons we have included it here. The story of the Bryant/Blount family on Ocracoke presented in the next chapter is an example of how individual African Americans in these areas have uniquely enriched our understanding of the critical role that African Americans had in development of the speech of white and Black people in earlier America.

*Chapter 21*

# WHAT DOES AN AFRICAN AMERICAN FAMILY ON OCRACOKE SOUND LIKE?

As described in the previous chapter, there were a number of important African American enclaves along the Outer Banks. African Americans have made many important contributions to the history of the region. For example, the life of Richard Etheridge is a fascinating one. Born an enslaved man in Manteo in 1842, Etheridge worked after the Civil War as a "surfman" at the Bodie Island lifesaving station. The Lifesaving Service and its surfmen were a precursor to the US Coast Guard. They would do all they could to save anyone who experienced a marine disaster. Etheridge was so accomplished that in 1879 he became the first African American head of a lifesaving station, when he took over the role of keeper (i.e., commander) at the Pea Island Lifesaving Station. The white surfmen refused to serve under him, and so Pea Island became the first all-Black lifesaving station in the nation. Such stories are typically invisible to the tourists who descend upon the Outer Banks, and this is no less true of the important African American history in Ocracoke.

## A SOLITARY TRADITION

On different Outer Banks island communities, a solitary African American family has sometimes resided in the midst of an overwhelmingly Anglo population. In some cases, a formerly enslaved African American family simply continued living in the community on the island. For example, on the neighboring island of Portsmouth, intimately connected to Ocracoke, Henry Pigott, a descendant of an enslaved family, was the last male resident of the island. His ancestors first came to the island as enslaved people. He was born in 1896 as one of seven children of Leah Pigott, one of the few African Americans who remained on Portsmouth after the Civil War. Henry and his sister, Lizzie, lived there for most of their lives. Lizzie served as the town's unofficial barber, and many people recall going "down the banks" to Lizzie's for a haircut. While both Henry and Lizzie continued to fish and oyster for a living, Henry became the "mailman," poling out to the mail boat and retrieving mail and passengers. In 1967, Henry sold his property to the State of North Carolina, enabling the creation of Cape Lookout National Seashore, but he retained a life estate to the house. In an article by the National Park Service, "A People, A Place, A Community That Time Forgot," the authors wrote of an exchange between a reporter from New York City and Henry Pigott:

> A reporter from New York City once came to Portsmouth to write an article about the village. She was given a tour of the village, and was later introduced to Henry. The reporter began to criticize the island lifestyle, telling Henry that he was

> crazy to live among the mosquitoes with no electricity and no running water. Pigott thought for a moment, then replied that he had done some traveling. He had been to New York City. He had even seen all the modern innovations. Then he paused and added, "And I'm not sure which one of us is crazy."

In 1971, Henry Pigott fell ill and died. The funeral service was held in the Methodist Church on Portsmouth Island, where he is buried in the church cemetery. His tombstone epitaph reads, "Gone but Not Forgotten." The two women who were still living on Portsmouth at the time left shortly thereafter, and Portsmouth has not had permanent residents since then.

On Ocracoke, the Civil War marked a brief end to the African American presence on the island, as all 100 to 150 enslaved Africans left the island following the war. But it was not long before a new African American family arrived. Winnie and Harkus Blount, formerly enslaved on the mainland, came together to Ocracoke after the Civil War as free people. They came from Blounts Creek, near so-called Little Washington, by a steamboat with a family named Williams. Winnie worked on Ocracoke as a domestic and Harkus worked as a carpenter and boat builder. As enslaved people, they did not have last names when they came, and simply adopted the last name of place where they came from. Historian Philip Howard reports that "Aunt Winnie," as she was known to many people on the island, may have lived on Portsmouth Island before emancipation, but this is unconfirmed. Today, the street in Ocracoke by the bank off Cedar Road is named Winnie Blount Road in her honor. Only two of Harkus and Winnie Blount's twelve children lived to adulthood, and one of them, Elsie Jane, married Leonard Bryant from the mainland Hyde County town of Engelhard. Their family lived on the island of Ocracoke for the rest of their lives.

## THE BRYANT FAMILY

Jane and Leonard Bryant had nine children who lived (thirteen in all), five boys and four girls, but only three of them made Ocracoke

FIGURE 21.1. Muzel Bryant. Photograph courtesy of the Ocracoke Preservation Society.

their home once they reached adulthood—Muzel Bryant, Mildred Bryant, and Julius Bryant. Muzel was the second-oldest child, born in 1904, and she lived with her sister Mildred in a small home behind the Island Inn, where the gravesite of the Blount family can still be found (see fig. 21.1). Julius lived in a trailer. We interviewed and recorded Muzel a number of times in the 1990s, both by herself and with her sister Mildred. Julius died in 1960, long before we arrived, but we managed to secure a recording of his singing and a limited amount of his talking to compare his speech with that of his sisters. After Mildred died in 1995, Muzel spent the last fourteen years of her life living with islander Kenny Ballance; she passed away several weeks prior to her 104th birthday.

Near the time of Muzel's passing, the Ocracoke Preservation Society worked with the Language and Life Project (LLP) to dedicate a room at the museum to her life, but unfortunately she passed away a couple of weeks before the actual celebration on her birthday. Nonetheless, the exhibit stood for two years as a tribute to this special woman. Muzel was known for her prodigious memory, as she remembered islanders' birthdays, the kinds of cars people drove and the years people purchased them, and other facts that many islanders had long forgotten. She was also known for her daily midday walks and her kind, gracious spirit to those she encountered.

One of the special events celebrating Muzel Bryant was the occasion of her 100th birthday in the gymnasium of the Ocracoke School. It was attended by more than 200 people in what was described by some residents as the largest social gathering ever held in the gym. It was a stunning sight to witness Muzel arriving to the event in a limousine. People lined the entrance to the steps into the gym, and friends and relatives gave speeches that would never be forgotten. The LLP was invited to film the occasion, some of which can be seen in the linked footage.

To watch a vignette from Muzel's 100th birthday celebration, visit www.ocracokebrogue.com/chapter/21/QR21-1.mp4.

After the main celebration, Muzel went with friends to Howard's Pub, where she and her friends continued to celebrate until nearly 1:00 a.m., chatting with well-wishers and listening to the music of the Ocracoke Rockers. It was a memorable celebration. But it was also a bit sobering to think that the celebration took place in the same school that she could not attend herself because of segregation. She was, however, quite literate, being taught by volunteers after school and learning from other children with whom she interacted. In fact, we would often notice reading material like *Reader's Digest* and other magazines and books in her home.

## A LINGUISTIC TREASURE

As a linguist who had been studying African American Language since the mid-1960s, Walt Wolfram found the speech of Muzel

Bryant and her siblings on Ocracoke a sociolinguistic treasure. The speech of an isolated African American family living in the context of a unique, historically isolated Anglo dialect situation might give important clues about the influence of surrounding dialects on a single Black family without an active community of other African Americas. Would a single Black family simply adopt the language of the community in which it was living, or would vestiges of an ethnic dialect from an earlier African American community still be heard? Naturally, linguists cannot set up an experiment in which they ask a Black family to move into an Anglo community for 150 years to observe the language effects of a surrounding community. But when we find this situation occurring naturally, it provides a great opportunity for linguists to see how social forces may affect language over a long period of time.

A sample from our first interview with Muzel Bryant, recorded in the early 1990s, is given below. We urge the reader to listen to the spoken version, since it gives clues about the kind of dialect she is using.

> A black cat was go—jump up in the window. And anybody go out of that house, and one of the black cats jump up in the window, and so people say that you couldn't stay there, or some way it were. Then one night, the preacher, he taken his Bible, and he said he was going down to study. And see, that night the preacher went in, was down in the living room and was sitting down in his rocking chair, and hdad his Bible. By the time he start reading his Bible, the black cat, he jumped up there in the window, and the black cat said to the preacher, says, "Ain't nobody here but you and me tonight." The old man told him, "Gee, ain't gonna be nobody here, I reckon, but you."

To listen to this passage from our first interview with Muzel Bryant, visit www.ocracokebrogue.com/chapter/21/QR21-2.mp3.

We played this passage to a group of listeners from Raleigh, and about 70 percent identified her as sounding African American. This surprised us, as there are a number of features of her speech that are *not* distinctly "Black-sounding." After 125 years, there were still a number of elements that sounded more African American than they did like the Brogue, meaning neither she nor her family had fully shifted to island speech patterns. At the same time, there are a few things that echoed the Brogue, and so we asked her more about the speech of the rest of her family. Part of the conversation went as follows:

> INTERVIEWER (I): Did your daddy sound like the other islanders? Or did he sound different?
>
> MUZEL BRYANT (MB): He sounded a little bit different than what the uh, uh—
>
> I: Do you think your family talked a little different from the other islanders?
>
> MB: Yes, I do, yes, uh huh.
>
> I: What was it about it that was different?
>
> MB: I don't know, they just speak a little bit different than us in a way I guess.
>
> I: And your mom—your mother also spoke a little different?
>
> MB: Yes, she did.
>
> I: Sometimes people say that the islanders speak a Brogue. Have you ever heard that?
>
> MB: Yes, I have heard 'em say.
>
> I: Do you think you have a Brogue?
>
> MB: Me? I don't know, I may have.

To hear this conversation about how Muzel's family sounded, visit www.ocracokebrogue.com/chapter/21/QR21-3.mp3.

Muzel Bryant is certain that she and her parents spoke differently from some of the residents of Ocracoke, but she is more uncertain about her status with respect to the Brogue. These perceptions were confirmed by several O'Cockers whom we queried about Muzel's dialect. All of them said she sounded different from the Anglo residents, citing her pronunciation of words and other language traits in general.

During our conversations about Muzel's speech with long-term O'Cocker men, we were told that we should have heard Muzel's brother Julius (who went by Jules), who had a different social interaction with locals. For example, he fished and shrimped regularly with some of the men, played poker and pool with them, and seemed to spend a lot more time engaging in local social activities with the men of the community than his sisters did, though of course this was still restricted because of racial barriers (see fig. 21.2). Unfortunately, because Jules died long before the LLP arrived on the island, we have no sociolinguistic interview with him. Fortunately, one of the men we were discussing language with said he recalled that Jules had made a few recordings of his singing on his old guitar that he loved to strum and shared them with some of the men. If only we could get one of those recordings! We started pleading with the men who had been given a copy of his tape, and sure enough, Dave Esham, then the owner of the Pony Island Motel, went home, found the recording, and let us copy it. This was one of the greatest gifts we linguists had ever received. We immediately started listening to it. It was mostly singing, with only a limited amount of speaking. Though songs are not the same as conversational speech, some linguistic features still might give us clues about Jules's speech. Listen closely to a couple of songs linked to below to find these clues. In the first song, a local version of the country song "They Cut Down the Old Pine Tree," listen to his pronunciation of the vowel in *pine* and *mine*.

FIGURE 21.2. Jules Bryant shrimping with O'Cocker Corkey Mason. Photograph courtesy of the Ocracoke Preservation Society.

*(Oh y—, oh yeah, I got you now, think of something,*
*oh yeah).*
*When we cut down the old pine tree,*
*Haul it away to the mill,*
*we go gather up pine*
*for this sweet gal of mine,*
*When we cut down the old pine tree.*

To listen to Jules Bryant's rendition of "They Cut Down the Old Pine Tree," visit www.ocracokebrogue.com/chapter/21/QR21-4.mp3.

Jules's pronunciation of *pine* and *mine* as "poin" and "moin" adopts the traditional pronunciation of the iconic vowel of Hoi Toiders in a way that indexes the local Ocracoke pronunciation, and anyone who hears it recognizes it. Jules's speech was definitely more like the Brogue than that of Muzel.

Now consider Jules's rendition of the traditional folk song "She'll Be Comin' Round the Mountain." Notice the fact that Jules sings the song without ever pronouncing the *-s* on the word "comes."

*She'll be comin' around the mountain when*
*she come, oh yeah!*
*Comin' around the mountain when she come,*
*She'll be comin' around the mountain,*
*She'll be comin' around the mountain,*
*She'll be comin' around the mountain when*
*she come.*
*She('ll) be drivin' six white horses when she come,*
*She('ll) be drivin' six white horses when she come,*
*She'll be drivin' six white horses,*
*She'll be drivin' six white horses,*
*She'll be drivin' six white horses when she come.*
*Oh yeah!*

To hear Jules singing of "She'll Be Comin' Round the Mountain," visit www.ocracokebrogue.com/chapter/21/QR21-5.mp3.

Jules never attaches the *-s* suffix to the verb *come*. Other renditions currently performed by singers or groups of singers, including those in Ocracoke, have the *-s* suffix. It is not accidental that Jules does not apply the *-s* since the absence of this suffix is a characteristic trait of African American English, which we presume his ancestors spoke when they arrived. While most of the O'Cockers we spoke to about Jules's dialect noted that he was primarily a Brogue speaker, they also acknowledged that he did have some language traits that were not quite like other islanders. So, we can assume that even he had more subtle remnants of a dialect associated with African American speech.

The Blount/Bryant family language legacy offers a couple of important insights about social effects on language. For one, we see that some of the earlier traits of African American English have persisted over generations that spanned a century and a half. That seems like an amazing legacy of persistence. While both Jules and Muzel Bryant adopted some of the local forms, Jules clearly assimilated much more of the local flavor than Muzel and her sister Mildred did. In large part, this is probably due to his regular, continued interaction with islanders outside of his familial networks, including social activities beyond work. While men routinely gathered to fish, play poker, make wine, and other activities, women traditionally spent more time alone in homemaking activities. So, part of the difference between the speech of Muzel and Jules may simply be gendered.

We may further speculate that the Bryants, a large, self-contained family unit of nine children and two adults, could have been a small community unto themselves, where the children primarily interacted with each other and their parents. Remember that the children could not attend the segregated school, so they were around each other most of the day, every day, acquiring and interacting mostly with the language used in their home. In this setting, they could have maintained some of the language that their grandparents brought with them and used regularly within the home.

By contrast, we would expect that an Anglo family that moved to Ocracoke in the mid-1800s would fully acclimate the Brogue, given their routine interaction with the rest of the island in work, school, church, and a full range of social activities open to them and their children. In that period, the dialect that an Anglo family brought to the island would likely be given up by their children, who would be exposed to the Brogue at school, church, dances, and other community activities. The same opportunity was not available to the Bryant family.

The story of Bryant/Blount family is a complicated one in the historical context of race relations in the United States. But it is also an encouraging one, as Ocracoke has come to celebrate and remember the legacy of Muzel Bryant, Jules Bryant, and Mildred Bryant, the three members of the last African American family to live their entire lives on the island, and especially Muzel Bryant, as the last member of this family. It is a story to be remembered.

We are encouraged by efforts of the community to remember this legacy over the years since Muzel has left us. In February 2021, Ocracoke's Facebook page posted a remembrance of Muzel Bryant, and there are other audio and video recordings of her archived in different social media accounts preserved by the Ocracoke Preservation Society and the Language and Life Project. The February 1, 2021, Facebook note reads:

> Who Am I? I am Muzel Bryant. I was born on March 12, 1904, only 39 years after slavery ended and fifty years before the civil rights movement began. I was one of nine children to Leonard and Elsie Jane Bryant. My parents both worked at the Doxsee Clam Factory at the turn of the century.
> I celebrated my 100th birthday in March of 2004 with over 300 guests at the large community party. I was fortunate to live out my last years with Kenny Ballance. I took care of him as a child and then he took care of me. When I passed away in March of 2008, I had lived a full life on Ocracoke.
> My thoughts about living on Ocracoke, Grandma (Winnie Blount) always said that when they first came here that everybody treated them alright. My grandfather (Harkus) was a boat builder—and a good one, so I've heard. While he was doing this, my grandmother use to help different ones in their homework. . . . You see, in them days, everybody was just alike. Nobody had anything, so one would give to the other if they needed something, and they would help each other with this or that. I've heard that when different ones around would kill a cow or pig, they'd usually let other people know about it and let them have some.

As Philip Howard put it, "Everyone agrees that Muse was an island treasure: She will be greatly missed." Gone but not forgotten.

*Chapter 22*

# HOW HAS SPANISH CHANGED THE LANGUAGE LANDSCAPE OF OCRACOKE?

MARIA COADY, PHD, AND JODIE ROBERSON

Language contact occurs in communities across the United States. Not even isolated islands like Ocracoke are an exception. The world we live in is increasingly mobile, and people move in search of social or economic opportunities, to escape war or violence, or due to impending climate disruptions. They also change locations as relatives and friends outside of the United States join them, and they bring their languages, cultures, and identities with them. When people arrive in a new community, their languages come into contact with the existing languages of that community. This contact can result in a language shift, which occurs when an individual or a community of speakers switch their language use from one language to another. Language shift is neither unusual nor rare, but it can evoke strong and sometimes conflicting emotions that range from a sense of change or loss to hope. Language shift is complex and can happen in various ways, depending on the community's circumstances. It is, therefore, crucial to understand the linguistic and social context in which language shift occurs and the motivations that drive it, as these factors can have important implications for the maintenance of minority languages and the cultural identities they represent.

Like other remote rural communities, Ocracoke has undergone significant language contact over the past decades. The local Ocracoke Brogue, once the primary language variety spoken on the island, has come into contact with other dialects of English, resulting in a shift in local language patterns. In more recent years, the island has experienced further language contact and shift as Spanish-speaking Latinos have migrated to the island in search of work and better opportunities in various industries, including construction, lodging, and food service. This has led to a significant change in language use on the island, with Spanish used in oral and written forms. According to the 2022 American Community Survey, the percentage of Hispanics on Ocracoke was 28 percent (*Hispanic* is the official census category, which we use here; elsewhere we use *Latino*, which is the label most of the local community uses for self-identification). For emerging Hispanic communities, census data can be difficult to compile accurately for various reasons, but the school, which compiles these records each year, is a good source for profiling ethnicity of the younger population. As of fall 2024, 54 percent of the 164 students attending the K-12 school were identified as Latino or Hispanic. More was said about the language use of these students in the next chapter. That is a dramatic transformation on an island that was monolingual just a quarter of a century ago. As a result, the island's public spaces, signs, and material artifacts have transformed, reflecting the island's changing linguistic landscape. With the increasing influence of the Spanish language and Latino culture on the island, we have to consider how this contact and shift in language patterns manifest in the day-to-day life of the island's inhabitants.

## THE LINGUISTIC LANDSCAPE

In the past thirty years, there has been an increase in research on what is referred to as "linguistic landscape" and there is even an academic journal, *Linguistic Landscape: An International Journal*, that publishes papers on linguistic landscapes worldwide. Most of these studies focus on urban communities or cities, and there are few papers on rural communities and even fewer on remote rural locales. With the repopulation of many rural communities across the United States by Latino immigrants providing much-needed labor, it is largely unknown how immigrants' languages are used in those areas. The fact that remote islands like Ocracoke are relatively isolated and often cut off from mainland communication due to storms and inclement weather makes studying the local linguistic landscape even more interesting.

As educators, we understand that schools can reflect their communities and are microcosms of society. While some schools are inclusive and welcoming of all cultures and languages, others may discourage students from expressing their home languages and cultures. This also holds true for community spaces where people live and work. For example, in a community with a significant percentage of Spanish-speaking Latinos like Ocracoke, it is important to consider how the Spanish language appears in public spaces. Do newcomers have access to information in their native language? Are resources available to support print-literate individuals who may need to improve in English? We can explore these questions by considering the material artifacts in public spaces on Ocracoke Island.

## SEARCHING FOR SPANISH ON OCRACOKE

During an off-season week, we traveled to the Swan Quarter Ferry and drove our car onto the barge traversing Pamlico Sound. As we waited in the car queue to embark on the trip, we heard Mariachi music from across the parking lot, where young men were listening in elevated pickup trucks. We noted the sounds of spoken English and Spanish by people playing games in the waiting area. We booked rooms in a hotel and were greeted upon arrival by the bilingual receptionist, the US-born daughter of one of the earliest Mexican residents on the island. We were off to an exciting start.

We spoke with US-born and non-US-born residents living full-time on the island. We visited them in hotel kitchens and reception areas, in the local grocery store, working in restaurants, and at Taqueria 504Suazo's food truck parked on West End Road. We examined signage inside the community center, churches, the health clinic, and the local post office. We walked the Story Walk trail on Robbie's Way and read the placards describing the island's rich history, including the lighthouse, the preservation society, and Blackbeard's demise in 1718. We read stories from the local newspaper, the *Ocracoke Observer*, and its online section of *Noticias en Español*. Because we visited in the offseason, some buildings and seasonal tourist shops were closed, including some Latino-owned businesses. This allowed us to observe how the island functioned without the bustle of tourists traversing on bikes and in golf carts. When we visited in 2023, we specifically sought out any signs or material artifacts, flyers, documents, advertisements, instructions, applications, maps, newspapers, menus, and so on that were in Spanish or bilingual. We took over 150 images of artifacts that painted the *linguistic landscape* of written language use over a week-long period. After analyzing the percentage of Latinos residing on Ocracoke Island and the length of time they have lived there—over twenty years—we discovered surprisingly low usage of written Spanish on the island. This means that despite the significant number of Spanish-speaking and bilingual residents and a couple of decades of language contact, Ocracoke still presents itself as a monolingual destination for tourists rather than a multilingual one.

## SPANISH IN COMMUNITY SPACES

Signs, images, flyers, and food packaging all contribute to the linguistic landscape of a place, revealing the languages used by its inhabitants. During our visit to Ocracoke, we noticed that the post office and the grocery store were the locations with the most print-based multilingual examples, with Spanish being the most-represented language other than English. These locations had bulletin boards with locally created materials, such as event flyers and business cards. The grocery store stood out in particular, as it had a significant number of food labels and flyers in Spanish displayed at the entrance.

One bilingual flyer posted at the Ocracoke post office caught our attention. The flyer's top was written in English (indicating its higher status), and the bottom was in Spanish. Not all of the information on the English side appeared in the same format as Spanish. For example, the top indicated that public library hours were "Monday–Friday 3 p.m.–7 p.m." However, the Spanish below indicated "Lunes–Viernes 3 p.m.–19:00." Standard Spanish would not capitalize the names of the week, *lunes* (Monday) and *viernes* (Friday). This small example demonstrates different ways of using everyday language and how using one language (or language norms, such as using 19:00 instead of 7 p.m.) is influenced by other languages. It is worth noting that the flyers positioned near the bilingual library information flyer were all in monolingual English. This suggests that there are approximately three times more English signs than Spanish or bilingual signs in the area's linguistic landscape.

A second observation, from the island's single grocery store, offers a different insight into our landscape study. Located on the main road, Irvin Garrish Highway (a section of NC Highway 12), the Ocracoke Variety Store housed interesting material artifacts in print form, and we noted that this was the place we were most likely to hear both Spanish and English spoken by bilinguals or by Spanish monolinguals. The products on the shelves of this store reflected the linguistic and cultural diversity we experienced on the island but did not find in artifacts in other locations. For example, we noticed in the grocery store a wide range of *galletitas* (cookies) from Mexico and other Spanish-speaking countries. These included Spanish and typical Latino brands such as Principe and Marinela and types such as *submarinos* (submarines) and *penguinos* (penguins), but the descriptions of the cookies were in English: "strawberry crème filled snack cakes" and "sandwich cookies with chocolate filling."

On the store's shelves, we noticed an interesting juxtaposition of two different brands of black beans. One of the brands was La Preferida, and the package was labeled "frijoles negros"; Luck's "black beans" offered an "authentic southern taste!" Interestingly, both brands are positioned side by side on the same shelf in the store, indicating that there is no separate "Latino" or "International" food section. Both brands were equally and fully stocked.

## WHEN DID THE LINGUISTIC LANDSCAPE ON OCRACOKE BEGIN TO CHANGE?

Perhaps the first Latino-owned community mainstay was Eduardo's Taco Stand, established in 2010 by Eduardo Chávez Perez as a food truck adjacent to the Ocracoke Variety Store's parking lot. Eduardo used the truck to begin sharing his love of Mexican food with the community. He proudly hung a Mexican flag outside the truck, and used the flag's green, white, and red stripes as the background to his first sign. Though his first sign was entirely in English, it did use both familiar and unfamiliar Mexican foods to draw in customers. It read:

eduardos' [lowercase, with the apostrophe
represented by a chili pepper]
TACO STAND
Authentic Mexican Food
Try Our Huaraches & Tortas

FIGURE 22.1. Eduardo Chavez inside his eponymous taco truck and the truck's current design, which combines Mexican iconography with Ocracoke and beach themes. Photograph by Jeffrey Reaser.

Eduardo's now occupies a much larger plot on Irvin Garrish Highway, closer to Silver Lake. While its signage is entirely in English, the visuals merge traditional Mexican and local iconography (see fig. 22.1). For example, in the nearby gift shop, tourists can buy T-shirts or stickers that feature a Dia de los Muertos–style skeleton with the famous Blackbeard emblem as a heart driving a golf cart, the mode of transportation for many dingbatters. You can also find a skeletonized Ocracat (a stray cat) with a taco in its mouth, a mermaid and salsa, or Blackbeard holding a burrito. In fact, virtually all the merchandise includes images that present mashups of island mainstays (beach cruiser bicycles, the lighthouse, a marlin, etc.) and Mexican images (chili peppers, avocados, sombreros, quesadillas, etc.). Eduardo's maintains an active Facebook page, with updates nearly every day they are open. The page's intro text is mostly in English, with an appended bit of Spanish: "Come join me for an authentic taste of Mexico on Ocracoke. Bienvenidos." His postings follow this pattern of being mostly in English with some infusion of Spanish, especially with greetings, as in, "Buenos Dias Amores." Other infusions of Spanish are found in the prose itself, but these tend to be limited, such as changing out the English *more* for the Spanish *muy* in their slogan, "Where life is *muy* flavorful." These linguistic and cultural mergers reflect well the new linguistic landscape of the island: mostly English, but with some Spanish unabashedly included to signify Latino identity.

The linguistic landscape of a community is impacted when speakers of different languages come in contact with each other, particularly in remote rural areas. On Ocracoke Island, the linguistic landscape reflects an image that the island wants to present as an English-dominant space for English-speaking tourists who visit during the summer months. In all the areas we visited, there were fewer material artifacts in Spanish than in English. The grocery store was an important location on the island where Latinos—a significant part of the population—can buy familiar foods that sustain their culture, so this was naturally the place where there were more Hispanic foods and products for sale. It is also a place where Spanish-speaking locals who can read and write can advertise services such as handyman and tutoring services.

The profile of the Latino imprint on the material culture of Ocracoke is selective in terms of the Spanish-language impact, but it is also significant in terms of the transition of the community into one that has become increasingly bilingual in its educational, social, and religious activities. The subsequent chapter explores some of the personal and interactional effects of the Latino population on Ocracoke.

*Chapter 23*

# WHAT IS THE OCRACOKE LATINO COMMUNITY LIKE?

In this chapter, we consider some of the more personal and interactional aspects of the Latino community in Ocracoke, including the use of Spanish in everyday life. How did this migration start, and how has its growth progressed? What is the day-to-day status of Spanish, and how has the Ocracoke community responded to it? How has the school responded to the influx of Spanish-speaking students, and how have Latinos integrated into the social community? What is the significance of another language on Ocracoke, after three centuries as a monolingual community using a distinctive dialect of English?

## LATINOS COME TO OCRACOKE

When we started visiting the community in the early 1990s, there were no native Spanish speakers living on the island. By the end of the decade, a few Spanish speakers had come to Ocracoke, in most cases not intending to stay permanently. There were obvious opportunities for work in the tourist and construction industries, and even a few jobs related to the fishing industry. We conducted our first interview with a Latino in 2002. For confidentiality reasons, we will use a pseudonym, Franco Garcia, whom Walt and Jeff interviewed for about an hour on one of our trips. We initially asked him how and why he came to Ocracoke. At the time, he was middle-aged, and although his English was accented, it was quite understandable:

> Well, I come from Mexico and I'm coming here find, looking for job, you know what I'm saying? Well, I'm working first in Germantown [mainland Hyde County], yeah, in one plant open oyster. I don' like this work, you know and I coming to Little Washington. Somebody going to Little Washington and I tell him, "Man, where you from?"
>
> He say, "From Ocracoke," he say.
>
> "Oh, you see job over there? Man, give me one favor. Give me ride to Ocracoke."
>
> He said, "Okay I give you ride, but I don't give you my house."
>
> "Hey man, you just put me in Ocracoke and I'm survival, okay?"
>
> "All right," he say, the guy.
>
> He give me the ride to here, to Ocracoke. My first night I'm sleeping in bushes, yeah, in the bushes. Yeah, it's fine. In 2000 I coming here, I think so, in March, something like that. I'm working, well, I'm listen, know somebody, the guy needed people, you know, for work, you know, for packing fish, and I'm see him and he told me yeah, "I give you job," pero he told me, "I no give you place for sleep, you know?"

> I don't care. I'm thinking I don't care, I gonna sleep in the bushes, maybe two weeks. I like it, for me it's no problem. When you, when you coming from Mexico, you know, when you say bye to your family, you ready for everything, you know. Maybe die, survive, or whatever. No sé. Now I no good but I'm stay okay, and I got a job, I got a friend in Ocracoke, yeah, it's good, I think so for me.

To listen to Franco Garcia describe his arrival to Ocracoke, visit www.ocracokebrogue.com/chapter/23/QR23-1.mp3.

Franco Garcia heard from a friend in Washington, North Carolina, that there might be work on Ocracoke Island, so he put his belongings in a backpack and hitched a ride to the island. Once there, he slept in the bushes, out of sight of residents, for several weeks. At daybreak, he would walk the island in search of work. Arriving at the onset of the tourist season, he had little trouble finding work as a busboy, in the fish house, and at a variety of other jobs. He lived on Ocracoke for more than two decades, mostly residing in a permanently docked sailboat in Silver Lake, the small harbor where ferries from Swan Quarter and Cedar Island dock. He supported himself with jobs that ranged from painting houses to construction, repair work, and net-mending. We would see him coming to the gas station early in the morning, which had a small breakfast area where some of the men gathered and socialized in the morning. The island men that gathered there in the mornings were always welcoming of Franco. We found him friendly and gregarious, not unlike the O'Cockers that hung out, drinking coffee and eating biscuits. Franco was not hesitant to talk to us in his accented English, openly discussing the path that brought him to the island.

Ironically, Franco's living quarters his first weeks on the island were probably not unlike those of the first Spanish travelers who set foot in North Carolina. Centuries earlier, the lawyer and nobleman Lucas Vázquez de Ayllón sponsored several explorations to the New World that included an expedition that landed on the coast of North Carolina near the Cape Fear River. Their stay in the Carolinas, however, was much briefer than Franco's, due to their general disenchantment with the region and the diseases that plagued their attempts at settlement. Today, the most enduring Spanish legacy of the early expeditions along the coast of North Carolina is probably the wild horses that roam on Shackleford Banks and other Outer Banks communities. Ocracoke still has some ponies that are descended from an early Spanish shipwreck; the ponies are now confined to a pen about seven miles north of the village.

Franco Garcia's initial destination point was Germantown, a cluster of houses at an intersection of roads in mainland Hyde County, where he shucked oysters in one of the few remaining plants. Following a short stay in Washington in Beaufort County, often referred to as "Little Washington" to avoid confusion with the nation's capital, he made the trip to Ocracoke, where he lived until he returned to Mexico in the early 2020s. The first modern migrants came based on word-of-mouth promises of work—mostly from the landlocked state of Hidalgo, Mexico, and many are from the same extended families. Their intention was to return to their home or to be joined by their families in the United States once their financial situation allowed, but they often stayed for extended periods, and now some have even become homeowners in Ocracoke—quite an accomplishment, given the price of housing on an island mostly oriented toward wealthy, mainland tourists. Franco Garcia described his experience with the family he left in Mexico:

> Garcia (FG): No problem. Yeah, I'm, I'm good here in Ocracoke. I think so working couple more years, go home Mexico.
>
> Interviewer (I): Do you have family back in Mexico?
>
> FG: Yeah, I got a wife. I got, uh, two kids. Yeah, two kids.
>
> I: How old are they?

FG: Yeah, I got my first—my older son, he have twenty-six. My daughter have twenty-two. Eh, my younger son have sixteen year old.

I: Do they ever come up? Do they ever come up to visit you?

FG: He is in Mexico. Yeah, my wife and him, she no like here. Well, I'm talking with her every two week, every week, and I tell 'em, "Hey, come here." And she told me, "No, you come back here." Yeah, she loves too much the babies.

I: Do you have a place of work back there? Work back in Mexico? What part of Mexico are you from?

FG: Tabasco. Yeah, in Tabasco. Yeah, I'm thinking work a couple more year and go home. Maybe no come back anymore.

To listen to Franco Garcia describe his family and the challenge of living away from them, visit www.ocracokebrogue.com/chapter/23/QR23-2.mp

## SPANISH GAINS A FOOTHOLD ON OCRACOKE

When Franco Garcia arrived, Latinos made up less than 2 percent of the island's population. Spanish is now heard daily among Latino workers in motels and restaurants, and it is also regularly taught in the schools. There were also classes in English and Spanish for the community that were started by Peter Vankevich, a retired employee of the Library of Congress in Washington, DC. At the time, Peter was serving as the librarian and Spanish speakers sometimes came to the library to improve their English and chat with him in his "passable" Spanish. He organized a language exchange program based on one he had organized at the Library of Congress for speakers of different languages. In an interview as part of the article "Two Cultures Come Together on Ocracoke," in

*Our State* magazine (February 7, 2017), he noted, "After religion, you probably have more tension around language than anything else. . . . Getting people to talk to each other—it's so basic and necessary, but it's complicated by so many factors. . . . On a barrier island, where the only exit is by boat, where there's one post office and one car repair shop, where every child attends the same school, there's no avoiding your neighbor."

In the winter of 2013, following the tourist season, Peter set up sessions for up to forty adults—twenty English speakers and twenty native Spanish speakers—to gather in the library, the nearby Methodist church, and other local places to talk. The participants focused on the words and phrases that would be most useful to both groups in their jobs and daily lives. In the aforementioned *Our State* magazine article, Peter described this collaboration: "'That's what's beautiful about this island,' Peter says. 'You come down here, and, if you want to, you can have a real impact.' He invited everyone in the program to his house for a potluck—potlucks being 'our lavish dinner parties on Ocracoke.' Kids and spouses mingled, too. 'Someone observed that it was the first time many of these families had gotten together socially to really get to know each other,' he says."

The conversations continued, and many of the friendships have endured. As Peter said, "Sometimes people just need a place to start." Some Ocracoke residents learned minimal Spanish that might be useful in their work relations and ritualistic greetings, but it was also symbolic that these folks had made an attempt to accommodate Spanish. Of course, there was also a small minority of English speakers on Ocracoke who had studied Spanish in school and used it previously, and who were much more fluent. For both groups, it was an opportunity to sharpen their language skills in conversation. However, today there are precious few conversations in Spanish between Ocracokers and members of the Latino community. At least some native islanders who employ or work with Spanish speakers know a few useful phrases that they use in instructions related to work or in their social interactions.

## SPANISH TODAY ON OCRACOKE

The situation is quite different for Latinos who now live in Ocracoke. Most Latino children born in Ocracoke are quite proficient in English and use it as their primary language in their regular interactions in the community, though they may use more Spanish at home with their parents and grandparents. In fact, Ocracoke's Latino population is experiencing a fairly typical three-generational shift to English in many cases. This pattern has held for immigrant communities across the country, including groups that spoke Italian, Polish, Vietnamese, Somali, or any number of other languages. The parents come as primary speakers of their heritage language—in this case, Spanish—and use English to some degree with their children, who become more proficient in English than Spanish. The next generation of children, born and raised in Ocracoke, will retain little Spanish, used primarily with their grandparents, with English becoming dominant in their lives. This is the usual situation of many immigrant communities. In these cases, despite fears to the contrary, there is no threat to English posed by the new language. In fact, it is always the heritage language that is endangered by the dominance of English. If anything, on Ocracoke, the acquisition of English over Spanish is an accelerated version of this pattern, condensing what had traditionally been a three-generation shift into two generations. In recent years, a number of the Latino students we have taught—students whose parents arrived to Ocracoke from Mexico or other locations—claim they know only a little Spanish and speak almost exclusively in English despite their parents' attempts to support their bilingualism.

Though this is the typical situation, using Spanish can be problematic in terms of new arrivals, who may know little English to begin with. For example, in one situation in an eighth grade classroom we were teaching, there were six Latino students. Five of them had been Ocracoke residents for years and were fluent in English and most retained some Spanish. However, the sixth student had just arrived a few weeks earlier from Honduras and was, for all intents and purposes, monolingual in Spanish. Happily, a couple of fluent bilingual students sat by her and translated for her as she was immersed in the monolingual English classroom. Fortunately, one of our graduate students was semi-fluent in Spanish and could help her with the linguistic information. Of course, English as a Second or Other Language services are now available in the school, but these services do not have the resources to do what the students were doing for the least English-proficient student in the classroom. We were inspired by how natural and gracious the students were to the student struggling in English, as the Latino community rallied around to assist in her struggle to learn English.

In Ocracoke, there is now a spectrum of Spanish speakers. Recent arrivals who are still largely monolingual Spanish speakers (but who are quickly learning English) make up one pole. At the other end of the spectrum are Latino children born in Ocracoke who have only very limited Spanish ability; though they were born to bilingual parents, their Spanish is often restricted to listening competency. In the middle are a range of folks, from now-permanent-resident Latino adults with more accented English to bilingual Ocracoke natives who are equally fluent in Spanish and English, and whose speech reflects their peer's influence more than then family's provenance. This is the nature of shifting language communities, and it is hardly unique to Ocracoke, but our long-range concern is the threat to Spanish-language heritage on the island rather than Latino children's acquisition of English.

## LATINO INSTITUTIONS ON OCRACOKE

In the last chapter, we mentioned a couple of the eating and shopping establishments on Ocracoke that offer delicious Mexican foods. Some Mexican options are now available in a few of the established Ocracoke restaurants of the community as they adapt to the expanded palates of the residents. But there is more that is Latino about Ocracoke than just the food. The community is establishing more Latino traditions as Latino residents highlight their culture while acknowledging the broader community. The

Latino community started an annual Latino festival in 2017 and in 2023 celebrated its sixth annual Festival Latino de Ocracoke. The two-day festival has now moved to Ocracoke's Berkeley Manor and features food, games, performances from Trio Los Chavales de Hidalgo, Larry Bellorin & Friends, and even Ocracoke's own Ballet Folklórico de Ocracoke. The school's basketball, volleyball, and baseball teams include Latino players, and they now have a majority-Latino soccer team. Finally, Ocracoke has a new Catholic chapel, named Stella Maris, Latin for "star of the sea.," dedicated in the fall of 2023. Institutionally, socially, and personally, the community is becoming more bicultural than at any time in its three-century history, although the Latino community is certainly not proportionately represented in the governance of the community. These kinds of institutional roles take time, but the prediction for continued participation in the wider community is optimistic.

In the first decade of the Latino community, one of the Latino families became homeowners on Ocracoke. Though the number of homeowners is growing, it is not proportional to the percentage of the population now made up by the Latino community.

Within the United States, immigrant status is often controversial and highly politicized, and there are many communities where tensions between Latino and Anglos have been intense. Having examined coexisting language communities in other regions of North Carolina and in the United States, we can honestly say that these kinds of tensions seem to be relatively minimal on Ocracoke. The community has greatly appreciated the assistance of Latinos in supporting the tourist industry, and we have heard many employers sincerely say they don't know what they would do without the Latino workforce on the island. We have heard very few concerns or suspicions, compared to many other communities we have examined. This, however, does not entirely exempt the community from misunderstandings, tensions, and social issues. For example, Eduardo Chávez Perez, owner of the island's first Latino food truck, reported that on his business's opening day he hung a large Mexican flag on the front of the truck, thinking it would be a good way to advertise. This decision was misinterpreted. Eduardo recalled,

"A man came, a customer, and he tore down the flag. . . . He said to me, 'Put up the American flag.'" Happily, Eduardo reported, "The man has since been back—to eat. . . . He misunderstood. I was trying to say what kind of restaurant—he did not understand I have family here. This is my home."

On Ocracoke Island, where old-timers claim ancestors from Blackbeard's day, a new community is taking shape. As the subheading of the 2017 article in *Our State* magazine in which Peter Vankevich was quoted, states, "The two cultures may not speak the same native language, but they understand that the best way to weather change is together." Ocracoke has not achieved a perfect integration of Latinos into the older, European-descended community, but it is certainly a model for other communities to emulate. And everything we have observed in the community suggests that things will continue to improve. The Latino community has increasingly engaged with the traditional island community's history and culture, and the traditional residents have come to appreciate and celebrate the cultural traditions brought by the Latino community. It is a small island, but it is one that has always been welcoming of other ways of being and speaking.

*Chapter 24*

# WHAT WILL HAPPEN TO THE BROGUE?

Once an iconic trait of the 200-mile chain of Outer Banks islands, the Brogue is now merely a whisper in this region. Ancestral islanders are now outnumbered by transplants to the island and, in the summer, vastly outnumbered by vacationers. The dialect that was once heard along the barrier islands has disappeared in locations that experienced such tourist inundation earlier, such as Hatteras, Rodanthe, Nags Head, and Kitty Hawk. In regions still inhabited by some ancestral families, such as Ocracoke, Harkers Island, Cedar Island, and coastal mainland Hyde County, it still may be noticeable among older speakers, but it has become the exception. Observations by many residents and by linguists studying these dialects indicate that Hoi Toider speech will soon be largely meshed with other dialects. On the island of Ocracoke, we now estimate that between 100 to 200 folks still have some semblance of the traditional Brogue, though many use it only with other community members. This strongly suggests that the dialect is not sustainable in the long term. During the non-tourist season, Brogue speakers make up fewer than one in five residents, and this percentage continues to shrink each year. On a summer day, they may make up only one in 100 people on the island.

## THE BASIS OF CHANGE

Compelling geographical, historical, cultural, and linguistic facts support the observation that the Brogue is being washed away with the ever-rising tide of tourism and other changes along the Outer Banks. Social changes are one of the most obvious reasons for this language recession. When a small community inhabiting approximately four square miles on the island is inundated by as many as 10,000 to 12,000 dingbatters during a summer day, it may be hard to locate a person speaking the traditional Brogue in public spaces. You need to know where to locate them in shops and locations on the island run by locals. Even finding the locals, however, does not mean you will hear the Brogue. Many islanders have learned to turn off their Brogue when speaking to outsiders. Over time, that can result in those residents using the Brogue less in all parts of their life, including around their children, resulting in a break in the generational transfer that has been occurring for nearly four centuries.

Islanders estimate that only about 300 to 350 people of the 900 year-round residents are descended from the families that came to the island by the end of the 1700s, generally referred to as *O'Cockers*. Of those, it is estimated that only about a third to a half have any recognizable Brogue. As we have seen throughout this book, the term *O'Cocker* is a significant cultural designation reserved for those whose families have lived for centuries on the island. The rest will always be *dingbatters*, *tourons*, *from off*, *strangers*, *foreigners*, *woodsers*, or whatever term is in current use for those from off-island, even if they've lived there for more than a generation now or married into an island family. As we noted in earlier chapters, to be an *O'Cocker*, you have to be able to trace your ancestry on the island for at least a couple of centuries, and most of those with such roots have done so. Historically, the label typically implied a way of

FIGURE 24.1. Family trees on Ocracoke are extensive, as is seen by the scale of this ancestral family tree of Harry Walton O'Neal at the Ocracoke Preservation Society. Photograph by Amy Howard.

speaking as well, but this is no longer the case. Now it is possible to be an O'Cocker without a Brogue, and in the near future, it is possible that nearly all O'Cockers will be Brogue-less.

When the team of NC State researchers first arrived on the island in the early 1990s, we were impressed by the number of people on the island who had access to impressive genealogies that represented their family ancestry on the island, and the tradition of genealogical research continues to be popular. In fact, emphasis on ancestry has increased as more outsiders arrive. The Ocracoke Preservation Society's museum used to feature the ancestral tree of different prominent O'Cocker families (e.g., Howard, Garrish, O'Neal families, etc.) each season to highlight the settlement ancestry of the island (see fig. 24.1). Practically every ancestral islander has access to a genealogy that goes back to the early days of Ocracoke. As linguists, we were interested in how ancestral status might relate to language in determining who counts as O'Cockers, so we asked islanders about this relationship. And we learned that, as much as we love dialects, islanders value genealogy and community far more. As Candy Gaskill, a good barometer of how island folks feel, put it, "It's not the Brogue that's home, it's the people and the warmth, you know, the love and the community, the togetherness. I mean, I don't really think it's the Brogue or the dialect, I think it's more the people that makes it." In other words, O'Cockers are O'Cockers because of their family heritage, not because of their language. Their language is simply an index of that cultural heritage. While they may be concerned about the erosion of the dialect, ancestry clearly wins out over dialect in terms of significance.

The challenge to the traditional dialect started when the island began transforming from a marine-based society of people descended from the original English-speaking families during the mid-twentieth century. Prior to this time, although a few mainland families would visit for limited periods of time during vacation seasons, Ocracoke was still a remote, isolated outpost. This began to change when electricity came to the island in 1938. The first paved road, called Ammunition Dump, was constructed by the Navy in 1942, and Highway 12, the only road that extends from the northern end of the island to the village, was completed in 1958. The inception of a regular ferry that carried motor vehicles in addition to people in the 1950s was also a pivotal point in the history of the island—and the endangerment of the Brogue. The expanded ferry service began when the State of North Carolina purchased a private ferry (Frazier Peele's ferry) in 1957, and, since then, access to the island by ferry has steadily increased, starting with the establishment of the Cedar Island route in 1961 and now including a passenger-only hydrofoil ferry from Hatteras which allows easy access for day-trippers. Since the age of the 911 service and GPS, all the streets now have names and the houses have numbers, something unheard of before the late twentieth century.

There is now a free tram service that circulates through the village, moving tourists among the restaurants and shops.

The social shifts of the island have changed the community and its economic base—and the language situation has followed suit. As we noted above, the year-round population of the island is now composed primarily of families from the mainland, who outnumber ancestral islanders two-to-one. Further, only a small percentage of young'uns from ancestral families maintain the Brogue. There are now fewer and fewer Brogue speakers, and increasingly, most of them are older. These are sure signs that the traditional Brogue will soon become extinct. This fact is acknowledged by older islanders, and not without some remorse. For example, when James Barrie Gaskill, an O'Cocker who had a strong version of the Brogue, was asked by CBS News correspondent Mo Rocca if it would sadden him if the island lost the Brogue, he replied, "To a certain extent, it would. Every generation now is losing it, and probably by another generation or so you won't even notice it." Chester Lynn, a tenth-generation O'Cocker, offered a similar response when asked by a correspondent from WRAL, a state television station, about the unique dialect: "A few of us, your know, when we're gone, it will die, you know." He then adds, with a sense of island pride, "The thing I am really happy about is that I have been a little bit of its heritage and its knowledge, and, you know, keeping it as long as we could."

To hear Mo Rocca's interview with James Barrie Gaskill, visit www.ocracokebrogue.com/chapter/24/QR24-1.mp4.

To hear excerpts from WRAL's "Exploring Ocracoke Island," visit www.ocracokebrogue.com/chapter/24/QR24-2.mp4.

Residents such as James Barrie Gaskill and Chester Lynn, along with many other O'Cockers, do not see a future for the traditional Brogue and predict its imminent death as the older residents pass on. The Brogue has certainly been a significant symbol of the island, and it is one of the indexes of residents' island heritage, but they recognize that it is continually receding, and that family heritage rather than linguistic repertoire will remain the primary designation for O'Cocker status. At the same time, the Brogue is also now a token of a proud tradition, as expressed above by Chester Lynn, who is happy to keep it as an active voice on the island for as long as he can.

When James Barrie's son, Morty, was born, James Barrie lamented the fact that Morty would probably never speak the Brogue. We interviewed Morty shortly after he had returned to the island following college to become the eighth generation of Gaskill family fishermen. As you can hear in the linked video, Morty does not speak the Brogue of his father, but his speech is still different from that of mainland North Carolinians.

To hear James Barrie talk about his son's language prospects, and then to hear Morty as a young adult, visit www.ocracokebrogue.com/chapter/24/QR24-3.mp4.

As the island changes, so do the families. A century ago, practically all islanders married others from the island, but now there are an increasing number of "mixed marriages"—that is, marriages between ancestral islanders and partners from the mainland. In fact, in previous times, the few people from outside who married into island families were never quite considered to be Ocracoke insiders. Notice how James Barrie Gaskill refers to his wife as a dingbatter in the vignette linked to below, even though they had by then been married for decades and she had been active in community affairs.

To hear James Barrie Gaskill discuss the term *dingbatter*, visit www.ocracokebrogue.com/chapter/24/QR24-4.mp4.

Of course, people from the mainland may pick up some local terms for locations and people, such as *up the beach* referring to "off the island to the north," *taking a scud* for "taking a ride in a boat or car," *dingbatter* for "outsider," and *O'Cocker* for "ancestral islander," but the pronunciation and grammar of parents from off island tends to remain different, and children pick up these different patterns. In the first eighth grade class that we taught in 1993, there were four students, all with at least one parent who was an ancestral islander. In our most recent class in 2024, there were twelve students; only one of these had at one O'Cocker parent. Perhaps more significantly, six of the students in the class had at least one, and in most cases two, parents from a Latin American country, usually Mexico.

The addition of a different cultural-linguistic population adds a completely new language dimension to the community. More than 50 percent of the students in the Ocracoke School in 2024 identified as Latino. When we discuss a number of the linguistic traits of the traditional Ocracoke Brogue in our annual course with eighth-graders, the students from ancestral island families often recall their grandparents or parents using some of the dialect features we describe, even if they themselves do not use the Brogue. But most of these features are completely unknown to the Latino students, whose familiarity with the dialect is much more limited.

As discussed in more detail in chapters 22 and 23, the significance of the Latino settlement in Ocracoke adds another critical social factor to the island. Several popular places for dining now feature Mexican cuisine exclusively, and Latino culture is becoming a part of the landscape, manifested clearly all over the island but especially in the construction of the its Catholic church. The Latino students learn English inside and outside school, but they do not learn the grammar or pronunciation of the Ocracoke Brogue and often find it alien and confusing. There is currently a vast difference in terms of what the children of ancestral islander parents know and what the Spanish-speaking population knows about the island's distinct dialectal heritage. At the same time, the

Latino students do know the most famous parts of Ocracoke's history, including its connection to pirates, so it is possible that future generations will learn more about and contribute to the island's living history.

## HOW IS THE BROGUE SHIFTING?

Up to this point, we have discussed the recession of the Brogue as though it were a straight line descending on a graph that ends when a generation no longer uses it. But the situation is not quite that simple. Complicated factors such as occupation, gender, and attitude all contribute to the dissipation, which instead of a charting the course of a line, may be more like the fog created by warm breath on a cold morning: the edges disappear first, but eventually, every bit of the cloud is dispersed; it is no longer distinguishable from the surrounding air. For example, in chapter 12, we discussed how the dialect is affected by gender. The oldest generations did not show much of a difference in the speech of men and women, although some of the older women had a stronger dialect than the men because of women's and men's different roles on the island. But this has now changed; in the younger generations, the Brogue has become more associated with traditional watermen, thus becoming more associated with the male gender for younger speakers. The younger men are now more likely to retain at least a few features of the Brogue since it now carries traits associated with rugged masculinity, while younger women will avoid the Brogue because of these same associations. Furthermore, it is men rather than women who perform the dialect for reporters, journalists, and other outsiders. We know a couple of women whose Ocracoke dialects are pretty strong, but they tend to be reticent about performing their speech for outsiders. Even when we do convince them to talk to news reporters, they are often cut from the segment that airs, perhaps because they do not fit the waterman archetype that outsiders have come to associate with the Brogue. The performance routines associated with men thus enhance its correlation with gender.

Recall also the groupings of middle-aged men we described in chapter 18. We noted that the Poker Game Network men in our initial study and the Pelican Network men in our subsequent study had stronger Brogues than did their peers. In both cases, these men would regularly hang out together for conversations, games, and a few drinks, creating a close-knit social group. They also regularly participated in fishing and other marine-based activities such as ferrying tourists to Portsmouth or taking them out on fishing boats. We found that the speech of the men in the Pelican group still resembled that of the Poker group. It was different in some ways, but the younger guys still retained some of the older vowel sounds, used selected grammatical features such as "it weren't me" or "he weren't there," and were readily familiar with some of the traditional Ocracoke vocabulary.

Cases like these demonstrate how the recession of a dialect can be tempered by group associations, gender roles, network associations, and identity. Women do not talk like men not only because traditionally they have not belonged to the same social (and occupational) groups as men, but also because the Brogue has recently become more associated with a traditionally masculine image, as noted above. The lesson from these kinds of observations is that dialect recession is not a straightforward process; instead of a single decline, there are a number of trajectories with different levels of dialect maintenance and recession for different subgroups of speakers. Women may take different paths than men, and some men may take different paths than other men, all influenced by the speakers' involvement in in traditional island activities and pride in traditional island identity.

## WHAT DIALECT REPLACES THE OCRACOKE BROGUE?

Folks do not simply go silent when they lose their language or dialect; instead, one dialect or language is replaced or meshes with another language variety. That is why some linguists prefer to talk about "language shift" rather than "language death" when a language variety is no longer used. Chapter 18 discussed in detail the kinds of dialects that are replacing the traditional Brogue as it recedes. The simplified conclusion is that it is complicated, as some parts of the Brogue are replaced by a mainland southern dialects, while others parts seem to be replaced by northern or midwestern dialects. Why this is the case is not something we can answer definitively, but our research does allow us to speculate as to what is happening and why. The answer, we believe, is found in demographics and culture, just as are the reasons for the Brogue's demise in the first place. By focusing on the receding features of the Ocracoke Brogue, we can make a few interesting observations.

We can get some demographic information about who visits the island from the state-run ferry system, since this is how just about everyone arrives. When the vehicles are registered by the ferry system, they are designated as being from either North Carolina or "another state." Unfortunately, the names of the other states are not officially registered. To get more specifics, we might look at the license plates of visitors' cars. As reported in chapter 18, Walt Wolfram once assigned his students the task of going to all the hotels, restaurants, and other places where visitors might park to tabulate what states outside of North Carolina were represented. Cars with plates from states south of Ocracoke, such as South Carolina, Georgia, and Alabama represented less than 5 percent of the vehicles, but states such as Ohio, Pennsylvania, New Jersey, and Virginia were common, making up the bulk of states other than North Carolina. These also happen to be the states outside of North Carolina from which most newer inhabitants arrive. These demographic patterns suggest that non-southern dialects might have a stronger influence on new ways of talking in Ocracoke than southern ones.

One observation we have made involves the vowel of *high tide*, which on Ocracoke was traditionally produced more like "hoi toid." The iconic southern pronunciation of the vowel, as "hah tahd," is still common in in rural mainland North Carolina and throughout the general South. For the most part, O'Cockers traded in their "hoi toid" for "high tide," the dominant non-southern dialect variant, rather than the southern "hah tahd." We compared this change in Ocracoke with the change in Harkers Island, a fishing island south of Ocracoke on the Outer Banks that also uses the Brogue. We found that people there favored the "hah tahd" pronunciation rather than "high tide." But Harkers Island is not a prominent tourist site, and most folks who go there for fishing are from North Carolina. For this vowel pronunciation, it seems that the best way to predict the direction of change is to investigate which other language models are most commonly available.

Another trait that helps us think about the question of which dialects are replacing the Brogue is the pronunciation of *pin* and *pen*. In the South, the vowels in pairs like *bin* and *Ben*, *kin* and *Ken*, and *Lynn* and *Len* are pronounced the same. In non-southern dialects, these vowels are pronounced differently. Just about every year, we take a survey of the students in our eighth grade class to hear how they pronounce these words, and we have found that about half of the native islanders of this generation have the southern merger of *pin* and *pen*. While many southern dialect features are waning in the mainland, the *pin/pen* merger is one of the more persistent. It is noteworthy, then, that only about half the young people in Ocracoke use it. This feature suggests that it is not possible to say there is a single dialect replacing the Brogue. Instead, speech on Ocracoke is taking pieces from a number of dialects.

Some of the pronunciation features taking over the Ocracoke Brogue are non-southern, but many vocabulary words and a few grammatical structures that have long been part of the dialect remain quite southern. On the island, it is still common to hear double modals such *might could* (e.g., "I might could do it") and southern vocabulary terms such as *y'all* for plural *you* (e.g., "y'all come back"), *carry* for *take* (e.g., "they carried us to the movies"), and *fixin to* (e.g., "he's fixin' to go to the creek"). In fact, the current dialect used on the island by younger folks is a unique mixture of southern and non-southern dialect traits, along with the retention of a couple of features of the traditional Brogue. It may not be as noticeable to outsiders coming to Ocracoke in search of the traditional Brogue, but the Ocracoke dialect is still unique in its own right. And even while some non-southern features are adopted, it is our prediction that the southernisms that remain are enough to preserve the perception that Ocracoke English is a variation of Southern English, even while the linguistic story is a bit more complicated.

## WHAT CAN WE DO?

Linguists are generally sad when a language or a dialect dies, because they are intrigued by language variation and they know that languages and dialects can be a rich part of people's cultural heritage. But sometimes dialect loss is inevitable—and it is not up to linguists to decide whether a community keeps its dialect or not. Even if Ocracoke residents wanted to maintain the traditional Brogue, it would be a near-impossible task given the demographic, economic, and cultural obstacles they would face. However, as languages change, there are some things that linguists and communities can do together to celebrate and to preserve the heritage of the traditional language.

Over the years, we have conducted sixty- to ninety-minute interviews, similar to oral histories, with more than 120 O'Cockers. All of our interviews are presently archived in one of the largest websites ever compiled for language varieties, the Sociolinguistic Analysis and Archive Project, housed at North Carolina State University (https://slaap.chass.ncsu.edu/), along with more than 5,000 other interviews of this type. Although they are not available to the public without explicit permission, we have given access to a number of people interested in this collection, including Ocracoke residents who may want simply to hear the voice of a loved one or learn about the island from the voice of a resident. These voices should never be lost. We are currently adding to our collection of dialect recordings stories of the destructive Hurricane Dorian in 2019. We have also compiled, with Ocracoke residents, two audio collections of oral histories, *Ocracoke Speaks* (2001) and *Ocracoke Still Speaks* (2011). Both of these projects are now available in their entirety on the website that accompanies this book. They include the voices of a number of island residents and cover topics like island history, weather, the way things were, changes in the island community, and Ocracoke today. There are also plenty of funny stories, since Ocracoke residents have always loved a good laugh.

Ocracoke was also the site where we started our now-extensive documentary initiative, when a couple of undergraduate students, Phyllis Blanton and Karen Waters, produced a twenty-minute documentary, *The Ocracoke Brogue*, in the mid-1990s. The Ocracoke Preservation Society's (OPS) "dialect room" plays either that documentary or our more recent documentary *The Carolina Brogue* (produced by Neal Hutcheson, 2008) on a continuous loop. (Both of these documentaries are linked from this book's website.) Because the OPS is a small place, for more than twenty-five years, all visitors have at least overheard some of the Brogue during their visit. The robust YouTube channel for the Language and Life Project at NC State, with more than 23 million views, features many vignettes from Ocracoke, so examples of how Ocracokers speak, or at least how they once spoke, remain quite accessible to the public. Television features have been produced by CNN, BBC, and CBS's *Good Morning America*, among others, that document and celebrate the Brogue. Such public outreach has contributed to the unique appeal of the island now twice celebrated as the "Best Beach in America." We have also done a special museum exhibit at the OPS on the dialect and on the life of Muzel Bryant (see chapter 21), the last member of one African American family who lived on Ocracoke since the Civil War. We have further given annual Porch Talks for the summer tourists at the OPS for a couple of decades now. We connected with the OPS on our first trip to the island by our crew in 1992, and it has been a synergistic partnership ever since. We also host a dinner each spring called the Brogue Banquet as a way of thanking our friends in Ocracoke. Despite the community's partnership celebrating the dialect, none of these efforts will revitalize the Brogue.

To watch a vignette about the annual Brogue Banquet, visit www.ocracokebrogue.com/chapter/24/QR24-5.mp4.

Perhaps the most essential aspect of our celebration of dialects and the Ocracoke Brogue is the dialect curriculum we teach each spring in the Ocracoke School. We started in 1993, and we are still going strong at the time of this writing. We have worked mostly with two legendary classroom teachers and community residents, Gail Hamilton and Gwen Austin, who have been extremely supportive, as has the entire school leadership. We bring our graduate students, who love interacting firsthand with Ocracoke residents they have learned about in their classes at NC State. Both the students from NC State and the eighth-graders treasure this week of classes about the dialects of North Carolina, with a focus on Ocracoke. It is a tossup as to which group learns more, but we tend to think it is our graduate students. Over the course of three decades, we have seen the attitude of residents shift from dialect uncertainty and insecurity to dialect pride and celebration. Even as the dialect disappears, the students are proud to know the linguistic history of the island.

To watch a brief vignette from our teaching about dialects in Ocracoke School, visit www.ocracokebrogue.com/chapter/24/QR24-6.mp4.

Our test case of a formal dialect awareness program has assured us that attitudes about dialects in the United States can shift over time—if students in classrooms are given the opportunity to learn about dialects. Students in the Ocracoke School consistently write in their journals, during the week we are with them, about the new perspectives they are learning about language, as in the following: "Studying dialect is a lot more involved than what I realized. It has a lot of dialect rules in it. I do think dialect is important here. I'm glad I got to study more on the situation with the class. I feel like our dialect is dying here and with you coming here, you will hopefully make us realize that our dialect is unique. I'm very interested in dialects." The first teacher we worked with, Gail Hamilton, from an O'Cocker family, had this to say about the dialect awareness program: "I appreciate it personally, not just for the student's perspective of learning about their own language, but I didn't realize the there was a pattern. As an English teacher, I would cringe at what I considered 'bad grammar.' Showing me that there is a specific pattern, a method of speech, is something that now I'm really proud that they know." Though also quoted in chapter 19, we return to the thoughts of the second teacher to welcome us at Ocracoke School, Gwen Austin, a social studies teacher married to an O'Cocker and a long-term resident of the island, who noted, "I feel we are at the heart of our community. We must teach our past and explain how, as we grow, we are losing so much of what we used to be. We are so unique, and I am so glad that NC State feels that we are, too. . . . The community has changed so much; many have no clue about our rich past and especially the native Brogue. Many just come to Ocracoke without knowing a thing about our rich history. As we grow, I think we *have* to educate our youth and our changing community."

The *Voices of North Carolina* curriculum is now the longest-running school-based program on dialect awareness in the country. The success of the program demonstrates that students are curious and excited to learn about dialects, that learning about dialects helps students and teachers learn about the patterned nature of language variation, and that dialect awareness programs change community attitudes about community dialects and language in general. It may seem surprising, but we are convinced that the residents of Ocracoke lead the nation in education about language diversity: there is no community anywhere in the United States that knows more about its dialect history and about dialectology than Ocracoke. We look forward to a day when the United States follows the example set by this small, exceptional island. As Gail Hamilton noted, "Before, when foreigners, tourists, would come down, it was something that [Ocracokers] were ashamed of, because they talked differently. And so now, with pride, they say, 'Hoi toid on the sound soid.'"

## A LITTLE MORE SPECIAL

It would be easy to end this volume with a paragraph in which Jeff and Walt wax linguistic about the importance of the dialect to the culture. But such a choice puts the spotlight too brightly on us linguists. Instead, we sign off humbly, by thanking the community for its ongoing gift of trust, knowledge, stories, and voices. We have published more on the Ocracoke Brogue than anyone in the world, but we are reminded on each visit that the true experts are the community members who have lived what we only glimpse. It is in this spirit that we close with the voice of one community member and our co-author, Candy Gaskill, who has been deeply invested in preserving in many forms all aspects of Ocracoke's history, from places to people to food to music to traditions—and everything in between.

> I guess they realize that, yes, they do have a accent but it's a little bit more special than other people's accents. And I think that, you know, they really, I guess maybe appreciate it more, and appreciate the island more, and maybe, where they come from, and their family, you know, grandparents and stuff and everything a little bit more. I mean I know that I have; I mean I've always loved Ocracoke and I always loved my family and stuff and everything, but it just seems that it's another little special piece that goes, you know, to the puzzle and stuff and everything, to have the dialect and to have the accent and stuff and everything, that makes Ocracoke, another little special, more special place than what it already is.

QR 24.7. To hear Candy's conclusion about what makes Ocracoke a special place (from *Ocracoke Still Speaks*), visit www.ocracokebrogue.com/chapter/24/QR24-7.mp3.

# INDEX